AVICENNA

AVICENNA

His life and Works

SOHEIL M. AFNAN
Ph.D. (Cantab.)

Ruskin House
GEORGE ALLEN & UNWIN LTD
MUSEUM STREET LONDON

FIRST PUBLISHED IN 1958

Printed in Great Britain
in 12-point Fournier type
BY UNWIN BROTHERS LIMITED
WOKING AND LONDON

PREFACE

THIS is an attempt to present to the general reader the life and works of Avicenna, who is beyond doubt the most provocative figure in the history of thought in the East. It is not a defence of him and his system, nor a critique of his philosophy. During his lifetime he was deliberately scornful of defenders and critics alike; he could not think better of them now that a thousand years have gone by. With his position amply justified, and after that extended period when his name hung on the lips of physicians and philosophers from the borders of China to the cloisters of mediaeval Paris and Oxford, it seems best to let him speak for himself. The painted frieze only lately discovered behind a coating of plaster at the Bodleian, is sufficient evidence that he is no newcomer to the Western world.

We have felt no temptation to adapt him to modern thought; or to graft his conceptions on to those that belong distinctively to an experimental age. We have wished to give the right historical perspective, and to show him as the product of the impact of Greek thought on Islamic teachings against the background of the Persian Renaissance in the tenth century.

The legitimate question whether there is anything of permanent value in his thought has been left for the reader to decide. Yet it has been emphasized that the problems he was confronted with resulted from the conflicting disciplines of two separate cultures brought face to face. He is therefore of more than historical interest. His attitude can be of guidance to those in the East who are meeting the challenge of Western civilization; and to those in the West who have yet to find a basis on which to harmonize scientific with spiritual values.

There remains the pleasant task of expressing our thanks to Dr S. Pines with whom we have discussed Avicenna frequently, and who has read some of the chapters of this book, and made valuable suggestions.

S. M. AFNAN

Pembroke Cellege, Cambridge, July 1956

CONTENTS

INTRODUCTION

MANY factors helped to introduce the remarkable 'Abbāsid Age under the aegis of the Caliphs of Baghdad. Their newly-founded capital had gathered together men from distant countries, and the stimulating *élan* of Islam was everywhere at work. The change from the Umayyads of Damascus and their tribal loyalties held fresh promise for the non-Arabs who had adopted the new Faith. It was a case of religion uniting people and giving purpose and direction to their lives.

The Arabs contributed a high sense of mission; the Persians their culture and sense of history; the Christian Syriacs their linguistic versatility; the Ḥarrānians their Hellenistic heritage and the Indians their ancient lore. All mixed freely and joined in an earnest quest for knowledge. The Persians became particularly favoured. They had done most to establish the new regime; they had much experience to offer in the field of administration and State finance; and they consequently filled many of the government posts. An unfortunate consequence of this was that racial rivalry reappeared. It led to the unhappy Shu'ūbīyya movement with its emphasis on the superiority of the non-Arab races, leading to occasional violence and bloodshed. The association, nevertheless, proved eminently fruitful. All branches of art and literature flourished as never before or since in the Islamic world. A new civilization was being created, and members of all the nations involved made vital contributions.

The Caliphs themselves set the pace. Al-Manṣūr (d. 775) added to his liberal outlook a deep love of learning. Hārūn al-Rashīd who reigned after him established the library known as the *Khazānat al-Ḥikma* (The Treasure-house of Wisdom) under the direction of competent and earnest scholars. Material prosperity enabled the people to take an increasing interest in cultural pursuits. There was an intensive study of the Arabic language and grammar, already associated with the two rival schools of Kūfa and Baṣra. The whole corpus of pre-Islamic poetry including some of doubtful authenticity came to be recorded. Rules of prosody were laid down and carefully studied; poetry took forms hitherto not attempted. Public and private libraries began to multiply,[1] and high prices were paid for manuscripts.

Two factors were to prove of great importance to the subject of our inquiry. In the field of thought there was the emergence of a rationalistic school of theologians who came to be known as the Mu'tazelites and whose views eventually influenced profoundly some of the Islamic philosophers. In literature there was the gradual development of an as yet hardly existing secular prose as distinct from the purely religious, or the mystical or even the Mu'tazelite style of writing and terminology. This secular prose was to become the model of Arabic philosophical language and a chief source of its technical terms. It first appeared in the late Umayyad period in Syria and 'Irāq, and was created by Muslims of foreign extraction, mostly Persians. At first it was used for correspondence concerned with the administration of the new Empire and the organization of secretarial offices. Its chief exponent was 'Abd al-Ḥamīd al-Kātib, a school-master who rose to high office under the Umayyads.[2] With the establishment of the 'Abbāsid Caliphate in 750 (132 A.H.) it developed in the form of court-literature and *belles-lettres*. The Caliphs from the time of Umayyad Hishām realized the necessity of some guide to help them to formalize their relations with the various communities they were now to rule. This they found in the court-literature of the erstwhile Sāsānian Empire which although at the time of its conquest was hopelessly divided within itself, deeply impressed the Arab conquerors by its outward majesty and efficient system of administration. 'It was from them [the Persians] that we took the methods of royalty and government, the organization of the

[1] Cf. Miss Pinto: *La Bibliotheche degli Arabi* . . . *Bibliofilia*, XXX, 1928.
[2] *Fihrist*, p. 117.

chosen and the common classes, and the suitable policy towards the governed. . . .'[1] Consequently the secretarial *kātibs* undertook the translation of some of these Persian court-books, describing the duties of the monarch to his people and the proper procedure at court.

Together with epistolary and court-literature came *belles-lettres*, to be known as *adab*. The outstanding writer in this genre, if not its actual originator, was Ibn al-Muqaffa' (killed in early age). One of the creators of Arabic secular prose, he was also perhaps the earliest to introduce Aristotelian Logic to the Islamic world.[2] This author has grown in stature since modern scholarship began to devote attention to him and recognize the valuable services that he rendered to the Arabic language. It has been possible to show[3] that some of the happiest philosophical terms in Arabic that are not of Qur'anic origin, borrowed by the translators and philosophers alike, are first met with in his writings and are presumably of his coining. Discussing this aspect of Arabic literature and the advent of secular prose, Professor Gibb remarks that 'in the second century therefore there were in 'Irāq two schools of Arabic letters, entirely distinct from one another, deriving from different sources, animated by a different spirit, serving different purposes, and almost entirely negative towards each other.'[4]

It was, however, during the Caliphate of al-Ma'mūn (d. 833), which might from the political point of view be considered the beginning of that general decline in the fortunes of the 'Abbāsids, that learning flourished most. His special interest in foreign culture and philosophy is commemorated in the story that Aristotle appeared to him in a dream and spoke words of encouragement to him.[5] Thus inspired, al-Ma'mūn sent groups of scholars to Asia Minor and Cyprus to bring back Greek books. He wrote to

1 Jāḥiẓ: *Kitāb al-Tāj . . .*, edit. A. Zakī, p. 23.

2 *Fihrist*, p. 242; Ibn al-Qifṭī, p. 220.

3 Cf. S. Afnan: *Greek Philosophical Terms and Their Arabic and Persian Equivalents.*

4 *Social Significance of the Shu'ūbīya. Studia . . . Pederson*, p. 107.

5 *Fihrist*, p. 243.

the Emperor of Byzantium asking him to send some of those fine collections of Greek learning that were still stored and treasured in his country, and the Emperor after some hesitation complied. Al-Ma'mūn also made the old medical and philosophical school of Gundīshāpūr in southern Persia the object of his special care; and he lavishly rewarded poets, scholars, and translators.

The general intellectual climate of this time is typified by the literary and philosophical gatherings in the homes of wealthy patrons or learned men, and the heated discussions that took place there. Very engaging accounts of these have survived in the writings of an unappreciated but gifted *littérateur*.[1] Men went on journeys in search of knowledge; linguists hastened to the heart of Arabia to learn the pure tongue; geographers went to visit the lands conquered by Islam; and Ḥunain arrived in Syria to study Greek and search for books to take back with him.

The generous support of literary men by the Caliphs set an example to the members of certain old and well-known families who had attained power and wealth. The Barmakids, although primarily concerned with government and administration, paid thousands of *dirhams* to medical men and translators of books.[2] The Nowbakht family, less interested in politics, were distinguished authors themselves, translated books from Persian, and supported those who translated from Greek.[3] Furthermore they held regular meetings in their homes at which religious as well as literary subjects were discussed. One of them 'entertained a group of those who translated books on philosophy';[4] and himself wrote a detailed commentary on the *De Generatione et Corruptione* of Aristotle. The Munajjim (astronomer) family who, as their name shows, were interested in astronomy, became perhaps the most famous patrons of literature in Baghdad. They also were authors themselves, held meetings and, we are told, were enterprising enough to help their wealthy friends to start private libraries; 'they used to provide for a group of translators . . . about five

[1] Cf. Tawḥīdī: *Muqābasāt; Imtā'*.
[2] Qifṭī, p. 143.
[3] *Fihrist*, pp. 177, 238, 274.
[4] *Ibid.*, p. 177.

hundred *dīnārs* per month for translations; and for their company.'[1] And Zayyāt, the son of an olive-oil merchant of Ṭabaristān, who became the vizier to three different Caliphs, did not fail in the patronage of literature. His 'bounties to the translators and copyists was nearly two thousand *dīnārs* every month. And many books were translated in his name.'[2] There were also some Arabs equally interested and enthusiastic about the new learning.

It was in this brilliant *milieu*, at a time when the age of Arabic prose and poetry was approaching its zenith, that Islamic philosophy began to take shape with a free and vigorous exercise of reason.

* * * *

The sources of Islamic philosophy are not far to seek, but they are numerous and complex. The main stream comes from classical Greece, with a strong current of Muslim religious thought associated with the Mutakallemūn and the Mu'tazelites. To these were added varying measures of Stoic, Neo-Platonic, Gnostic, Manichaean, Hermetic and other ideas proceeding from the different schools that flourished in the late Hellenistic age. This is not to say that Islamic philosophy is a sterile hybrid denied the capacity to produce any characteristic thought of its own. It is only to stress the contrast with Greek philosophy as a secular discipline, not much influenced by foreign and conflicting views, occupied with the problems of analysis, not synthesis, and addressing itself to a people with a common culture and heritage.

It may well be asked whether there is such a thing as Islamic philosophy proper. The term philosophy has admittedly had different connotations at various periods of history and in various parts of the world. This is as true today as it was many centuries ago. Philosophy meant one thing to the pre-Socratics, another to Aristotle, and still another to the Stoics and the thinkers of the Hellenistic age. It is not surprising therefore that what actually developed in Baghdad during the 'Abbāsid Caliphate, differed

[1] *Fihrist*, p. 243. [2] I. A. Uṣaibī'a, Vol. 1, p. 206.

materially from the classical conception of that subject. But it was philosophy inasmuch as it aimed at the establishment of a system rationally conceived, logically argued, and based on the general principles of the Greek discipline, even while attempting to harmonize it with the fundamentals of religion. In outlook it was deeply influenced by Stoic and Neo-Platonic thought in addition to the thought of classical Greece. And it was in turn to influence, far more than is generally conceded, Christian philosophy in the Middle Ages. It will be noted that almost all the translators of Greek works into Arabic were Christians; and there were a few who wrote philosophical treatises of their own; nevertheless the term Islamic philosophy is justified because although its outstanding figures were often of different countries, they were either Muslims by birth or converts from Christianity, Judaism, and Zoroastrianism. Furthermore their chief aim was the application of reason to revelation, and the reconciliation of Greek thought with the tenets of Islam. None of the Christian thinkers of Baghdad grew to the same stature. Not until mediaeval Europe and the rise of Scholasticism, do we find a corresponding intellectual effort.

Greek learning reached Baghdad by different routes. The teaching of classical philosophy from its source in Athens established itself in the *museia* and academies of Alexandria; and when the Arabs conquered Egypt, these institutions were still flourishing. Fārābī does not say why, but he is quoted to the effect[1] that 'it was transferred from Alexandria to Antioch, and kept there for a long period, until there was only one man to teach it. Two others studied with him, one was from Ḥarrān [Carrhae] and the other from Marw. . . .'[2] After a stay in his home town, the first went to teach in Baghdad. The second also eventually left Persia for the same destination; and Fārābī studied Greek philosophy under a pupil of the latter by the name of Ibn Ḥailān. The chief route of Greek learning, however, led through the Christian

[1] Cf. Meyerhof: *Von Alexandria nach Baghdad.*

[2] I. A. Uṣaibī'a, Vol. 2, p. 135.

communities of Syria and northern 'Irāq. In opposition to the pagan origin of the school of Alexandria and in imitation of it, Eustathius, Bishop of Antioch, founded a school there not long after the Council of Nicea in A.D. 325. The language of the Church was Greek and religious problems were debated in that language with the support of classical learning and philosophy, thus making it a Hellenizing institution.[1] And soon after, Bishop Jacob founded a school at Nisibis. It was headed by St Ephraim, a noted poet and theologian in Syriac. Because of political uncertainties, it was later transferred to Edessa, capital of Osrohene, and since the second century centre of Christianity in 'Irāq.[2] The institution became known as the school of the Persians, perhaps because the students and teachers were mostly from that country.

The schism which broke up the Eastern Church into Orthodox or State Church, Jacobite or Monophysite, and Nestorian, had important literary consequences for the Aramean world. Although Syriac translators from the Greek had been active even before the schism, the Nestorians, to break away from the other two Churches, helped the development of the Syriac language by the translation of many important works, including those of Aristotle, Hippocrates and Galen, as well as writings by the Christian Fathers, thereby stimulating if not actually originating that movement, until it was superseded by the more virile and resourceful Arabic. Their centres were at Nisibis, Edessa Seleucia on Tigris and Gundīshāpūr, not to mention minor places; while those of the Monophysites were Alexandria, Antioch and Amida. It was from these towns and from their convents that some Syriacs moved to Baghdad to teach and to translate Greek classical learning into their mother-tongue and into Arabic. To them must be added a few notable translators from the Sabean community of Ḥarrān who rendered valuable services particularly in the translation of Greek mathematical texts into Arabic.

[1] Cf. Matter: *Histoire de l'École d'Alexandrie*; Barhadsabba 'Arbaya: *Cause de la Fondation des Écoles*.

[2] Cf. Hayes: *L'École d'Édesse*.

There was still another route to which some reference has already been made above. Although one scholar has entertained doubts, it is hardly disputable that Ibn al-Muqaffa' did translate some parts of Aristotle's *Organon* from the Persian (presumably in its Pahlawi form). And Ibn al-Qifṭī calls him 'the first person in the Islamic nation to occupy himself with the translation of the Logic books for Abū Ja'far al-Manṣūr . . .';[1] then proceeds to specify and enumerate them. It has not yet been established whether the two manuscripts so far traced, and purporting to be an abstract of some of the books of the Aristotelian *Organon*, are by him or his son.[2] Various sources have testified to the acquaintance of some of the Sāsānian kings of Persia and particularly Chosroes I (531–578) with the works of Plato and Aristotle;[3] the Syriac version of the treatise[4] which Paulos Persa wrote for him on the logic of the Stagirite, as well as a Latin rendering of Chosroes' discussions with Priscianus, the Greek philosopher who had sought refuge at his court, have remained.[5]

Yet another route by which Greek learning reached Baghdad and the Islamic world was by way of the medico-philosophical school of Gundīshāpūr in southern Persia. This institution had very much declined by the time of the early 'Abbāsid Caliphs; but the names of the many physicians who left it to settle in the capital of the new Empire, and who attained considerable wealth and renown, have been recorded.

If these were the routes, the *Kitāb al-Fihrist* composed in 987 gives us valuable information about the extent to which Greek learning was rendered into Arabic. Source-book for almost all our knowledge of the works written and translated in Baghdad, whether from Syriac, Greek, Persian or Indian, it shows that Greek scientific, medical and philosophical writings were far more

[1] *Tārīkh al-Ḥukamā'*, p. 220.

[2] The Mashhad copy is in the name of himself, and the Beirut copy in that of his son.

[3] Cf. Agathias: *Patrologia Graeca*, Vol. 88, Col. 1389.

[4] Land: *Anecdoton Syriacorum*, Vol. IV.

[5] Edit. Bywater: *Supplementum Aristotelium*, Vol. 1, p. 2.

appreciated and studied than the purely literary, such as poetry and tragedy.

The currents of orthodox and Mu'tazelite religious thought are explained by the fact that the *Falāsifa*[1] were true Muslims even though unable to subscribe to all the dogmas expounded by the theologians of the time; and themselves had received a thorough training in the tenets of their Faith. Furthermore their fundamental problem—sometimes called the scholastic problem—was the reconciliation of religion and philosophy. It was therefore only natural and necessary for them to devote equal attention to the often conflicting principles of the two disciplines. The significance of the term *kalām*, as denoting theological speculation, may be disputed; and the name Mu'tazila for those who professed 'a state intermediate between two states'[2] may not be quite clear; but their religious views became the official theology of the 'Abbāsids for a hundred years, and had considerable influence on the climate of thought at the time. The Caliph al-Ma'mūn infuriated orthodoxy by publicly joining them. Although these were intellectually inclined, and attempted to explain all things rationally, they were neither philosophers, nor free-thinkers, nor always very liberal; they were good theologians. Nevertheless their influence proved profound and widespread.

As regards Stoic, Neo-Platonic and other currents in Islamic philosophy, it should not be supposed that it is always easy to detect them. The *Fihrist* attests to the fact that such works were translated into Arabic, and that justifies the supposition in doubtful cases that these influences were in fact operative. Very often there is no direct link between the two, yet the traces seem undeniable.

* * * *

With Ḥunain (Ioanitus) as the central and dominating figure,[3]

[1] It applies to all those who followed the Greek discipline as distinct from the religious.

[2] Cf. Nallino: *R.S.O.*, Vol. VII, pp. 429 ff.

[3] Cf. *Fihrist*, p. 298.

the professional translators, most of whom were Christians, fall into three groups. There was first the pre-Ḥunain school; second, the school of Ḥunain, his relatives and pupils; and third the post-Ḥunain school. The nature of their activities may be deduced from a valuable report by Ḥunain on the translation of the works of Galen.[1] In this we find that there had been cases of:

translations from Greek into Syriac;
translations from Greek into Arabic;
translations from Syriac into Arabic;
translations from Arabic into Syriac;
separate translations of the same work by different persons;
separate translations of the same work by the same person;
revision of previous translations by their authors or by others;
translations by one person into both Syriac and Arabic of the same or different works;
translations by different persons of different parts of the same work;
some translations remaining incomplete due to the absence of the necessary texts.

He further informs us that in Alexandria there were daily meetings at which a specific book of Galen was carefully studied and discussed. And that in Baghdad the Christians were in the habit of copying that practice, and meeting every day in their school which bore the Syriac name of Eskol, an adaptation of the Greek *scholé*.

Another document[2] establishes the fact that they had for aid suitable compilations in the form of *instruments de travail*; among them were lexicons called by the Persian name of *Chahār Nām* which, as the title implies, gave equivalents in the four languages more often employed in their work, viz. Greek, Syriac, Arabic and Persian. And it may be assumed that at least some of the translators were proficient in all four. They also had glossaries

[1] Cf. Bergstrasser: *Hunayn . . . über die syrische und arabischen Galen-übersetzungen.*

[2] Bērūnī: *Kitāb al-Ṣaidana*, edit. Meyerhof.

for special books 'covering strange words and the explanation of the difficult among them.'

The list of their translations is enumerated in three Arabic source-books[1] of great value. And their careful collation of different copies of the text, their faithfulness to the original, and their painstaking effort to find suitable equivalents have won the admiration of modern scholars.[2] In some cases they could be used to correct present-day Greek texts the originals of which reached the West by way of Constantinople. But they blundered also, and lamentably sometimes. In the translation of Aristotle's *Poetics*, tragedy was thought to be panegyric poetry, and comedy was understood as invective; with the result that none of the Islamic commentators, even centuries afterwards, ever realized that tragedy and comedy are acted on a stage. They considered them parts of logic and studied them together with rhetoric. The actor[3] was in one rendering translated 'the hypocrite' (*al-munāfiq*), and in another 'the taker of faces.' And Avicenna speaks in despair of 'this thing they call the taking of faces.'

The literary value of the Arabic versions varies. The cultural background of the translators could be Greek, Syriac, Arabic or Persian, and they could be more influenced by one of these languages than by the other. There were those who knew no Greek at all and translated only from Syriac. The Arabic style of Ḥunain was accepted with some reluctance, while that of Quwairī was declared dreadfully complicated and unnecessarily involved. The same applies to terminology which was of course more important because of its adoption by their successors. In the Paris manuscript of the Arabic translation of the *Organon* there are three different renderings of the *Sophistics*; and a comparative study of their terms has produced some very interesting results.[4]

1 Al-Nadīm: *Al-Fihrist*, edit. Fluegel, 2 vols.
Ibn al-Qifṭī: *Tārikh al-Ḥukamā'*, edit. Lippert.
Ibn Abī Uṣaibi'a: *Ṭabaqāt al-Aṭibbā'*, edit. Muller, 2 vols.

2 Cf. R. Walzer: *The Arabic Translations of Aristotle, Oriens*, 1953.

3 ὑποκχριτής.

4 Cf. C. Haddad, O.P.: *Thèse presentée a la Sorbonne*, 1953.

Among the pre-Ḥunain group we have the case of Usṭāth, about whom very little is known except that he was a contemporary and associate of Kindī. His version of a large part of the *Metaphysica* of Aristotle has survived in a commentary of Averroës.[1] Arabic sources speak of him as a mediocre translator; and yet historically his work is worthy of note because his terms sometimes differ from those of the Ḥunain school which were later adopted by the *Falāsifa*. We find these in the writings of his friend Kindī, and curiously enough in the history of Ya'qūbī. He may well have been the originator of some of the neologisms that shocked Arab purists and delighted the followers of the new school of writing. The terms *annīya* and *huwīyya*,[2] we believe, were coined by him.

Of all the translators none attained greater renown and had more works to his credit than Ḥunain (d. 873). He had the good fortune to have a gifted son who not only shared his interests but surpassed him in ability; and another close relative and numerous pupils all devoted to the task of translating Greek and Syriac books. But he had the ill-fortune to incur the displeasure of his Church, and was eventually excommunicated and forced to choose suicide. In him are united all the four traditions already referred to. Arab sources claim that he was the most proficient of his time in Greek, Syriac and Persian; and had a command of these languages that none of the other translators could equal. He constantly endeavoured to improve his Arabic, which was not particularly strong. His son came to write much better and was more appreciated by the Arabs. The terminology of Ḥunain's renderings, and that of his son and pupils, is very important. Though sometimes different from that of his predecessors, it was adopted by almost all the *Falāsifa* who helped to establish it as the technical language of philosophy. After Kindī, who was still attached to the earlier school, the terms of Ḥunain are invariably employed by those writing in Arabic. And today, after the lapse

[1] Averroës: *Tafsīr ma ba'd al-Ṭabī'a*, edit. Bouyges.

[2] Greek *τό τί ἦν εἶναι* and *τό εἶναι* respectively.

of centuries, they still constitute the basis of all books on logic, metaphysics, and even psychology. In spite of the fact that there is very little originality in them, and that it may be doubted whether he himself coined a single new term, they are universally accepted. It is otherwise in the case of medical works. There he was often obliged to use Syriac and Persian terms for lack of an Arabic equivalent.

On the whole, early versions abound in transcriptions from Greek. Whenever the translator is in a difficulty and cannot find an Arabic word suitable to the context of the treatise, he gives the original Greek term. Among later translators we find the transcription side by side with a tentative translation whenever the writer is in doubt. And lastly come those who give a definite Arabic equivalent of their own, or a term borrowed from some literary author, for every Greek expression. Very often Syriac is made use of in an Arabized form. Even among these there is very little linguistic boldness, and hardly any coining; and when not using a Qur'anic or classical term, they show a decided inclination to benefit from the writings of some celebrated stylist. This is why so many of the words found in the *Kalīla wa Dimna* of Ibn al-Muqaffa', are met with in the translation of Greek philosophical writing. None of the translators was a pure Arab sure of his language and with the courage to coin new expressions. The Arabs themselves were not interested in linguistic innovations and frequently showed marked disapproval of neologisms. Among some of the *Falāsifa*, and especially with Fārābī, we find two alternative renderings of the same Greek term used together as synonyms; for the simple reason that the author not knowing Greek could not make the proper choice, and preferred to give both terms. It may also be noted that there is a slight difference in style and terminology between books translated directly from Greek and those translated first into Syriac. The translation of mathematical works, associated with the people of Ḥarrān, among whom was the highly competent Thābit ibn Qurra, needed a different terminology; but they succeeded in overcoming this difficulty, and were notably successful in their choice of terms.

* * * *

The field of Islamic philosophy is dominated by three figures: Kindī, an Arab; Fārābī, a Turk, and Avicenna, a Persian. The *Falāsifa* stand in sharp contrast to religious thinkers such as Ghazālī and Ibn Taimīya, to philosophers of history as Ibn Khaldūn, and to those who were primarily commentators like Averroës and his Andalusian school.

Of the works of Kindī, a pure Arab of princely lineage, born in Kūfa (middle of the ninth century A.D.) where his father was governor, educated in Baṣra and Baghdad, and a member of the Mu'tazelites, regrettably little has survived. The source-books[1] quote over two hundred titles but what remains fills two small volumes.[2] A man of means associating with Caliphs and Amirs, he was in close touch with the early translators and may well have supported some of them. 'He was famous in the Islamic nation for his profound knowledge of the Greek, Persian and Indian arts of wisdom, and he was an expert astronomer.'[3] He became known as 'the philosopher of the Arabs,' but it is not certain that he had many pupils or formed a school of his own.

From the list of his works it may be inferred that he was most interested in the natural sciences though he also left treatises on Logic and Metaphysics. Like Plato he was devoted to mathematics and wrote a book entitled *In that Philosophy cannot be Attained except by way of Mathematics*.

Some early Arabic sources have stressed that Kindī was the first to introduce Aristotelian thought into the Islamic system. Whether that can be taken as a fact or not, there is no doubt that in the field of secular thought as distinct from religious speculation, he is the first of the *Falāsifa* to be deeply influenced

[1] *Fihrist*, pp. 255 ff.; Qifṭī, pp. 366 ff.; I. A. Uṣaibi'a, Vol. 1, pp. 206 ff.

[2] *Rasā'il al-Kindī al-Falsafiya*, edit. Abū Raida, Cairo, Vol. 1, 1950. Vol. 2, 1953.

[3] Qifṭī, p. 367.

by the Stagirite, and is the author of a treatise still extant *On the Number of the Works of Aristotle and those Necessary to the Study of Philosophy.*[1] There is no reason to believe that, as has often been asserted, Kindī translated Greek works into Arabic. Admittedly his terminology differs sometimes from that of the *Falāsifa* who followed him, but that is only because he was using the versions of Usṭāth to whom reference has already been made, whereas his successors used the versions of Ḥunain and his school. The new terms[2] thought to have been coined by him are actually those chosen by Usṭāth.

But there is also Platonic thought in Kindī. His cosmology owes a great deal to the *Timaeus* and his theory of the soul is derived from the *Phaedo*—a book deeply appreciated by Islamic thinkers. He may have been the first in Islam to be inspired by the personality of Socrates on whose exemplary life he is supposed to have written some treatises.[3] His mathematical writings are based on the Neo-Pythagorean principles which he considered the fundamentals of all the sciences. His theory of the intellect has been traced back to Alexander of Aphrodisias, and in true Neo-Platonic fashion he felt he could combine Plato with Aristotle.

Two books proved to be most confusing elements in Islamic philosophy, and Kindī was associated with one of them. The first was a work that became known as the *Theology* of Aristotle,[4] though it was actually parts of the *Enneads* of Plotinus (Books IV–VI). This was translated by Ibn Nā'ima, and Kindī probably helped him in polishing up the Arabic. The other work was what the Occident called *Liber de Causis*,[5] actually comprising parts of the *Elementatio Theologica* of Proclus. With occasional doubts, as will be seen, it was throughout believed that they were both by the Stagirite; and in this manner Neo-Platonic thought was unknowingly introduced into Islamic philosophy.

Kindī's treatises on logic have been lost, but we have a short essay on the intellect (*'aql*) which was translated into mediaeval

1 Edit. Abū Raida, Vol. 1, pp. 362 ff.   2 Ex.: '*aisa, aisīyya; laisa, laisīyya.*'
3 *Fihrist*, p. 260.   4 Edit. Dieterici.   5 Edit. Bardenhewer.

Latin under the title of *De Intellectu et Intellecto*. In this he proceeds to discuss the intellect and its varieties according to what he supposes to have been the opinion of the early Greeks and also of Plato and Aristotle 'the most esteemed of them.'[1] He then goes on to state that in the view of Aristotle intellect may be divided into four kinds. There is first the intellect that is always *in actu*; second comes the intellect that is *in potentia*; third is the intellect that has passed in the soul from a potential to an active state. And towards the end of his essay he speaks of the fourth kind which he says is apparent (*ẓāhir*)[2] in the soul once it has appeared in the active state.

This short treatise exemplifies problems typical of many passages of Islamic philosophical writing. The fourfold division of the intellect is not to be found in the *De Anima* of Aristotle and scholars have searched in vain for its source. One distinguished author[3] has claimed that it comes from the *De Anima* of Alexander of Aphrodisias, but there the division is threefold only. The fact is that Islamic philosophers made much use of Peripatetic and Stoic commentaries on Plato and Aristotle and very often what they thought was genuine Platonic or Aristotelian thought was actually the interpretation or the personal opinion of some commentator. They were particularly well acquainted with the works of Themistius of which Arabic translations have recently begun to be found and studied. Another difficulty is that whenever an attempt is made to put a particular passage from Arabic into some European language it is found that it often defies translation altogether, and when scholars have taken it upon themselves to infer the original Greek of some Arabic philosophical term without reference to the actual translation on which the *Falāsifa* worked, they have fallen into serious errors. The 'apparent intellect' (*al-'aql al-Ẓāhir*) of Kindī is a typical example. What could the original Greek be?

[1] *Rasā'il*, Vol. 1, p. 353. [2] Scholastic '*demonstrativum*.'

[3] Cf. Gilson: *Les Sources gréco-arabes de l'Augustinisme avicennisant. Archives d'Histoire doctrinale et littéraire du Moyen Âge*. Paris, Vol. IV, 1929.

Kindī's treatise on Metaphysics—the longest of his extant writings, and addressed to one of the 'Abbāsid Caliphs—is important because it deals with one of the main themes of Islamic philosophy. Aristotle had said that the world was eternal, whereas the *Mutakallemūn* (Loquentes) vehemently protested that it was created *ex nihilo* by an act of the Almighty. How to reconcile these two conflicting views expressed in the terms *qadīm* (old, eternal) and *muḥdath* (created)?

Metaphysics he calls 'the highest in honour and rank . . . because the science dealing with the cause is more honourable than the science dealing with the caused,'[1] and this is typical of the attitude of all the *Falāsifa*. He pays tribute to 'philosophers before us not of our tongue. . . . We should not be timid in praising truth and in seeking it, from wherever it may come, even if it be from distant races and people different from us.'[2] This marks the dawn of the true scientific spirit in Islamic philosophy and is perhaps its first enunciation. 'We maintain in this our book our custom . . . to recall what the ancients have said . . . and to amplify what they have not discussed conclusively . . . to the extent to which we are capable . . . avoiding the interpretations of those . . . who trade in religion and have none of it themselves, for he who trades in something sells it, and he who sells something loses it . . . for the true prophets, upon whom may God's benediction rest, came only to confess the divinity of God, and the necessity of those virtues pleasing unto Him . . . man's existence is twofold . . . a sensual and an intellectual existence.'[3]

With these introductory remarks, Kindī enters into the discussion. Contrary to the views of Aristotle, he argues at length to show that Time and Movement are not eternal and infinite for 'Time is the period of the existence of a thing so long as it exists,' and again in an early Latin translation 'Tempus ergo est numerus numerans motum.'[4] If Time and Movement are not infinite, and creation is only a form of Movement, then the world cannot be

[1] *Rasā'il*, Vol. 1, p. 101.
[2] *Ibid.*, Vol. 1, p. 103.
[3] *Ibid.*, Vol. 1, pp. 103–4.
[4] *Ibid.*, Vol. 2, p. 35.

eternal either. It must have had a beginning and might have an end. Its beginning was in the hand of God, He created it *ex nihilo* by His own divine Will and will end it when He wills. And again in proof of God, if the world is finite it had a beginning, if it had a beginning it was created, if it was created, it must have a Creator. All caused things must have a cause and the chain of causation cannot go back indefinitely, because that would be absurd. It goes back to God who is the Primal Cause. Thus in this difficult problem he takes the religious view in opposition to Aristotle.

Kindī was known to the Mediaeval Latins; Gerhard of Cremona was among his translators and Cardan, a Renaissance philosopher, considered him one of the twelve subtlest minds.[1]

With Abū Naṣr al-Fārābī (d. 339/950–951) we enter into the field of Islamic philosophy proper. Not much more is known of him[2] than of Kindī, though more of his works have survived and his influence was much greater. Called 'the second teacher' (Aristotle being the first), he was born in Transoxiana, grandson of a pagan Turk. Educated in Baghdad, *protégé* of the Ḥamdanite dynasty in Aleppo, he wrote only in Arabic and left a valuable heritage for all Islamic thinkers after him. Modest and of a retiring nature, he was intellectually bold and tireless. He eclipsed Kindī and except for Avicenna, who was greatly indebted to him, stands foremost among the *Falāsifa*.

Fārābī was in many ways different from Kindī and has more in common with his successor. He did not belong to the same social class and although he had come in his early youth to Baghdad he was always known as a Turk. He did not share Kindī's particular admiration for Socrates nor was he very much inclined towards mathematics and the natural sciences. Ibn al-Qifṭī[3] calls him 'the unrivalled philosopher of the Muslims' while Ibn Taimīya calls him 'the greatest of the *Falāsifa* in the exposition

[1] Cf. Gilson: *La Philosophie au Moyen Âge*; 2nd edit., Paris, 1944.

[2] Cf. *Fihrist*, pp. 248, 263, 264; also Brockelmann: *G.A.L.*, Vol. 1, pp. 210 ff.; *Supp.*, Vol. 1, pp. 375 ff.

[3] P. 277.

of Logic and its branches.'[1] Andalusian commentators also regarded him as a great logician, but unfortunately very little of his work on that subject has survived, though there are already traces of Stoic logic, which were to become more marked in Avicenna.

In thought Fārābī is not lacking in originality. His was a very suggestive restatement of the speculative thought of his day, with all the different influences that were shaping it. Yet there is nothing new or peculiar in his terminology; it is that established by the Ḥunain school, and there is no evidence that he knew any Greek. As his language includes terms associated with the theologians, the mystics, and the Isma'īlī heterodoxy, we may presume that he was familiar with their literature. His intellectual background is wholly Islamic, but he is far better informed than Kindī about Greek philosophy in both its classical and its Hellenistic form. His is a more comprehensive attempt to reconcile religion with philosophy. He considers the personality of a prophet as a social and intellectual leader, apart from his spiritual mission, and he shows a strong interest in political science.

If Islamic philosophy is by nature synthetic when compared to the analytical method employed by the Greeks of the classical age, it is also theocentric in contrast to the anthropocentric conceptions of the Athenian thinkers. Both trends are distinctly reflected in the systematic speculations of Fārābī, for whom philosophy had two sides, one religious and the other secular, with no fundamental opposition between the two. There was also, he thought, an agreement on essentials; and where there is an apparent divergence, it is only due to our faulty understanding. To demonstrate that principle, he wrote a whole treatise to prove the complete agreement and unity of thought between 'Plato the godly, and Aristotle.'[2] The Neo-Platonists before him had done the same. There is nothing in the world with which philosophy is not concerned, he claimed. By contrast with Plato, the method

[1] *Al-Radd 'ala al-Manṭiqīyīn*, p. 41.

[2] Cf. *Alfarabi's Philos. Abhand*, edit. Dieterici.

which Aristotle chose involved observation, classification, clarification and exposition, all conducted with remarkable insight into the nature of things. The commentators, Fārābī thought, helped us to understand Aristotle better, and among those whom he mentions are Ammonius, Themistius and Porphyry. On the vexing question of the eternity of the world, however, he tries to show that Aristotle never really meant that the world was eternal; adding—and here comes the source of confusion already referred to—'he who looks into his statements on the Deity in the book known as the *Theology*, will not fail to understand his position, and his proof for an original creator of this world.' He was thus asserting that a creation must have an original creator, as the theologians insisted.

God as the efficient cause was the originator of all things. He is the One and the True. Fārābī proceeds to quote from Plato's *Timaeus* and *Politeia*, as well as from Book Lambda of Aristotle's *Metaphysica*, what he regards as proofs for the existence of God as the first cause. But his chief source is always the *Theology*. Some had had doubts with regard to the authenticity of this work. Fārābī confidently asserts that it is not true that only some parts of it are by Aristotle, whilst others are not. Avicenna, however, was among the doubters,[1] though he nevertheless continued to make full use of it, in spite of its obvious disagreement with other writings of the Stagirite.

The contribution of Platonism to Islamic thought was certainly not inconsiderable, though it still awaits careful assessment; but Aristotle soon became the chief guide and continued so ever after. The nature of his writings and their subject-matter helped to give him that paramount influence. His logic and his metaphysics supplied a great want; and his natural philosophy was a source of information unobtainable elsewhere. His doctrine of the eternal nature of Time, Movement and the world was indeed a stumbling-block, though attempts were made to explain it away by some of the passages of the *Theology*, as has been said. Plato,

[1] Cf. Badawī: *Arisṭū 'ind al-'Arab*, p. 121.

on the other hand, held some very attractive and congenial views, especially on the immortality of the soul. Nevertheless he seemed to the Islamic thinkers to be occupied with aspects of human life which properly belonged to the domain of religion. For them it was God and not man who is the measure of all things. The *Republic* was studied, and much was borrowed from it, but Aristotle was in general preferred.

Like Kindī, Fārābī devotes a whole treatise[1] to the various meanings of the term Intellect. It is often used, he thinks, without properly specifying the sense intended. According to him, Intellect could have six possible meanings. First there is the intellect the common man has in mind when he says somebody is intelligent; second is the intellect the theologians speak of; third is the intellect that Aristotle discusses in the *Analytica Priora*; and fourth is the intellect he expounds in the sixth book of the *Ethics*. Fifth is the intellect he analyses in the *De Anima*; and sixth is the intellect he mentions in his *Metaphysica*. It should not be supposed that this list is meant as a strict classification by Fārābī; it is rather a set of illustrations of the different meanings that can be given to the word intellect, and he explains each in some detail. Curiously enough when he reaches the fifth sense of the term, he remarks that 'the intellect which Aristotle mentions in the book on the soul [*De Anima*], he makes of four modes, an intellect *in potentia*, another *in actu*, an acquired intellect, and an active intellect.' So here we meet again the fourfold division found in Kindī and the problem of how it entered Arabic philosophy.

Intellect is, however, distinct from the soul which is an entity entirely separate from the body, yet—contrary to Plato—it could not have existed before it, nor can it transmigrate by metempsychosis which is a conception abhorrent to the Islamic mind. In accordance with the views of Aristotle, he teaches that the soul has parts and faculties through which it acts and that these parts and faculties form a single soul. It is the human soul that is endowed with the reasonable faculty and it is this that is respon-

[1] *Risālat fī al-'Aql*, edit. Bouyges.

sible for our acts of cerebration. Hence intellect is one of the faculties of the rational soul.

In expounding his metaphysics, Fārābī raises two points which were to be developed by Avicenna who made it the basis of his own thought and connected it with his proof of the existence of God, whom he calls the necessary being. First is the division of all beings into two kinds. One kind, upon contemplation of itself, finds that its existence does not follow necessarily; so it is called a possible being. The other kind when it reflects upon and considers its own self, finds that its being is duly necessitated; so it is called a necessary being. This division is found in a treatise[1] so similar in style and context to the writings of Avicenna that he may well be its author: just as another work commonly attributed to Fārābī has been proved to be by his successor.[2] Second is the distinction among created things between their essence and their existence which differ from one another as different entities. Only in God do they become identical. None of these two points, however, should be over-emphasized in Fārābī's system, as has sometimes been done. They do not constitute a fundamental element in his speculations, and it is not until we reach Avicenna that they become metaphysical essentials and play the role of an ontological distinction of great significance.

The most representative work of Fārābī that we now have is his *Ideas of the Inhabitants of the Virtuous City*.[3] It is one of the very few books in Islamic philosophy to be directly inspired by and modelled on the *Republic* of Plato; nevertheless it is not wholly Platonic in substance. As will be seen, there is plenty of Aristotelian and Plotinian thought intermixed. Nor is the influence of the commentators entirely absent. Fārābī begins by enunciating a form of theodicy rather than advancing proofs for the existence of God. The first being is the first cause, and the creator of all other beings. It is he who gives them existence. He is different

[1] *'Uyūn al-Masā'il.*

[2] *Fuṣūs al-Ḥikam.* Cf. Pines: *Rev. Et. Islam*, 1951.

[3] Edit. Dieterici.

in substance from all others besides himself. He has no opposite; it is in fact impossible that he should have one. He cannot be defined, because he is not divisible into elements constituting his substance. His oneness is his actual essence. He is the knowing and the wise, and the true and the living and the life. He is not corporeal, and does not reside in matter. In essence he is an intelligence *in actu*. And as such he is the first from whom being proceeds. From the being that is his due other beings proceed necessarily. His existence is not governed by the will of man nor by his choice. He transcends all and everything. But how and in what manner do other beings proceed from him? Here Fārābī maintains that it is by way of emanation (*faiḍ*) from God's own essence that all existent things come to be. And the process is not direct but takes place through successive stages until it reaches this sublunary world of ours.

Thus Fārābī develops his theory of emanation clearly along Neo-Platonic lines, though differing in some details. From the first being there emanate successively ten different intellects or intelligences; and from each of these when 'substantially constituted in its proper essence,' there results a sphere. The intelligences are absolutely incorporeal substances and in no way reside in matter. And the spheres that come into being from them are: the first sphere, the sphere of the fixed stars, the sphere of Saturn, the sphere of Jupiter, the sphere of Mars, the sphere of the Sun, the sphere of Venus, the sphere of Mercury, and the sphere of the Moon. This comprises all the beings that in order to exist in this fashion have no need whatever of matter in which to reside. They are separate beings, intelligences and intelligibles in their substance. And the sphere of the Moon is the last of those in which heavenly bodies move by nature in a circle. From the Moon there proceeds a pure intelligence called 'the active intelligence' which bridges the gap between heaven and earth. We thus have God as the First Being, a species by himself, governed by the principle of complete unity. From him emanate the ten intelligences with their nine spheres as a second species of being which represent plurality. Then comes the active intelligence as a third, and none of these species are corporeal themselves. Finally, in the last stage come Soul, Form and Matter. There have been many modern attempts[1] to trace the origin of this theory of the ten intelligences to Christianity, Mazdaism, Manichaeism, Sabeism, Ismā'īlī doctrines and various others, but no conclusive proofs have emerged.

Fārābī, though strongly inclined towards mysticism and himself an ascetic, also touched upon two subjects that reveal a more practical turn of mind. Unfortunately his commentary on the *Nicomachean Ethics* has been lost and we have no clear idea of his views on morals and human conduct; but he elaborates at length a theory of prophetism, and politics and State organization. In these he was much influenced by the *Republic* and perhaps by some Isma'īlī doctrines. Society, he thought, was composed of the common class and the *élite*. The common class are those who confine themselves, or are led to confine themselves in their theoretical knowledge, to what the initiator of public opinion requires. This division, so modern in its application, constitutes an entirely new conception in Islamic political thought and State administration. The whole idea is novel, and the function of an initiator of public opinion (*bādī al-ra'y al-mushtarak*)[2] as a counterpart to *consensus omnium* (*ijmā'*) is to our knowledge not found anywhere in Islamic literature before him. This is an interesting point that has not been noted so far. The qualifications of the head of the Virtuous City, whom he calls the *Imām*, are described along the lines of those required for Plato's philosopher-king. He should be well versed in the science of the intelligibles, while the public is to be taught 'by methods of persuasion and imagination.' The terms philosopher, first head, king, lawgiver and Imām all mean the same because they represent different functions of the same individual.

Fārābī's classification of the sciences[3] was translated into Latin

[1] Cf. Madkour: *La Place d'al-Farabi.*

[2] *Taḥṣil al-Sa'āda.* [3] *Iḥṣā' al-'ulūm*, edit. Amīn.

and widely used in mediaeval Europe; and various scholars have traced his influence upon Scholasticism. His treatise on music[1] has been called the most important Oriental work on the theory of that art. And yet in spite of many modern attempts, it seems difficult to arrive at a proper general estimation of his contributions to Islamic philosophy. Not until the Arabic translations of different Peripatetic and Stoic commentaries are traced and studied, can we with certainty determine in how far his ideas were original. His position in the Islamic world was undisputed for centuries after him; and an eminent theologian of much later times confidently asserts that he was 'the leader of the philosophers.' What is not clear is whether he founded a school of his own, and what particular aspect of his thought had most appeal for the men of his time.

One of Fārābī's contemporaries chose to take a different path. Rāzī, known to the Europeans as Rhazes[2] and considered 'the greatest clinical genius amongst the physicians of the Islamic world,' was also an independent thinker bent on speculation, and fearless in the expression of his views. Born in Raiy (Rhages), a poet, singer and musician in his early youth, he left Persia to study medicine in Baghdad, and stayed long enough to become the head of a hospital there. He then returned to his native country where he won both fame and notoriety before he died blind from cataract.

Very few of his philosophical works, which were numerous, have survived complete; and what remains are fragments, some gleaned from the books of his detractors.[3] It is therefore difficult to form a proper estimate and say with certainty whether he developed a coherent system of his own. He took the then unusual step of championing the cause of Plato against Aristotle. He expressed strong disapproval of the latter, and blamed him for parting company from his master, and for 'corrupting philosophy

[1] Cf. Baron d'Erlanger: *Grand Traité de la Musique.*
[2] Abū Bakr Muḥammad ibn Zakarīa al-Rāzī (d. 925 or 935).
[3] Cf. Nāṣir Khosrow: *Zād el-Musāferīn.*

and changing many of its principles.'[1] And like Kindī he had a deep admiration for Socrates, his life and teachings, calling him 'our Imām.' When people accused him of leading a worldly life himself, he answered back that Socrates had been no ascetic, and that there was no reason why *he* should be one. Socrates had even gone to fight for his country, and that is not easy to reconcile with the principles he declared.

The second and more important point on which Rāzī dissented from the views of Kindī and Fārābī, was his outspoken denial of the possibility of reconciling religion and philosophy—a theme they not only consistently maintained, but one which constituted the whole purpose of their thought. Yet he was no atheist, and we must believe his repeated invocations of the Deity, 'the bestower of intelligence'; nor was he 'the Voltaire of Islam,' as some have called him. Nevertheless his theism was not considered sufficient. He was denounced as a heretic and never gained a following.

Acquainted with the Greek Atomists, Rāzī was much influenced by Democritus. His, however, was a very different form of atomism from that which had been adopted by the Muslim theologians. His Platonic thought stemmed mostly from the *Timaeus* on which he had written a commentary. For some obscure reason he became the object of violent condemnation by Isma'īlī authors who bitterly attacked his theories of Time and Space, and his definition of pleasure.[2] Pleasure, he had said, was 'nothing but a return to the normal state.' Space, according to him, was infinite, but there is an absolute (*muṭlaq*) space which is the void, and a partial (*juz'īy*) space. In like manner there is on the one hand absolute Time, independent of the revolutions of the celestial sphere and co-existent with eternity, and on the other hand limited Time (*zamān maḥṣūr*). In this he seems to have gone contrary to the views of one of his teachers by the name of Irānshahrī, of whom practically nothing is known.[3]

[1] *Opera Philosophica*, edit. Kraus.
[2] *Ibid.*, p. 143. [3] Cf. *Albiruni's India*, ed. Sachau, pp. 252–4.

There exists an impressive list of the works of Rāzī;[1] but perhaps his most interesting theme, on which he is supposed to have written a book, was what he called the five eternal substances, viz. God, Soul, Matter, Space, and Time. The source of his theory is not clear. Some Arab authors thought that the notion originated with the Ḥarrānians; Rāzī himself claimed that it came from some early pre-Aristotelians; and Ibn Taimīya has stated that he acquired it from Democritus. The idea, however, is typical of Rāzī's unorthodox views; and it surprised and annoyed Islamic philosophers and theologians alike, providing yet another reason for condemning him. Nor had he any scruples about rejecting the metaphysics of the *Falāsifa* with its elaborate conception of successive cycles of emanation, developed under Neo-Platonic influence. While they maintained that matter (*hayūla*) had only a potential existence, he saw no reason why it should not also have an actual existence of its own.

Nor were Rāzī's political and religious views any more orthodox; and he must have deeply shocked Muslim society by his assertion that there is no necessity for prophets whatsoever; and that any man who is sufficiently endowed with intelligence can use it to fashion his own life and achieve his own salvation. Hence it is hardly surprising that although they called him the Galen of the Islamic world and studied his medical works assiduously, his philosophy evoked horror, and his non-medical works have almost entirely disappeared.[2]

Early in the tenth century, there was another philosopher of Persian extraction in Baghdad by the name of Sajistānī.[3] Because of a physical deformity he rarely appeared in public, but his home became the chief literary and intellectual meeting-place of his time. He was called the Logician, and is supposed to have written many commentaries on Aristotelian logic and kindred subjects.[4] Princes as far distant as the Sāmānids of Transoxiana addressed

[1] Cf. Bērūnī: *Risālat . . .*, edit. Kraus.
[2] Cf. *The Spiritual Physick of Rhazes*, trans. A. J. Arberry.
[3] Cf. Qazvīnī: *Abū Sulaimān Manṭiqī Sidjistānī.* [4] *Fihrist*, p. 241.

philosophical questions to him 'by the hundred.' Practically all of his works have perished. We know that he was the author of a compilation of biographical notes[1] on Greek philosophers; and extracts from this have survived in a later work that provides some useful information.[2]

If we exclude Rāzī as primarily a physician, Sajistānī may be considered the most distinguished thinker between Fārābī and Avicenna. Most of what we know about him is found in the writings of his pupil and friend Tawḥīdī; and from these accounts it appears that on the crucial point of the relation between religion and philosophy, Sajistānī took a position midway between the sanguine confidence of the *Falāsifa* that a reconciliation or synthesis is possible, and the outright repudiation of any such possibility by Rāzī. 'Philosophy is true,' he says, 'but it is in no way a part of religion; and religion is true, but it is in no way a part of philosophy. . . . One is concerned primarily with inspiration and the other with the search for truth. . . . One says "I was ordained, and taught, and told, and do not say anything from my own self"; and the other says "I saw, and observed, and approving accepted, and disapproving rejected." One says "the light of intelligence is what I seek guidance from"; and the other says "I have the light of the Creator of creatures, by its illumination I walk. . . . He who wishes to philosophize must turn his gaze away from religion; and he who chooses religion must avoid all attention to philosophy . . . and neither one destroys the other." '[3]

These statements appear in an account of a discussion between Tawḥīdī and his master over a collection of some fifty-two semi-religious, semi-philosophical essays by a group of anonymous writers that had become the talk of Baghdad. The authors were supposed to have come from Baṣra, and the book was entitled *Epistles of the Brethren of Purity*.[4] It had been placed quietly in the bookshops, presumably for free distribution, and constituted

[1] Cf. Plessner: *Beitrage . . . Islamica*, IV, p. 534–8.

[2] Baihaqī: *Tatimmat Ṣīwān al-Ḥikma.*

[3] Tawḥīdī: *Imtā'* . . ., Vol. II, pp. 18–19. [4] *Rasā'il Ikhwān al-Ṣafā*, ed. Zirgalī.

an invitation to join what was perhaps a secret fraternity of 'seekers after truth' uncommitted to any particular faith or philosophy. Tawḥīdī was among the very few who knew some of the authors personally.[1]

When questioned by one of the prominent citizens of Baghdad as to the religious faith of that member of the fraternity whom he happened to know, he replied that it was typical of that person (and apparently of his companions), that they did not officially attach themselves to any particular religion, nor join any special group. They regarded themselves as completely independent, keenly interested in everything, and free to examine all that might be said or written. They attached great importance to the principle that if Greek philosophy was properly introduced into religion, perfection would be attained. In the account of this discussion Tawḥīdī takes a copy of the epistles to his master, and Sajistānī after perusal turns to explain to his pupil that the attempt is in vain. What they had imagined they could accomplish was to introduce philosophy into religion, others had tried before them and all had failed. Nor could religion be attached to philosophy, seeing that each had its separate domain and they could never merge. Philosophy was based on logical reasoning and religion on premisses that the intelligence 'sometimes demands and sometimes allows.' He expatiates on the distinctions between the two disciplines and ends by saying: 'Where is religion, and where philosophy? Where is that which proceeds from revelation, and where that which is based on an opinion that may change . . .? The prophet is above the philosopher . . . for the prophet is delegated, and the philosopher is delegated unto him.'[2]

This collection of essays has failed to impress students of Islamic thought; and very few have taken a favourable view of it.[3] It is undoubtedly an extraordinary mixture of Greek, Persian, Islamic, Gnostic and even Indian ideas. But it should be remembered that originality was not the purpose or claim of the group.

1 *Muqābasāt*, pp. 45–51. 2 *Imtā'*, Vol. II, p. 10.

3 Cf. 'Awwa: *L'Ésprit critique des Fréres de la Pureté.*

They were avowedly eclectic, seeking a synthesis of some sort; and they put forward allegorical interpretations of some of the passages in the Qur'ān which must have deeply disturbed the orthodox. They presented their ideas in an encyclopaedic order under the various headings and in a language easy for the common man to understand, which methods upset Baghdad literary circles and caused much speculation as to the authorship of the essays. The group's recently found *Kitāb al-Jāmi'a*, supposed to be only for the initiated, has unfortunately added little to our knowledge. It is a barren and disappointing work devoid of particular interest. Historically, however, the essays are important, because they reflect far better than the writings of the *Falāsifa* the religious and intellectual ferment that was working in Baghdad under the impact of various religions, philosophies and ways of thought. It is difficult to say how much politics was involved in these tractates; but some scholars have undoubtedly gone too far in accusing the writers of deliberately subversive aims. They have, however, always been rightly associated with the Isma'īlī heterodoxy; and it is among its adherents that they were most popular. Avicenna, his father and his brother are supposed to have studied them either in the original or in a Persian translation. Modern Arabs while objecting to almost all that they assert, have nevertheless appreciated their simple style, free from artificiality, ornamentation or obscurity.

The purpose of this brief historical survey was to indicate the forces which were active in the Baghdad of the 'Abbāsid Age. Here the conquering power of religion meets the restraining discipline of rational analysis and explanation, and active minds are immediately engaged in attempts at reconciliation or synthesis. Their failures and successes are part of the history of ideas, but the problem remains perennial and has to be met in every age. Its importance is compelling for a civilization on the march, and it constitutes the *raison d'être* and the justification of Islamic philosophy, which culminates in the person of Avicenna. It is to Avicenna, then, that our attention must now be directed.

CHAPTER I

PERSIA IN THE TENTH CENTURY

THE age of Avicenna differed from that of Kindī and Fārābī. When the Umayyad Caliphate was succeeded by the 'Abbāsid, this meant a continuation of Arab rule; and when literature and learning deserted Damascus to flourish as never before in Baghdad, they were developed in the language of the conquerors and of the new Faith. But tenth-century Persia was to witness a change in the political scene and the re-emergence of prose and poetry in its own tongue. Kindī and Fārābī were the products of the golden era of Arabic; and Avicenna belonged, in time if not in sentiment, to an historical period and a national phenomenon known as the Persian Renaissance. Nevertheless the fundamental problems of Islamic philosophy persisted—the needs and purposes having remained the same.

Decline had set in over the 'Abbāsid Caliphate; and the weakening of central control was encouraging the rise of local dynasties in regions that had indeed never been very submissive. The Persians, who had suffered a stunning defeat at the hand of the Arab conquerors, were gradually recovering and the time seemed auspicious. The awakening of the new spirit was not at first widespread and sustained; and the original impulse may have come from the personal ambition of local commanders who found it expedient to exploit the sense of frustration of a people who, though devoutly Muslims, had never forgotten their ancient heroic history.

The first to establish their authority, preserving only a nominal allegiance to the Caliph, were the Ṭāhirids in Khurāsān who reigned some sixty-five years, from 809 to 873 (194–259 A.H.). They were of Arab extraction, but in time had become thoroughly

Persianized. 'It is a matter of common observation that settlers in a country, often after comparatively brief residence, outdo those native to the soil in patriotic feeling.'[1] From their capital at Nīshāpūr, and with two other provinces annexed, their rule extended eastward as far as the frontiers of India.

During this period there was a revolt against the Caliph in Ṭabaristān. This region which, as the name implies, is 'the Mountain Land' along the south coast of the Caspian, was under Zoroastrian *ispahbuds* long after the conquest of Persia and the extinction of the Sāsānians. The last Persian rulers there were the Qārinids who claimed descent from the national hero, the Blacksmith. The first Qārinid had successfully raised a combined army of local chiefs against the army of the Caliphs, and had then been defeated and carried to Baghdad; but on his return he had resumed his independent attitude. Now his grandson, Māzyār, was raising the standard of revolt both against the Caliph and against his personal enemies, the Ṭāhirids.[2] Attacked from two directions, and betrayed by his supporters, he was captured, carried to Baghdad, and died in Sāmarra in 839 (224 A.H.).

It was left to a humble coppersmith to revive the true spirit of independence among the Persians. Ya'qūb the son of Laith, known to his people as al-Ṣaffār (the Coppersmith), a man of 'unknown antecedents,'[3] founded a dynasty which, though short-lived, extended its rule over the greater part of Persia and almost as far as Baghdad.[4] From Sīstān, his place of origin, Ya'qūb marched triumphantly from one province to another, and in the year 873 took captive the last of the Ṭāhirids, thereby becoming master of a vast realm. His conquests gave him confidence, and he began openly to defy the Caliph. At the head of an army he marched towards Baghdad with the intention of deposing him and installing another Caliph in his place. But his camp was

[1] Browne: *A Literary History of Persia*, Vol. 1, p. 346.
[2] Cf. Ṭabari: *The Reign of al-Mu'taṣim*, trans. Marin, pp. 85–107.
[3] Cf. *Zain al-Akhbār*, edit. Nāẓim.
[4] Cf. Barthold: *Zur Geschichte der Saffariden, Nöldeke Festschrift*.

flooded with the waters of the Tigris; a considerable part of his army perished helplessly; and he had to retreat to Gundīshāpūr, where he died, unrepentant, in 879. When his brother and successor was finally defeated by the Sāmānids in 900, the dynasty practically ceased to exist. It had nevertheless succeeded in reviving the national feeling that had languished for so long; and had helped to detach permanently the history of Persia from that of the 'Abbāsids of Baghdad.

The Persian Renaissance, however, was more closely connected with the court of the Sāmānids, who rose rapidly to power in Transoxiana, and made Bukhārā their capital.[1] The dynasty was founded by a certain Sāmān Khudāt, a Persian Zoroastrian converted to Islam by the Arab governor. It was soon able to defeat the Ṣaffārids and to extend the frontiers of its rule from the Jaxartes almost to Baghdad, and from the Caspian to the borders of India. This dynasty reigned for a period of over a hundred years, and its members were distinguished by a liberality that made them famous throughout Central Asia. The name of the father of the dynasty is usually interpreted as 'the lord of the village of Sāmān,' but *sāmān* also means frontier; and so their ancestor may well have been the warden of that frontier region between Persia and Chinese Turkistan which produced some of the most celebrated poets, theologians and philosophers, including Avicenna himself. This explains why some have called them 'the Wardens of the Marches.'

Late in the tenth century, which is the period in which Avicenna was born, there were besides the Sāmānid rulers three other local dynasties in and on the eastern borders of Persia proper which were to determine many of the events of his life. In the region around the Caspian, including the rather restless Ṭabaristān, which had been one of the last strongholds of Persian nationalism and culture, the Ziyārids had seized power in 928 and established a local dynasty that endured for more than a century. Some of them were men of accomplishment and literary

[1] Cf. Narshakhī: *History of Bukhārā*.

taste who played a notable part in the promotion of learning.[1] To their west were the Būyids who were also of Persian stock and claimed descent from a renowned family; and who also reigned for over a hundred years. These grew far more powerful, conquered and controlled the whole of western Persia, and eventually took Baghdad itself in 945. The dynasty reached the height of its power under 'Alā' el-Dowleh, the great patron of scholars and poets who helped the progress of the Persian Renaissance, though along somewhat different lines from the Sāmānids at whose court creative literature and poetry were most highly appreciated. Under 'Ala 'el-Dowleh theology and jurisprudence were more in favour.

The Ghaznavid dynasty which appeared on the eastern borders of Persia and eventually succeeded in pushing back the Būyids, absorbing the Ziyārids and overthrowing the Sāmānids, was of very humble origin. It was founded by one of the Turkish slaves of the Sāmānids who had fled from Khurāsān to Ghazna and established himself there in defiance of his old masters. On his death another Turkish slave who had married his daughter was elected Amir. And it was Maḥmūd, the son of this second slave, who conquered practically the whole of Persia, and some parts of India, and proclaimed himself Sulṭān.[2] The rise of this dynasty of Turkish origin may be seen as part of the struggle that lasted many years between the Iranian and Turkish races for the mastery of that important border-land already referred to. Yet Sulṭān Maḥmūd, either out of vanity or from genuine appreciation of the arts, rendered a great service to Persian literature by gathering around him at his court most of the famous poets and scholars of the time, and generously spending some four hundred thousand *dīnārs* every year upon them. To this noble gesture he sometimes added force, and a modern author has called him, not without justification, 'the kidnapper of literary men.' His powerful dynasty reigned ruthlessly for about a hundred and fifty years

[1] Cf. Ibn Isfandiar: *History of Tabaristan*, trans. E. G. Browne.

[2] Cf. Nāẓim: *The Life and Times of Sultan Mahmud of Ghazna.*

until, as with all the others, rapid decay set in. One of the important effects of this dynasty upon literature was that it carried the use of the Persian language far towards the East, and was for many years its sole patron.

Baghdad continued to be the centre of Islamic culture in the tenth century, but the enthusiasm for the new learning—for such indeed was Greek science and philosophy—was waning. The period of the Translators had come to an end long before; and the general attitude of mind had become more sober and reserved, with even a tendency to be critical of all that was of foreign origin. There developed a violent reaction towards orthodoxy, and the Mu'tazelites were persecuted at the urgent instigation of the Caliphs. In Baghdad intellectual activity seems eventually to have come to a complete standstill; and what remained was shifting eastward, particularly in the direction of Persia and Transoxiana.

There is no reason to believe that force had been employed in the conversion of the Persians to Islam, and they had always maintained some freedom of thought. It was for that reason that there had been numerous semi-social, semi-religious movements during the first three centuries after the conquest by the Arabs of that country[1]—a sign of continuous unrest. As to literature, the Persians were using the Arabic language for all forms of literary composition—perhaps to the total exclusion of Persian. There were some Pahlawi writings that continued down to the ninth century,[2] but in the form of religious tractates, only for the use of those who had remained in the Zoroastrian fold.

The history of the Persian language and the different stages through which it has passed has yet to be written. It is not clear how and when it accepted defeat and left the literary field almost entirely to Arabic. And the accounts of its revival in its post-Islamic form are fragmentary and obscure. When the two languages came face to face after the Arab conquest of the country,

1 Cf. Sadighi: *Les Movements religieux iraniens. . . .*

2 Cf. Bailey: *Zoroastrian Problems. . . .*

Persian had an extensive literature not only in prose but, as has been lately shown, in poetry also. Arabic, on the other hand, in spite of the fact that its valuable pre-Islamic poetry was not extensive, and not all the poems that have survived from that period are authentic, and although there are hardly any traces of the early prose in whose existence some scholars believe, was the language of the conquerors and eventually became that of the administration throughout the Islamic Empire. It reflected the remarkable *élan* which was the distinguishing mark of the early Arabs, and which the Persians had long since lost. And above all it was the language of the new Faith and compulsory for all forms of prayer. It was enshrined in the Qur'ān the like of which—even considered in its purely literary aspect—Zoroastrian religious literature did not possess. Admittedly there was some Christian Arabic poetry of a high order, particularly at the court of the Umayyads in Damascus; but in style it did not differ from the Islamic and reflected the same spirit. Persian as a medium of literary expression was therefore easily suppressed. It persisted only in the seclusion of the countryside and the intimacy of the home. Consequently all the literature produced by the Persians, the value and influence of which can hardly be exaggerated, was almost entirely in Arabic—a situation analogous to the use of Latin in mediaeval Europe. And just as the Reformation and the rise of European nationalism brought about the gradual disuse of Latin and the rapid development of the vernaculars, so now changes in the political situation were creating a suitable atmosphere for the revival of Persian. Although the *literati* must have been writing in Arabic for generations, their aims and sentiments were undergoing a change, and they were inclined to make more use of their mother-tongue. But when the Persian language finally emerged from this long period of virtual suppression—some early historians have insisted that this was done by force—some 80 per cent of its vocabulary remained Arabic, and a whole series of compound words were formed one part of which was Arabic and the other Persian. It is a distinctive feature of this literature that the proportion of Arabic words seems to increase or decrease according to the taste of the patron and the political situation in the country; and also according to the subject-matter. There was always a greater use of Arabic words in prose than in poetry, and in theological and philosophical works than in pure *belles-lettres*.

The few available source-books[1] dealing with this period have not much to say on the subject of language. The revival of Persian seems to have begun in Khurāsān, the province most distant from Baghdad. From the middle of the ninth century onwards, it gathers strength in proportion to the degree of Persian emancipation and self-assertion. And it is finally assured of success by the triumph of Firdowsī, who gives the movement its seal and justification.

The Ṭāhirids, we are told,[2] 'had no faith in Persian and the dialect of *darī*' which was to become the cultivated language of the country and which corresponds in name to 'King's English.' But this is not strange when it is remembered that they were of Arab extraction and their patriotism was confined to political supremacy. The Ṣaffārids, on the other hand, being of Persian origin were more attached to the language of their forefathers. And under them there was a poet who 'like gentle rain cleansed the Persian tongue of chaff and corruption.'[3] Evidently in the early stages of its emergence, the vernacular that had suffered such long and rigid suppression was not in a very happy state.

The cradle of this vigorous national rebirth was in fact the court of the Sāmānids; and its rapid growth owes much to their tender care and encouragement. It should not be supposed that under this dynasty, which maintained correct relations with the Caliphs of Baghdad, all prose and poetry was written in Persian. Corresponding to a similar development in Western Europe, there is a distinct period of bilingualism in the history of the Persian people and their literature.[4] Political, religious and social considerations induced them to continue writing for long in both

[1] Cf. Dowlatshāh and 'Awfī.

[2] Cf. *Lubāb*, p. 2.

[3] *Ibid.*

[4] *dhū al-lisānain.*

Arabic and their mother-tongue. But under the Sāmānids the movement gained consciousness and determination, enlisting the support of men of learning. Later under the capricious eye of Sulṭān Maḥmūd the Ghaznavid, it reached its full maturity. The Ziyārids of Ṭabaristān also took an active part in this literary revival. They extended a happy welcome within the limits of their restricted domain to scholars and poets, who in those days were often itinerants in search of fortune and fame. One of the rulers has himself left a good specimen of early Persian prose;[1] and some of them wrote prose and poetry in Arabic, illustrating thereby the bilingual stage.

Under the Būyids, though they were themselves of Persian stock, practically all that was written was in Arabic. The reason for that was their close proximity to Baghdad which, as we have said, continued to maintain its position as the directing centre of Islamic culture. And an additional reason was that the subjects that occupied them most were theology, jurisprudence and philosophy, which could be more easily treated in Arabic, and were addressed to a class usually well-versed in it. The anthologies covering the period[2] show the extent to which Arabic continued to be used throughout Persia. They also illustrate the change in theme and in sentiment, and the decline in merit from those Baghdad poets who, though of Persian extraction, delighted the most fastidious of Arab critics, and who were wholly devoted to that inter-racial Islamic culture which the early 'Abbāsid Caliphate promised and only partially fulfilled.

For those who had put their faith in the rebirth of a distinctive Persian literature, one important development was a growing interest in the pre-Islamic history of the country; and in the ancient traditions and festivals of the Iranian people. Such chronicles as had become by then rare, began to be translated into the gradually emerging new idiom, rather than into Arabic

[1] Cf. *Qābūs-Nāmeh*, edit. Levy.

[2] Tha'ālibī: *Yatīma . . .*; *Tatimmat al-Yatīma*, edit. Iqbāl; Bākharzī: *Dumiat al-Qaṣr*, edit. Ṭabbākh.

as had been the case in ʿAbbāsid days. And when they were put into verse, they took the form of epic poetry which incorporated oral tradition and folklore into what survived of the semi-legendary semi-historical accounts. Among the first authors in this genre was Daqīqī (d. 975), who may have been a Zoroastrian by faith, and who was eventually murdered by his Turkish slave. At the request of one of the Sāmānid kings, he composed at least one thousand verses dealing with King Gushtāsp and the advent of Zoroaster. But the man to produce what by common consent is one of the great epics of world-literature, was Firdowsī (d. 1020). A country squire born near Ṭūs—the modern Mashhad—living on the rent of his land with a daughter as sole companion, he laboured for some twenty-five or perhaps thirty-five years to write the Book of Kings (*Shāh-Nāmeh*), his only authentic work. Sure of riches and renown, he sought the court of Sulṭān Maḥmūd the Ghaznavid; but he fell victim to the intrigues of the courtiers and was denied the reward that he felt was his due. Thereupon he ridiculed the king and his slave-ancestry in a merciless satire, and died a fugitive from that enraged monarch.[1]

The *Shāh-Nāmeh* is a part-historical part-legendary story of the kings of Persia from the beginning of time to the Arab conquest. Reflecting a Sāsānian civilization with a feudal form of society that was rapidly disappearing, the work as a whole merits comparison with the best European epics, in particular with the Iliad and the *Odyssey*. It might be thought that judged by the standards of Aristotle's *Poetics* it fails because it is episodic; but that is not a universal principle. Firdowsī, like Homer, may occasionally nod, but he too has his purple patches. In that literary movement of which he was the culmination in the field of poetry, his contribution was twofold. By reviving the lays of ancient Iran, based on prose works in the old Pahlawi tongue, he succeeded as none other had done in reanimating the national spirit of a people already some three hundred years under foreign

[1] Cf. Nöldeke: *Das Iranische Nationalepos.*

domination. And by making a deliberate attempt to use as few Arabic words as possible, he gave new life and vigour to a language that had been declining with alarming rapidity. More than any other single work, the *Shāh-Nāmeh* made Firdowsī's countrymen conscious of their destiny; and fortified their resolve at a critical time in their history. The sad reflections in which the work abounds, expressed with a felicity rare in those days, were a reminder of the hard times they had all passed through.

More important for the purposes of the present inquiry was Firdowsī's incomparable service to the Persian language in its post-Islamic form. Like Daqīqī, whose one thousand verses he had incorporated in his *Shāh-Nāmeh*, he chose for his epic a strictly Persian metre, the *mutuqārib*; and he reduced the use of Arabic words to the barest minimum. In a modern study,[1] there is a highly instructive analysis of the Arabic terms occurring in the *Shāh-Nāmeh*, based on the exhaustive glossary of Wolff.[2] It shows that in some fifty thousand lines of poetry, the poet has been able to use no more than 984 Arabic expressions. When one realizes the extent to which Arabic had penetrated Persian, this remarkable achievement can be better appreciated. Its social and cultural consequences were of great importance and proved far-reaching. It constitutes the first major breach in the linguistic unity of the Islamic Empire from south of the Pyrenees to Transoxiana; and from the Caspian to the basin of the Indus river. In the accomplishment of this task Firdowsī was indeed not alone; but the *Shāh-Nāmeh* is a monumental work that in subject-matter and artistic merit stands far above the rest.

This Persian revival corresponds to the supersession of Latin, the language of the Church until the Renaissance, by the tide of national literature in the vernaculars which gradually overwhelmed it. In Italy as early as the year 1434, Alberti writes, 'I confess that the ancient Latin language is very copious and highly adorned; but I do not see why our Tuscan of today should be

[1] Humbert: *Observations sur le Vocabulaire arabe du Chahnameh.*

[2] *Glossar zur Firdosis Schahname.*

held in so little esteem that whatever is written in it, however excellent, should be displeasing to us. . . .'[1] These words and this sentiment could be the expression of the feelings of Firdowsī and his associates with regard to Arabic and Persian. In France in 1549 Du Bellay wrote his *Deffence et Illustration de la Langue Francoyse.* And in England a Headmaster of the Merchant Taylors' School says: 'for is it not indede a mervellous bondage, to become servants to one tung for learning sake. . . . I love Rome but London better. . . . I honor the Latin, but worship the English.'[2] In this same spirit Firdowsī deliberately tried to replace Arabic terms by others of Persian root.

One unexpected feature of this rebirth of letters was its wide influence. Although soon after the period under review the whole land was overrun, first by hordes of Turkish origin and then by Mongols, with a devastation rarely equalled in the annals of history, the Persian tongue became the official language at the court of the new conquerors; and also that of diplomacy and *belles-lettres* far beyond the borders of the country proper. This has caused a modern scholar to remark, 'cela symbolise le fait que le rôle proprement dit de l'Iran s'exerça moins sur le plan politique et militaire que sur celui de la culture et de l'ésprit.'[3] Firdowsī himself was not unaware of the significance and the far-reaching results of his contributions, and we find him saying:

> 'Henceforth I shall not die, alive I shall remain,
> For I was he who spread the seeds of speech again.'

It will later be seen how Avicenna after him also made a special effort, with notable results, to contribute to this linguistic revival, though not indeed to the same extent.

Daqīqī and Firdowsī had an illustrious predecessor in the person of Rudakī (d. 940), reckoned the first really great poet of post-Islamic Persia; and sometimes called the Chaucer of Iran. Among the creative artists who founded the Renaissance in

[1] Cf. Baugh: *History of the English Language.*

[2] *Ibid.*, p. 251. [3] Humbert: *op. cit.*, p. 6.

Europe, the poets were the chief among those who initiated and fostered the new spirit of awakening after years of torpor. And in Persia this mission was ably fulfilled by Rudakī, the most celebrated poet of the Sāmānid period. Little of his poetry has survived; but the few remaining fragments are sufficient to show the simplicity of his style and the limpid purity of his language.

In the field of science and scholarship, Bērūnī (d. 1048) occupies the foremost position. Traveller, historiographer, mathematician, astronomer, geographer, and teacher of Greek learning, he is considered one of the greatest scientists 'of all time.' Born of Persian stock in Khīva, then called Khawārizm, which is the Chorasmia of antiquity, he joined the council of state of the local prince. And when Sulṭān Maḥmūd conquered the principality, or perhaps even before, he was induced to go to Ghazna, the capital of the now powerful monarch. Shortly afterwards he left for India, just opened to the Muslim world, where he transmitted to Indian scholars Greek thought in its Islamic form. He also wrote an admirable work on the religion and philosophy of India.[1] On his return he dedicated to the reigning king, Sulṭān Mas'ūd, his *Canon Masudicus* on astronomy, which is his greatest work. 'In astronomy he seems by his *Canon Masudicus* to represent the height, and at the same time, the end of the independent development of this science among the Arabs.'[2]

Bērūnī, a contemporary of Avicenna who entered into correspondence with him and was closely connected with his associates and fellow-philosophers, like most other men of learning, had no very easy life. According to an anecdote, Sulṭān Maḥmūd twice commanded him to prophesy; and because in both cases his predictions turned out correct, he was cast into prison. The incensed Sulṭān explained that 'kings are like little children—in order to receive rewards from them, one should speak in accordance with their opinion. It would have been far better for him on that day if one of those two predictions had been wrong.'[3]

[1] Cf. *Albiruni's India*, trans. Sachau.

[2] *Ibid.*, Vol. 1, p. xliii.

[3] Browne: *Lit. Hist. of Persia*, Vol. 2, p. 98.

Bērūnī was a man of scholarly spirit and outlook, refusing to accept any belief blindly or on the strength of tradition; always trying to reason, to understand, and above all to criticize. He reproaches the early invaders for having destroyed the civilization of Iran,[1] and his accounts of Hinduism, Christianity and Judaism are such as to win him the gratitude and admiration of modern students of these faiths.[2] Using the comparative method so rare in his time, he delights in comparing the different religious beliefs; and he regrets that the conquerors killed off the priests of his own dear Khawārizm and its learned men and burned their books. 'It is rare before modern times to find so fair and unprejudiced a statement of the views of other religions, so earnest an attempt to study them in the best sources, and such care to find a method which for this branch of study would be both rigorous and just.'[3]

The intellectual background of Bērūnī, who in the words of an early author, had 'no equal except in Avicenna' and of whom some twenty-seven works have survived,[4] reflects the state of knowledge and the various intellectual trends towards the end of the tenth century in Persia and Transoxiana. Basically Islamic, it was deeply coloured by Greek learning in its Arabic form. The violent orthodox reaction that had set in in Baghdad, had driven away, mainly towards the east, the Mu'tazila and the adherents of the different heterodoxies. Included among them were Christian physicians versed in Syriac and trained in Greek philosophy. The period of the translators was past, and no new translations directly from the Greek are heard of till modern times—indeed the knowledge of that language must have become extremely rare. Yet both Bērūnī and, to a less extent, Avicenna, betray some familiarity with it, possibly acquired through association with certain Christian physicians who kept their company and shared their fate, and because of their Syriac antecedents and their

[1] Cf. *Chronologie . . .*, edit. Sachau.
[2] Cf. *Al-Bīrūnī Commemorative Volume.* [3] *Ibid.*, p. 160.
[4] Cf. Brockelmann: *G.A.L.*, Vol. 1, pp. 870 ff.

training in Baghdad, it may be presumed that they already knew at least some Greek. Some have claimed that Bērūnī could read Greek, Sanskrit, Syriac and Hebrew. All that he himself tells us is that he used to go to a Greek to learn the names of the plants, and that he had in his possession a philosophical lexicon giving the names in Greek, Syriac, Arabic and Persian.[1]

Greek learning in its Arabic version constituted one of the mainsprings of Bērūnī's thought. In his writings he quotes frequently from Plato's *Phaedo*, *Timaeus* and *Laws*; from Proclus' commentary on the *Timaeus*; from Aristotle's *Physics* and *Metaphysics*; from Alexander of Aphrodisias, Porphyry, Ammonius, Galen, Hippocrates, Aratos, Eudoxos and even Homer. But, as has been shown,[2] there is no question of his having read these in the original, or translated any of them into Arabic. On the question of languages suitable for translation, he is characteristically objective. His mother-tongue had been Chorasmian, an Iranian dialect, with a strong Turkish admixture, specimens of which have lately been found. He ridicules the possibility of discussing the sciences in that dialect; and as between Persian and Arabic, in both of which he admits to being an 'intruder (*dakhīl*),' he gives his unqualified support to Arabic, adding that the books 'were in Greek and Syriac, no one having access to them except the Christians, and they were then translated into Arabic so that the Muslims could benefit from them.'[3] While admitting that his patron Sulṭān Maḥmūd 'hated Arabic,' he himself was not prejudiced. But he wrote books in Persian also, and Avicenna was to follow the same practice. He had the initiative to study Sanskrit, and translate Indian books into Arabic and some works, such as those of Euclid and Ptolemy, from Arabic into Sanskrit. Of the two outstanding intellectual figures at the end of the tenth and the beginning of the eleventh century, Bērūnī chose science and scholarship and Avicenna medicine and philosophy. They shared an almost total lack of racial prejudice, a broad humanity, a fear-

[1] Cf. *Kitāb al-Ṣaidana*, edit. Meyerhof.

[2] Cf. Gabrieli: *Al-Bērūnī Commemorative Volume.*

[3] *Kitāb al-Ṣaidana.*

less devotion to truth, an insatiable intellectual curiosity, as well as a physical restlessness that kept them continuously on the move.

Another contemporary of whom, we are told, Avicenna was rather scornful and with whom he had some sharp exchanges, was Miskawaih (d. 1030).[1] He was of Persian stock, and his grandfather, or possibly his father, was a Zoroastrian. Miskawaih was, like the others, bilingual, and he left books in both languages. In his youth in Baghdad he attended the lectures of Sajistānī and befriended Tawḥīdī, who is the only person to tell us much about him.[2] Mean, worldly, and not particularly intelligent, he spent most of his life at the court of the Būyids in western Persia; and so Tawḥīdī insists, was incapable of understanding philosophy. His historical works are voluminous, but he is known chiefly for his ethics based on Aristotle and certain Persian traditions. In his Eternal Wisdom (*Jāvīdān Khirad*) he gives an *exposé* of the concept of wisdom severally according to the Persians, the Arabs, the Greeks and the Indians. In his book on ethics, in which he quotes Aristotle, Galen and the Stoics, he discusses happiness, justice, virtue and sophrosyné (*'iffa*), as well as the problem of the Good. It is however in his exchange of ideas with Tawḥīdī, as recorded by the latter,[3] that the personality of both is best revealed. Tawḥīdī with all his accomplishments and wide interests finds himself neglected and almost destitute; and Miskawaih, far less gifted, but in a secure and lucrative post, is able to talk patronizingly to him, chide him for self-pity and recommend forgiveness as a cure. Tawḥīdī asks why those who preach contentment are so greedy themselves; why jealousy is far worse among the learned than among simple people; why the ignorant pretend to greater knowledge; and why slim men and women are usually more virtuous than the fat. The whole volume is enchanting, reminiscent of the essays of Montaigne.

Many were the Greeks who combined medicine with philo-

[1] Cf. Qifṭī, p. 331. [2] Cf. *Al-Imtā'* . . .

[3] Cf. *Al-Hawāmil wa al-Shawāmil*, edit. Amīn and Ṣaqr.

sophy; and the tradition persisted among the Islamic peoples. It is known that Rāzī made notable contributions to medical literature;[1] and there were others in Persia from some of whom important medical works have survived.[2] There were also compilations on pharmaceutical preparations.[3] The language employed in these manuals was usually Arabic, but when for some particular reason Persian was preferred, the difficulties involved did not prove insurmountable. In fact Persian names of drugs and diseases had entered Arabic from very early days, partly because many of the physicians practising were of Persian and Syriac origin—and the Syriacs of Baghdad were very much Persianized through their religious centres in that country. The Persian names may also be explained by the influence of the medico-philosophical school of Gundīshāpūr, whence some celebrated teachers were deliberately transferred to the new capital of Baghdad by the Caliphs. There were many drugs and diseases that retained their Greek names, so that medical terminology really consisted of Arabic with a large admixture of Greek, Syriac and Persian.

These physician-philosophers, for whom medicine was a profession and philosophy an intellectual pastime, were numerous and scattered all over the Islamic world, a number of them in Persia and Transoxiana. Usually trained in Baghdad, they were held everywhere in high esteem, and treated with great respect by rulers and kings even when of foreign extraction or of a different faith. Ibn al-Khammār (the son of Khammār), so called either because he was the son of a wine-merchant, or after the name of the suburb in which he lived and practised, was a Christian educated in Baghdad. He visited the court of the prince of Khawārizm, and stayed there until he was carried off together with Bērūnī to adorn the *entourage* of Sulṭān Maḥmūd in Ghazna. There he gained his living by his profession, and taught philosophy to a small circle, and as the author of many

[1] Cf. Browne: *Arabian Medicine.* [2] Cf. *Firdaws al-Ḥikma*, edit. Siddīqī.
[3] Cf. *Kitāb al-Abnia* . . ., edit. Seligmann.

medical works became known as 'the second Hippocrates.'[1] He lived to a good old age; and became a Muslim towards the end of his life. Avicenna had a high opinion of him, and in one place says, 'may God grant us to meet him, either to benefit from him or to benefit him.'[2] Another physician-philosopher was Abū Sahl al-Masīḥī (the Christian), born in Gurgān, and brought up and educated in Baghdad.[3] He returned to his native country and was welcomed by the prince of Khawārizm who was then at the height of his power. In addition to carrying on his medical practice he wrote books, twelve of which are mentioned by Bērūnī. Among them was a compendium called *The Hundred* which became a manual of medicine used all over Persia. He soon became very intimate with Avicenna, and may possibly have been his teacher in some of the subjects that were of interest to both. When Sulṭān Maḥmūd ordered the prince of Khawārizm to send him the celebrities who had gathered at his court, Masīḥī joined Avicenna in his flight, and, as will be told later, died in a sandstorm.

Some mention may also be made here of a much younger contemporary who in his way was quite a remarkable figure. Nāṣir Khosrow (d. 1061) was born in Balkh, and was thus a countryman of Avicenna, if not from exactly the same district. A gifted poet, his extensive travels took him as far as Egypt where he was converted to the Ismā'īlī heterodoxy. He returned to his native land as a 'propagandist (*dā'ī*),' wrote a delightful book of travel,[4] and shares with Avicenna the credit of being one of the creators of Persian philosophical prose.[5] His terminology is even more rich than that of his predecessor; and he coined certain terms from pure Persian roots that can be profitably used today. (The time has now come when the Persians must develop a philosophical language of their own. In that necessary task they will find him very helpful.)

[1] Cf. Brockelmann: *G.A.L. Supp.*, 1, p. 378.
[2] Baihaqī: *Tatimmat . . .*, p. 13.
[3] Cf. Brockelmann: *G.A.L. Supp.*, 1, p. 423.
[4] *Safar-Nāmeh.*
[5] Cf. *Zād el-Musāferīn.*

No account of this creative period is complete without a reference to the chief ministers at the court of the various rulers who competed with one another in literary accomplishment, and in their patronage of men of letters. Of these Ibn 'Abbād was a distinguished poet, philologist and wit at the court of the Būyids in western Persia. He was such a lover of books that when the Sāmānid king invited him to become his vizier, one of his excuses for declining was that four hundred camels would be required to transport his library alone. Ibn al-'Amīd too was a writer of note and a stylist imitated by many authors. We are indebted to him for his wise measure of having the works of Rāzī collected and copied by his pupils, though much from the collection has since perished, for reasons that are not hard to guess. Bal'amī, the minister of the Sāmānids, rendered an invaluable service to the emerging language by translating the voluminous history of Ṭabarī, specimens of which are still extant.

Thus the Persian Renaissance had its roots in both Islamic culture and the ancient civilization of Iran; and its issue was a combination of both. Its hybrid nature is especially marked in its literature and philosophy, and with a conspicuous constancy has persisted down to modern times. Sometimes one, sometimes the other element predominates, depending on the circumstances, but both are always present. This has often caused a dichotomy in ideas that can be explained only with reference to the history of the country. It is to be noticed in Ṣūfism and such religious movements as the Isma'īlī heterodoxy. All this goes to show that Avicenna was not a lone star. A galaxy of poets and men of learning were already contributing their share to this brilliant epoch in the history of Persia and Transoxiana. But he rose, destined to shed an abiding light far beyond his own horizon.

CHAPTER II

LIFE AND WORKS OF AVICENNA

ALL accounts of the early life of the man whom Chaucer's Doctour of Phisik was so proud of having read, and whose name echoed in the cloisters of many a mediaeval monastery, are based on an autobiographical narration which he himself chose to dictate to the man who was his companion and pupil of twenty-five years[1] (about whom more is told hereunder).

Abū 'Alī al-Ḥusain ibn 'Abd-Allāh ibn Ḥasan ibn 'Alī ibn Sīnā, which by way of Hebrew became Europeanized into Avicenna, was born in August 980 (Ṣafar, 370 A.H.) in a large village near Bukhārā called Kharmaithan (The Land of the Sun). His father was from Balkh—a city known to the Greeks as Bactra, with the epithet 'the glittering' in Middle Persian literature. This was an important commercial and political metropolis, and an intellectual and religious capital, a centre of religious and intellectual life. As the seat of the Graeco-Bactrian kings, it was for a period the centre of Hellenic culture, then lost its importance for a while, only to recover its ancient glory under the Sāmānid and Ghaznavid dynasties. Here Zoroastrianism, Buddhism, Manichaeism, Nestorian Christianity and finally Islam met. This was the site of the Nowbahār, the renowned Buddhist monastery visited by pilgrims from far-away China, at the head of which was Barmak, the ancestor of the most powerful, able and enlightened minister at the court of the Caliphs in Baghdad.

From Balkh the father of Avicenna moved to Bukhārā, an old Iranian city known to the Chinese as Pu-ho, also the seat of a large Buddhist monastery and since the Arab conquest a centre of Islamic studies that produced some eminent theologians. At

[1] Cf. Qifṭī, pp. 413 ff.; I. A. Uṣaibi'a, Vol. 2, pp. 2 ff.

this time it was the capital of the Sāmānid ruler, Nūḥ the second, son of Manṣūr, who had ascended the throne in 977 at the age of thirteen. Avicenna's father was appointed as a local governor in Kharmaithan, and must therefore have been a man of some standing. There he married and had two sons of whom Avicenna was the elder.

The origin of the father is not quite clear; Arabs, Turks and Persians have in turn claimed the son. There is at least no reason to believe that he was an Arab. As the vast majority of the inhabitants of Transoxiana at that date were of Iranian stock, and the great Turanian predominance does not begin till after the Mongol conquest, an Iranian origin seems the most probable. To this may be added the observation that throughout all his wanderings, Avicenna deliberately avoided Turkish patrons, and sought the courts of Persian rulers. The view that he was of Chinese lineage which is based on the assumption that the whole region was formerly a centre of Chinese rule where many of their people had settled, and which had become a cultural and commercial thoroughfare between Persia and China, is rather far-fetched. As to his mother: she came from the nearby village of Afshaneh, and her name Setāreh, a pure Persian word meaning Star, suggests that she was Persian.

The family returned to Bukhārā, and here Avicenna's early formative age begins. When he was only ten years old he had read the Qur'ān and some *belles-lettres*, he tells us; and all marvelled at his talent. The religious atmosphere of his home was not orthodox—an important point that he himself tended to conceal, but which helps to explain some of the difficulties of his life. 'My father,' he says, 'was one of those who had responded to the invitation of the Egyptians [the Fāṭimids] and was counted among the Ismā'īlīs.'[1] He used to listen to his father and brother discussing the soul and the intellect 'after the manner in which they [the Ismā'īlīs] expounded them,' but he hastens to add that

[1] Baihaqī (*Tatimmat* . . ., p. 40) stresses that both Avicenna and his father were in the habit of reading the *Epistles of the Brethren of Purity*.

he felt he could not assent to their arguments. They asked him to join them in their discussions on philosophy, geometry and Indian arithmetic; but he does not say if he ever responded to the invitation. He was sent to a certain grocer who was in the habit of using that form of calculation to learn Indian arithmetic; and at the same time he was studying Muslim jurisprudence by himself, and visiting an old ascetic from whom he learnt the methods of religious argumentation. Presently a man by the name of Nātelī, professing a knowledge of philosophy, came to Bukhārā. Avicenna's father immediately engaged him to teach his son and invited him to stay in their house. No source tells us whether or not he was an Ismā'īlī also.

The lessons started with the *Eisagoge* of Porphyry; and one day, having heard his teacher define a *genus*, the young pupil set about verifying that definition in a manner that deeply impressed Nātelī, and caused him to advise the father that the boy should not engage in any other occupation but learning. Together they went all through the elementary parts of logic; and from then onwards Avicenna read the texts himself with the aid of commentaries, supposedly of Hellenistic authors translated into Arabic. Similarly with Euclid: he read parts with his teacher and the rest independently. Next he took up the *Almagest* of Ptolemy, and often it was beyond the powers of his teacher to help him. When Nātelī left for Gurganj, Avicenna took up the natural sciences and metaphysics alone, reading the texts and seeking help from commentaries. These supplementary books were to prove an important influence on his own works. He often depended upon them for his understanding of Plato and Aristotle. Much Peripatetic and Stoic thought found in his writings stems from this source.

At this stage he decided to take up medicine, and proceeded to read all the available books on the subject. He assures us that he did not find it 'a difficult science,' and that he excelled in it in a very short time, using methods of treatment often extremely practical. He also continued his study of religious law and disputation. By then, he says, he was sixteen years of age. Whether this statement is true or due to the excessive zeal of the disciple who recorded it, we are unable to say.

During the following eighteen months he went over logic and the various problems of philosophy once again. During this period, he tells us, he did not sleep one night through, and worked all day, reducing every statement and proposition that he read into its syllogistic premisses and recording it in his files. Whenever he found himself in a difficulty—he chooses to assure his pupil—he repaired to the mosque, and prayer gave him insight in solving his problems. In the evenings he sat by his lamp and worked late into the night; and when sleep began to overcome him, or when he felt weak, he took a glass of wine and went back to work again. This minor detail which he candidly relates is interesting. He likes to assure his pupil that he is a religious man, and he wants to explain just how it came about that he became addicted to drinking.

By working in this manner he mastered logic, the natural sciences and mathematics, but he felt he must return to metaphysics. He took up the *Metaphysica* of Aristotle, read it some forty times, but to his great disappointment still could not understand it. One day in the booksellers' street a broker offered him a cheap volume which he bought only reluctantly. It turned out to be a book by Fārābī on the objects of the *Metaphysica*. He rushed home and read it, whereupon the whole purport of Aristotle's treatise was revealed to his mind, and he went out to distribute alms to the poor in gratitude the next day.

It happened at this time that Nūḥ ibn Manṣūr, the reigning prince, fell ill. Unable to help him, his physicians suggested that Avicenna, of whose wide reading they had heard much, should be summoned. He was duly sent for, and in collaboration with the others successfully treated the royal patient, and as a result became enrolled in his service. Special permission gave him access to the library of the Sāmānid rulers. This he found to be a mansion of many chambers with chest upon chest of books in each. Each apartment was devoted to a special subject; and when he reached the section on Greek, Avicenna tells us, 'I saw books whose very names are as yet unknown to many—works which I had never seen before and have not seen since. I read these books, taking notes of their contents.' This taking of notes was very important, since 'my memory for learning was at that period better than it is now; but today I am more mature, otherwise my knowledge is exactly the same and nothing new came my way after that.'

This great library, collected by successive rulers all known for their passion for literature and learning, was soon afterwards destroyed by fire. Avicenna's enemies—and he never lacked them—hastened to accuse him of firing the library; 'so that he could attribute the contents of those books to himself,' they claimed. Historians may well search for the perpetrators and their purpose. It might well have been connected with the racial and religious struggle that was going on at that time in the capital of the Sāmānids and that ended in their downfall. Hellenists must always mourn the treasures that were reduced to ashes in the library of Bukhārā.

According to his own account, Avicenna's first attempt at authorship was made at the age of twenty-one, while he was still at Bukhārā; when in answer to the request of a certain prosodist, he wrote a comprehensive book which he called the *Majmū'* (Compendium). This *genre* of writing had gone into common use since Alexandrian times, and it will be seen that many of his works take that form. Next, one of his neighbours, much interested in jurisprudence, asked him to write a commentary for him, whereupon Avicenna wrote *al-Ḥāṣil wa al-Maḥṣūl* (the (the Import and the Substance) in about twenty volumes; as well as a work on ethics called *al-Birr wa al-Ithm* (Good Work and Evil) of which he never made copies but presented it to his learned friend in the original.

Then abruptly his life entered a new phase. He tells us 'my father died and my circumstances changed. I accepted a post in the Sulṭān's employment, and was obliged to move from Bukhārā to Gurganj.' This obscure passage throws little light on what must actually have taken place. If after his father died he found it necessary to earn his living and for that reason enlisted in government service, then why was he 'obliged' to leave Bukhārā and submit his allegiance to a different ruler in Gurganj? These were troubled times at the court of the Sāmānids. The Turks were gaining the ascendancy and they must have frowned on the son of an Isma'īlī, even though some of the Sāmānid rulers themselves had Isma'īlī connections. Avicenna might therefore have become unwelcome for both racial and religious reasons.

It is significant that even to his intimate friend and pupil, Avicenna did not wish to expatiate on this episode; but his words betray bitterness; and we know from other sources that he was actually accused to Sulṭān Maḥmūd of being *bad-dīn* (of evil religion). Furthermore the Turks were such a menace to the Persian element that Bērūnī, who was somewhat in the same position, wrote a book entitled *A Warning against the Turks*. In fact it is tempting to suppose that Avicenna's autobiographical narrative, with its emphasis on the study of Muslim jurisprudence and religious disputation at the feet of an ascetic, and his later commentary on that subject in some twenty volumes—matters remote from his chief interests—were meant to assure his pupil of his religious conformity and of the fact that he never acceded to the Ismā'īlī beliefs of his father and brother. It is not difficult to imagine that his enemies made capital of the heterodoxy of his family; and we find historians like Ibn al-Athīr, writing much later, levelling the same accusation against him in the most violent terms. In any case his departure from Bukhārā was in unhappy circumstances, and marked the beginning of a most troubled period in his life.

His arrival in Gurganj—a large and flourishing city along the banks of the Oxus—at first seemed fortunate and of happy augury. The minister of the ruling Ma'mūnid prince was a learned man by the name of Soheilī. He welcomed Avicenna and introduced him to the Amir, dressed in the garb of a theologian with scarf and chin-wrap. A salary was duly fixed for him which he describes as 'amply sufficient for the like of me,' only to add immediately afterwards, 'then necessity constrained me to move to Fasā and thence to Bāward and thence to Ṭūs, then Shaqqān, then Samanqān, then Jājarm the frontier-post of Khurāsān, and thence to Jurjān (Gurgān). My entire purpose was to reach the Amir Qābūs; but it happened meanwhile that Qābūs was taken and imprisoned in a fortress, where he died. After this I went to Dihistān where I fell very ill, then returned to Jurjān where Abū 'Ubaid al-Jūzjānī made friends with me; and I composed a poem on my condition in which there is a verse saying:

And great once I became, no more would Egypt have me,
And when my value rose, no one would care to buy me.'

Here ends the autobiographical note dictated to Jūzjānī. The life-long friendship between these two men is not surprising. His companion, as the name shows, was a fellow-countryman; Jūzjān being the western district of Balkh, his father's home-town; and like him he apparently had no family attachments. Yet again he does not tell us why 'necessity' forced him to leave Gurganj and embark on his peregrinations, though the tenor of the account is full of restrained self-pity, a mood also implicit in the surviving lines of his otherwise lost poem, with their reference to the story of Joseph in Egypt.

From another source[1] we have a highly coloured account of the reasons that forced Avicenna to leave Gurganj, which if not entirely true is not pure fiction either. It says that Sulṭān Maḥmūd was told that there were some highly gifted people at the court of the Ma'mūnid prince, who should be made to join his *entourage*. The king thereupon sent a special envoy asking the prince to send him Bērūnī, Khammār, Masīḥī, Avicenna and a painter by the name of 'Arrāq, 'that they may have the honour of being received in our meetings and we may be pleased by their know-

[1] Niẓāmī: *Chahār Maqāla*, pp. 76 ff.

ledge and accomplishments.' The prince, who had suspected the purpose of the envoy even before arranging to receive him, called these men 'for whom he had provided all their earthly wants' and acquainted them with the probable intentions of Sulṭān Maḥmūd. The Sulṭān, he told them, was very powerful and coveted his principality and he was therefore in no position to anger or provoke him. Bērūnī, Khammār and 'Arrāq, having heard much of the generosity of the Sulṭān, agreed to go; but Avicenna refused and Masīḥī decided to keep him company. On the advice of the prince, they terminated their ten happy years in Gurganj, and left by night with a guide to lead the way.

There is reason to suppose that it was primarily for religious reasons that Avicenna refused to comply with the wish of Sulṭān Maḥmūd, whose strict orthodoxy and ruthless treatment of the unorthodox had already become proverbial. This may well have been the motive of Masīḥī also, who unlike Khammār had remained a Christian; and according to one account even Bērūnī went reluctantly.

The story goes on to relate that Sulṭān Maḥmūd was very angry when he heard of Avicenna's flight; that he ordered 'Arrāq to make a portrait of him and that some forty copies were circulated throughout the land with strict orders that he should be arrested wherever found and sent to the Sultan under escort. Meanwhile Avicenna and Masīḥī who had left Gurganj with a relation of Soheilī, the minister, as guide, wandered from village to village until on the fourth day they were caught in a violent sandstorm and completely lost their way. Masīḥī could not survive the excessive heat of the desert, and died of thirst, assuring his companion, however, that 'their souls would meet elsewhere.' Avicenna together with the guide found his way to Bāward 'after a thousand difficulties.' From there the guide returned, and Avicenna went on to Ṭūs. It is thus seen that the itinerary corresponds with his own account as recorded by his pupil, and that this account may therefore well be true.

The story is then taken up by Jūzjānī. 'From this point,' he says, 'I mention those episodes of the Master's life of which I was myself a witness during my association with him, up to the time of his death.' In Gurgān, Avicenna seems to have been well received. One man 'who loved these sciences' bought him a comfortable house next to his own and lodged him there. And Jūzjānī used to visit him every day, to read the *Almagest* with him, and to listen to his discourses on logic. He here dictated a book on that subject which he called *al-Mukhtaṣar al-Awṣat* (The Middle Summary) which his pupil took down. He also wrote others; among them *al-Mabda' wa al-Ma'ād* (The Beginning and the Return), and *al-Arṣad al-Kullīya* (The General Observations) composed in honour of his benefactor. He began writing the first part of *al-Qānūn* (The Canon), his chief medical work; and one that he called *Mukhtaṣar al-Majisṭī* (Summary of the Almagest), and many other tractates on similar subjects of interest to him and to the man who had been so good to him. After a while, however, he chose to leave Gurgān and go to Raiy. Again the reasons for that decision are obscure. Admittedly he had originally gone there with the hope of offering his services to Qābūs, the celebrated Ziyārid prince and man of letters; and had instead found that the unlucky ruler had been betrayed by his army chiefs and died while imprisoned in a fortress. Yet the philosopher had been welcomed in that place, had been offered a home by one of the townsmen, had found a devoted friend and pupil in the person of Jūzjānī, and had occupied himself with the writing of books. What then made him leave? Was his departure again due to some religious hostility towards him or simply to his own ambition and the hope of doing still better for himself?

Raiy, the ancient Ragha, some five miles from present-day Tihran, had peculiar attractions. It was an old centre of communication between east and west Iran; associated with Zoroaster and the twelfth sacred place created by Ahura Mazda, with accommodation for the three estates of priests, warriors and cultivators. It had been fortified by Darius and destroyed by

Alexander; rebuilt by Seleucus Nicator and named Europos; reconquered by the Parthians and called Arsakia. It was from this city that the last Sāsānian king issued his farewell appeal to the Iranian nation before fleeing to Khurāsān. Here the Umayyads handed over power to the 'Abbāsids, and here Hārūn al-Rashīd, the Caliph, was born. The population though predominantly Persian included men of many lands; and the bishops of the Syriac Church in Persia had made it their seat. In 925 when the Būyids had established themselves there, Raiy was 'one of the glories of the land of Islam' and possessed a very large library. Under Fakhr el-Dowleh, the Būyid prince, it had become a great centre of learning; and the two accomplished ministers of this dynasty, Ibn al-'Amīd and Ibn 'Abbād, had made it a centre of attraction for men of letters.

When Avicenna came to Raiy, Fakhr el-Dowleh was already dead, leaving a son by the name of Majd el-Dowleh, still only a child, and the country was ruled by his widow—a princess in her own right—known as *al-Saiyyida* (the lady). This able and courageous woman had refused to hand over power to her son when he came of age, and had kept Sulṭān Maḥmūd at bay with the warning that should he conquer her principality he would earn the scorn of the world as the mighty king who made war on a woman.

Avicenna, as Jūzjānī tells us, offered his services to the *Saiyyida* and her son, and was welcomed because of the favourable letters of introduction he had brought with him. Who gave him these letters, he does not say. Majd el-Dowleh was not a happy man at the time. He had tried to win back power and establish his rightful position, but had failed. He had therefore taken to the pleasures of the *harem* and of literature. We are told that 'he was overcome by melancholia and the Master applied himself to treating him.' Avicenna remained for two or three years at Raiy, during which period he composed the *Kitāb al-Ma'ād* (Book of the Return). Then trouble once more overtook him. The city was attacked by Shams el-Dowleh, a brother of Majd el-Dowleh, and again 'circumstances conspired to oblige him to leave Raiy for Qazwīn, and from Qazwīn he proceeded to Hamadhān.'

Although the pupil is careful to conceal the 'circumstances,' Khondamīr—an historian of later date—informs us that Avicenna infuriated the *Saiyyida* by insisting on the legitimate rights of her son in the dynastic quarrel between the two. This had become a local issue of some importance and the moral indignation of the philosopher could not be allowed to interfere.

In Hamadhān yet another phase begins in the life of Avicenna. He decides to take an openly active part in local politics; and places himself at the disposal of another influential lady, who may have been the wife or the favourite of Shams el-Dowleh, 'in order to investigate her finances.' By this means he becomes acquainted with the ruler and is summoned to court to treat him for an attack of colic. The treatment proves successful and he departs 'loaded with many costly robes . . . having passed forty days and nights at the palace and become one of the Amir's intimates.' In a war against the Kurds, he accompanies the prince as his personal physician; and although the expedition proves a failure, he succeeds in winning the favour of the Amir, and on their return to Hamadhān is appointed a vizier with all the powers of that office. His *début* as a political figure and State administrator, however, was followed by further trouble. The army for some reason refused to have him, 'fearing for themselves on his account', whatever this statement means. They could not in any way be pacified and 'they surrounded his house, haled him off to prison, pillaged his belongings. . . . They even demanded that he should be put to death; but this the Amir refused, though he was agreeable to banishing him from the State, being anxious to conciliate them.' The fury of the army was such that Avicenna had to go into hiding for forty days in the house of a friend. However, Shams el-Dowleh was again attacked by colic and he was again sent for. When he appeared at court, the Amir apologized profusely for what had occurred. For a second time and with great ceremony Avicenna was appointed vizier.

At this juncture Jūzjānī suggested that he should not neglect his writing, and urged him to undertake a commentary on the works of Aristotle. The reply is revealing with regard to Avicenna's attitude and outlook. He said he had not much time at his disposal, but 'if you agree that I should compose a book setting forth those parts of the sciences that I believe to be sound, not disputing therein with any opponents nor troubling to reply to their arguments, I will do so.' He then began work on the physical section of the *Kitāb al-Shifā* (The Book of Healing) which is the longest of his extant works. He had already started on his *Qānūn* (Canon) of medicine, and here he finished the first book. Every night he held a circle of study at his home for his pupils. 'I would read the *Shifā*,' Jūzjānī says, 'and another in turn the *Qānūn*. When we had each finished our allotted portion, musicians of all sorts would be called in and cups brought out for drinking, and in this manner we spent the rest of the time. Studying was done by night because during the day attendance upon the Amir left him no spare time.'[1]

A different account[2] of his daily programme relates that during the period that Avicenna was a vizier, he used to rise before dawn every morning, write some pages of his *Shīfā*, then call in his pupils and with them read some passages from his writings. By the time he was ready to leave the house, all those who wanted him to attend to their work were waiting outside. At the head of them all he rode to his official *dīvān* and dealt with affairs of State till noon. He then returned home and invariably entertained a large number of guests to lunch. After the *siesta* he went to present himself at court, and alone with the Amir discussed matters of importance.

These two accounts which may well be taken together as complementary show that he was a man of extraordinary industry and varied interests. They also reveal some of the more personal sides of his life. Evidently he did not hesitate to display publicly his love of music and wine, and to share them with those who

[1] Qifṭī, p. 420. [2] Cf. Niẓāmī: *Chahār Maqāla*, pp. 82–3.

partook also of his intellectual pleasures. Such conduct must have seemed scandalous to his colleagues in the Government, particularly in the rigorous Islamic society in which he lived. But all throughout his life he appeared to find satisfaction in completely disregarding what the public thought and said of him. This unconventional way of life he continued for some time and it may have been the source of much of his unpopularity. In the meantime the restless Amir decided to go to war again, and took Avicenna along with him. A severe attack of colic seized the prince during what proved to be an exhausting campaign, and he refused to follow the directions of his watchful physician and take sufficient rest during the intervals of fighting. The army, apprehensive and fearing the consequences of his death, decided to convey him to Hamadhān, but he died on the way.

The son of Shams el-Dowleh was thereupon sworn in as Amir, and the army petitioned that Avicenna should continue as chief minister. This Avicenna declined and entered into secret correspondence with 'Alā' el-Dowleh, the ruler of Iṣfahān, offering his services. The reasons for this change of allegiance are not clear. It may be supposed that Avicenna's relations with the army were strained and his past experiences not altogether happy. Fearing the consequences of his refusal, he went into hiding in the house of a druggist. There again the pupil who seems to have valued his intellectual accomplishments far more highly than his political acumen, urged him to profit from this enforced leisure and finish writing the *Shifā*. Accepting this proposal, Avicenna summoned his host and 'asked for paper and ink; these being brought, the Master wrote in about twenty parts of eight sheets each, the main topics that he wanted to discuss, in his own hand, and he continued writing for two days until he had enlarged on all the topics without once asking for any book or referring to any text, accomplishing the work entirely from memory. Then he placed these parts before him, took paper, and pondering on every question, wrote his comments on it. Each day he wrote fifty leaves until he had completed the whole of the natural sciences and metaphysics, with the exception of the books on animals and plants. He also began with logic and wrote one part of it.'

Meanwhile he had been accused of corresponding with 'Alā' el-Dowleh and a search for him was instituted. His enemies betrayed his whereabouts and he was cast into prison in a fortress. There he again took to poetry, and wrote scornfully:

> 'My going in was sure, as you have seen,
> My going out is what many will doubt.'

But after some four months he did go out of that fortress. 'Alā' el-Dowleh attacked and captured Hamadhān, and the defeated ruler, together with his family, sought refuge in the very place where Avicenna was confined. When 'Alā' el-Dowleh withdrew with his army, they all returned home; and Avicenna accepted the hospitality of a friend and busied himself with the completion of the logical section of the *Shifā*. Nor had he been idle while in the fortress, for there he had written the *Kitāb al-Hidāya* (The Book of Guidance) and the *Risālat Ḥaiy ibn Yaqẓān* (The Treatise of Living, the Son of the Vigilant)[1] and the *Kitāb al-Qulanj* (The Book of Colic). The *al-Adwiyat al-Qalbīyya* (The Cardiac Remedies) he had composed when he first came to Hamadhān.

On his return the prince did his best to win back the allegiance of Avicenna and promised him handsome rewards, but all in vain. At the first opportunity he slipped out of the town in disguise accompanied by Jūzjānī, his own brother, and two slaves, all dressed as Ṣufis. After suffering many hardships they reached the gates of Iṣfahān, where his friends together with the courtiers went out to welcome him, and 'robes were brought and fine equipages.' He was lodged in a large house and 'his apartment was furnished and carpeted in the most sumptuous manner.' At court he was received very cordially and with all due ceremonial.

'Alā' el-Dowleh, who valued Avicenna's talents highly, decreed that every Friday evening a meeting should be held in his presence

[1] Cf. ζῷον ἐγρηγορός (A. Pr. 38 a 41) *Ḥaiy Yaqẓān* (Tazārī).

for learned men of all classes, to discuss scientific and philosophical topics. We are assured that 'at these gatherings he proved himself quite supreme and unrivalled in every branch of learning.' These were indeed the best days of his life, and in the introduction to his Persian logic he expresses deep gratitude to his patron for granting him 'all his wishes, in security, and eminence and honour.' Here in Iṣfahān he occupied no official position, and avoiding politics and its pitfalls, he devoted his entire time to writing. He now set about completing the *Shifā*. In his commentary on the *Almagest* 'he introduced ten new figures into the different observations,' and at the end, under the section dealing with the celestial sphere, 'he had things that had never been discovered before.' In the same way he introduced some new examples into Euclid; and in arithmetic 'some excellent refinements'; and in music 'matters that the ancients [the Greeks] had neglected.' At Isfahān he also wrote his first book on philosophy in the Persian language, probably something which had never been attempted since the Arab conquest of Persia. This work he called, after the name of his patron, *Dānish-Nāmeh ye 'Alā'ī* (The 'Alā'ī Book of Knowledge).

While accompanying the Amir on an expedition, he composed the remaining parts of the *Shifā* together with an abridgement of the whole work which he entitled *Kitāb al-Najāt* (The Book of Deliverance). By this time he had become one of the intimate courtiers of the Amir, and when the latter decided to attack Hamadhān—city of unhappy memories for Avicenna—he did not remain behind. One night while discussing the imperfections in the astronomical tables based on ancient observations of the stars, the Amir asked him to compile new ones, assuring him the necessary funds. He immediately started work and deputed Jūzjānī to select the instruments and engage skilled assistants. Many old problems were thus elucidated and the imperfections were found to be due to the fact that the observations had been made at irregular intervals and on different journeys.[1]

[1] Cf. Faddegon in *Archeion*, 1932, Vol. XIV, who calls it *un travail très soigné*.

At this stage of his narrative Jūzjānī, who had been repeating what Avicenna had related, breaks off to observe that 'one of the remarkable things about the Master was that I accompanied and served him for twenty-five years and I did not see him take up a new book and read it right through. Instead he used to look up the difficult passages and the complicated problems and see what the author had to say, so as to discover the state of his learning and the degree of his understanding.'

Avicenna had never been a master of Arabic. One day when in the presence of the Amir, he expressed an opinion on a difficult linguistic question. One of the scholars present who was particularly proud of his knowledge of that language, immediately turned to him and said, 'You are a philosopher and a man of wisdom, but not sufficiently well read in philology as to be able to please us by the expression of your views.' This rebuke greatly annoyed Avicenna; and he at once took up a thorough study of Arabic grammar and literature. He ordered anthologies from Khurāsān—in those days a great repository of Persian and Arabic books—and various literary works, and began reading extensively. Some three years later he composed three Arabic poems full of rare words; then three essays, one in the style of Ibn al-'Amīd, another in that of Ibn 'Abbād, and still another in the style of al-Ṣābī. He had all these bound in one volume, had the binding rubbed and soiled, and presenting it to the Amir asked that it be passed on to the learned man who had administered the rebuke with the request that he should determine the value and find out the authorship of a volume that had been found while he was out hunting. To the satisfaction of Avicenna and all those who had witnessed the disputation, the pretentious scholar was entirely baffled. It was after this incident that he began a work on linguistics which he called *Lisān al-'Arab* (The Language of the Arabs)—still only in the form of a rough draft at his death. What purports to be a copy of that treatise has lately been published in Persia.[1]

[1] Edit. Yār-Shāṭir.

Another story concerns an essay on logic written in Gurgān and called *al-Mukhtaṣar al-Aṣghar* (The Smaller Epitome), later placed at the beginning of the *Najāt*. A copy of this had reached Shiraz in southern Persia, where a group of scholars had taken exception to some of its statements. The judge of the religious court decided to send their objections together with a covering letter to one of the pupils of Avicenna, asking him to present them to his master and elicit an answer. This the pupil did just as the sun was setting on a summer day. Avicenna immediately asks for paper and ink, orders drinks to be laid out, and while a general conversation is in progress, sits there and by candle-light examines the points raised. While thus occupied he bids Jūzjānī and his brother to sit and drink with him, and when they become drowsy, orders them to depart. In the morning he calls up Jūzjānī and gives him what he had written during the night in some fifty sheets, saying, 'I made haste to reply so that the messenger should not be delayed.'

During this period the *Kitāb al-Inṣāf* (The Book of Equitable Judgement) was also written. This was destroyed by the invading army of Sulṭān Mas'ūd, but certain fragments have survived.[1]

The ruler of Raiy had been an astute lady who had usurped the rights of her own son and kept the ambitious Sulṭān Maḥmūd at bay. But after her death, the son proved unequal to the task. He injudiciously asked the assistance of Sulṭān Maḥmūd who seized the long-awaited opportunity to send an army, conquer the whole kingdom and dispatch its ruler and his son as prisoners to India. He showed his intolerance of heterodoxy in a ruthless manner. In the words of a modern historian,[2] he 'began to persecute the Carmathians, the Bāṭinīs and the Mu'tazelites, and thousands of them were gibbeted, stoned to death or carried in chains to Khurāsān to languish in captivity.' One authority is quoted to the effect that 'fifty camel-loads of books are said to have been burnt under the trees on which the Carmathians had

[1] Cf. Badawī: *Arisṭū 'ind al-'Arab.*

[2] Nāẓim: *Sulṭān Maḥmūd of Ghaẓna*, p. 83.

been gibbeted.'[1] And he concludes that 'An invaluable store of learning, which the liberal policy and scholarly zeal of the Buwaihids [Būyids] had accumulated in the course of years, was thus consumed in an instant to satisfy the enthusiasm of the puritan warrior.'[2]

The fall of Raiy had made the position of 'Alā' el-Dowleh in Iṣfahān very critical. He did his best to conciliate Sulṭān Maḥmūd, but the latter was adamant, and entrusted to his son the task of conquering all the Būyid possessions. When Mas'ūd, the equally ambitious son, entered Iṣfahān in 1030 (421 A.H.), 'Alā' el-Dowleh fled, and it may be presumed that Avicenna accompanied him. It was then that his house was plundered and his library carried off to Ghazna, only to be destroyed about a century later by the invading Ghūrid Turks.

Accounts of the sequence of political events during this period are contradictory, and the dates not very reliable. We are told that in the year in which 'Alā' el-Dowleh was fighting a Ghaznavid army chief, Avicenna, while in the company of the Amir, was seized by a severe attack of colic. Fearing the prospect of being left behind if the Amir were defeated, Avicenna took heroic measures to cure himself, and in one day injected himself eight times, with the result that his intestines were ulcerated. Nevertheless he accompanied his patron in his flight, and at their next stopping-place 'the epilepsy which sometimes follows colic manifested itself.' He continued to treat himself by injections, and one day when he desired to be injected with two measures of celery-seed, one of the physicians attending him put in five measures instead. Jūzjānī adds, 'I do not know whether purposely or by mistake.' The excess of celery-seed aggravated the abrasions. 'He also took *mithridatum* for the epilepsy; but one of his slaves went and threw in a great quantity of opium, and he consumed the mixture; this being because they had robbed him of much money from his treasury, and they desired to do away with him so that they might escape the penalty of their actions.'

[1] Nāẓim: *Sulṭān Maḥmūd of Ghazna.* [2] *Ibid.*, p. 160.

Such was the state of his health when Avicenna was carried into Iṣfahān. He continued to prescribe for himself, though he was so weak that he could hardly stand on his feet. When he felt a little better he once more attended the court of the Amir, and is said to have indulged in excesses for which he again suffered in health. Once again 'Alā' el-Dowleh marched on Hamadhān and again Avicenna accompanied him. On the way he had a severe relapse; and when they finally reached their destination, he realized that his strength was ebbing fast; his body had no longer the strength to repel the disease. It was then that he gave up all treatment and took to saying, 'the manager who used to manage me, is incapable of managing me any longer, so there is no use trying to cure my illness.' He lingered for a time in this condition and died not long after his return to Hamadhān. He was buried outside the town in June or July, 1037 (428 A.H.), at the age of fifty-eight.

* * * *

The autobiographical note and what his pupil had to add are obviously neither complete nor convincing; and this bare outline of an eventful life does not give a full picture of the man and all that he went through. Nor is the motive for reticence always clear. Was it himself or his pupil who thought it best to leave certain things unsaid? Casual remarks by later authors fill few of the gaps, but there is always a feeling that something has been kept back. Avicenna was never a popular figure, and his detractors succeeded in spreading all sorts of derogatory stories about him even during his lifetime; so that in popular Arabic, Persian and Turkish literature he often figures as a sorcerer and magician, a conjurer of evil spirits. No one would be expected to make a careful record of the events and circumstances of such a man's life.

The book that in our view gives the best background to much that Avicenna had to suffer, and helps to explain some of the obscure motives that influenced the course of his life, is a semi-historical semi-political tractate[1] by a renowned statesman who was eventually assassinated. In page after page he describes the persecution of the followers of the Ismā'īlī heterodoxy, and the ruthless suppression of all forms of unorthodox movement and belief. This puritanical revivalism and rule of rigid orthodoxy was particularly strong in Transoxiana and on the eastern borders of Persia, and extended in time from before the days of Avicenna till long after him. It was associated with the Turkish influence, and its victims eventually included the Sāmānian rulers of Bukhārā under whom Avicenna, his father, and his family had lived. With this situation in mind, one finds the tone of reticence both in the autobiographical account and the additions of his pupil more understandable. And we have in support the evidence of Shahristānī that throughout his life Avicenna was suspected of Ismā'īlī leanings. It is not surprising, therefore, that we find the pattern of his life so uneven from the very start—sometimes even tragically tortuous. Never long in one place, he is hounded from town to town for reasons that he does not care to tell. We suppose that he must have learnt early in his life to suppress and conceal; and it is clear that even a friend and disciple of twenty-five years did not enjoy his full confidence. A sense of futility and frustration seems to cast a shadow over all his doings; and this may have been one reason why his pupil urged him constantly to devote most of his time in writing. Hence the difficulty of uncovering the complexities of a character composed of deep and varied strains; to probe into a restless mind never at peace with itself or the world around it.

Yet Avicenna was no recluse given to solitary contemplation like Fārābī. He loved and sought company, and he possessed an infectious *joie de vivre* that delighted his companions. He does not seem to have had many close friends, and that may have made him unhappy; yet people were fascinated by his rare gifts and scintillating mind. It is in this connection that his pupil chooses to tell something that was repeated by all later authors

[1] *Siāsat Nāmeh* of Niẓam al-Mulk, edit. Schefer.

—not without malice. As a man of excessive passions, not given to moderation, he indulged in sexual relations far more than even his strong physique could stand. We are told that even in failing health he did not abstain; and on top of his political activities and intellectual pursuits this proved extremely exhausting. When reproached for such intensive living, he gave his famous reply that he wanted his years in breadth and not in length. Yet he never married, deliberately denying himself the pleasures of family life: he was a lonely man to his dying day. All these facts imply a deep-seated unhappiness, and a fundamental dissatisfaction with his lot.

Two different sources[1] attest to Avicenna's strikingly good looks and impressive figure. One relates that when supposedly in hiding, he ventured into the bazaar, and was immediately recognized by a man, who says, 'I could easily tell. I had heard so much about your remarkable face and attractive appearance.' We do not know how he dressed in his home town. He tells us that in Gurganj he chose the attire of a religious divine. And the other testimony to his fine appearance is in an account of how he attended the court of 'Alā' el-Dowleh in Iṣfahān, in a long robe with a short jacket and a turban of coarse cloth. 'He used to sit very close to the Amir, whose face became radiant with delight as he marvelled at his good looks, and accomplishment and wit. And when he spoke all those present listened attentively, none uttering a word.'[2]

He could not have been a modest man, nor, in some respects, a particularly endearing personality. His disputes with fellow-philosophers reveal a violent temper; and a merciless scorn for the mediocre. He dismisses Rāzī's philosophy as the lucubrations of a man who should have stuck 'to testing stools and urine.' He ridicules Miskawaih and his pitiful limitations—and thereby provokes the rather significant retort that he would do well to amend his own character. From everyone he demands both quick wits and application; and assures us that he himself always went

[1] Cf. Niẓāmī and Baihaqī. [2] Baihaqī: *Tatimmat* . . ., p. 59.

over what he wrote carefully, 'even though that is a very tedious task.' These sidelights may stimulate our desire to know more about him, but actually this man of genius keeps the secrets of his true personality and leaves us still guessing. Most of the books that mention him are full of praise for his knowledge and ability, but contain not a single kind word for the man himself. Often they half-mockingly remark that he was the person who died of sexual excesses, and whose Book of Healing (*Shifā*), and Book of Deliverance (*Najāt*) helped neither to heal nor to deliver him. This obvious ill-feeling had various sources. One was his Ismā'īlī origin which was never forgotten; another was that his many writings ran directly counter to religious dogma. To these may be added his behaviour in public and his utter disdain of conformity. Of what else could they accuse him? Power, except for a brief troubled period, he never gained; wealth, by the testimony even of his detractors, he never sought; and the quiet comfort of a home he confesses he never had. Often he lived under a cloud of menace, and in spite of great self-confidence he claims that 'events befell me, and such trials and troubles came rushing upon me, that had they befallen the mighty mountains, they would have cracked and come crashing to the ground.' In a Persian quatrain which, if authentic, must be considered a revealing *cri de cœur*, he says:

'How I wish I could know who I am,
What it is in this world that I seek.'

* * * *

Of the two hundred books or more attributed to Avicenna, some are spurious, others are sections of some major work appearing under a different title. The authentic writings run to about a hundred; and of these the most important have fortunately survived. It is to be regretted that his last detailed work, supposed to contain the results of his mature thought, and which he deliberately called *Kitāb al-Inṣāf* (The Book of Equitable Judgement), written with the intention of arbitrating between the conflicting views of contemporary philosophers, was lost in the sack of Iṣfahān, only fragments of it having survived.

Thanks to Avicenna's pupil, we have a general idea of the order and sequence of his writings. This helps to determine the development of his thought to some extent. But the account is not always clear nor sufficiently instructive. The books of Avicenna suffer from being often *œuvres d'occasions* addressed to a friend or patron and suited to his tastes and attainments. It was probably for that reason that he did not always trouble himself to retain copies of them; so that but for the devoted efforts of his pupil they would long since have been lost. Most of what he wrote was in Arabic, with a few works in Persian. In neither does he show felicity of language or interest in what might be called the magic of words (and of course the same could be said of Aristotle). Yet he rendered a great service to the development of philosophical style and terminology. Avicenna's Arabic is definitely more lucid than that of Kindī and Fārābī. The aphorisms give place to real philosophical argumentation. He is at his best in discursive rather than in assertive passages. He has, however, some serious defects of style. In particular he is too repetitive; and as he was not a true Arab, his writings abound in what may be called Persianisms, particularly where he tries to be 'expansive' as in the *Shifā*. These Persianisms can be detected in both the structure of the sentences and in his vocabulary. When compared to good classical Arabic prose, with which he must have been quite familiar, his sentences lack the compactness so characteristic of that literature; and sometimes they are even unidiomatic. His vocabulary is full of new abstract terms, which were shocking to Arab purists, and which were very reluctantly, if ever, used by Arab authors after him. These terms were derived neither from Greek nor from Syriac, as is sometimes supposed; they are the direct result of his knowledge of Persian, which has an easy way of forming them. Hence the reason why his own countrymen found them natural and even felicitous, while the Arabs considered them barbarisms. Nevertheless these neologisms helped to enrich Arabic philosophical language, and they constitute a far more valuable contribution than any made either by Kindī, the pure Arab, or by Fārābī. Avicenna's choice of terminology is also more extensive than that of his predecessors. Kindī and Fārābī followed one set of translators consistently, with the result that they had no choice of terms, while Avicenna had the good sense to compare alternative translations and choose such technical terms as he considered the best for his purposes. Consequently his language is more varied and interesting. There is no question of his having known Greek, and this he never claimed. But in the *Shifā* he makes various illuminating remarks about Greek linguistics and grammar which can only be explained by the supposition that he was in contact with someone who had a fair knowledge of that language: the most likely person is Abū Sahl al-Masīḥī, who was his close companion and as a Christian physician trained in Baghdad certainly knew Syriac and may also have known some Greek.

Another feature of Avicenna's style—characteristic of his writings and of his mode of thought—is his passion for classification. He divides and subdivides far more than any Greek author; and it is from him that mediaeval European philosophers copied that method. Classification was once considered a device of the Western mind, here we find it even more marked. Still another contribution of Avicenna in this field is his attempt to introduce more precision in the use of Arabic terms. There had already been tentative efforts in that direction by Kindī and Fārābī, but theirs had taken the form of aphorisms. Only in Avicenna do we find a special treatise[1] devoted solely to definitions and the specification of terms. This was a valuable service, and it is only since his day that most of the technical terms of logic and philosophy have acquired specific senses and values.

[1] *Risālat al-Ḥudūd.*

It stands to his credit that they continue to do so to the present day.

Arabic philosophical language was not easy to mould. Aristotelian logic is so bound up with Greek grammar that it is sometimes doubted if it can be faithfully rendered into any other tongue. The early translators, as well as the *Falāsifa* who followed, had some formidable obstacles to overcome. Of these perhaps the most intractable was the total absence of the copula in Arabic. A characteristic of the Indo-European languages, it does not exist in the Semitic tongues. Thus it was sometimes necessary to use almost a dozen different equivalents in different contexts in order to convey an idea, and even then the result was not always satisfactory.

Whilst Avicenna helped to establish Arabic philosophical terminology for a thousand years, and himself introduced into it abstractions never before used, he can claim to be the actual originator of Persian philosophical language. His *Dānish-Nāmeh* is the first book on philosophy, logic, and the natural sciences in post-Islamic Persian. It is highly doubtful whether any such work had ever been attempted before: if so, no mention or trace of it remains. It is difficult to say what motives inspired Avicenna to undertake this work. Jūzjānī only tells us that it was written at the request of his patron, 'Alā' el-Dowleh, who could make no sense of it because it was beyond his understanding. Arabic, as has already been noted, was the proper medium for theology and philosophy; and the innovation places Avicenna in line with all the other bilingual poets and prose-writers of the Persian Renaissance. Although there is nothing new in the *Dānish-Nāmeh* that is not to be found in his Arabic writings, it is linguistically one of the most important books in the history of Persian prose. It abounds in the most resourceful and happy equivalents for Arabic terms, coined from pure Persian roots. Although some of them sound rather archaic after the lapse of so many years, most of them can and should be used today. Reference has already been made to the fact that his initiative was copied by his younger contemporary, Nāṣir Khosrow, the Ismā'īlī poet and philosopher, who wrote a number of treatises in as pure a Persian as he could command on religious and philosophical subjects. And yet religious, social, and political exigencies militated against the development of this literary movement; and we find very few subsequent authors wishing, or venturing, to continue the effort. Ghazālī and Ṭūsī, writing not so long after Avicenna, preferred to use the Arabic terms, and the practice has continued since in all theological seminaries.

Avicenna wrote some poetry also. His Arabic poems, including the celebrated ode on the soul, are elevating in thought and in theme, but they cannot be considered of great literary value. It is clear that he used the medium of verse without any artistic pretensions; and his poem on logic has nothing to recommend it (except to remind us of Empedocles and the early Greeks who wrote philosophy in verse); and the same may be said of his poem on medicine. The Persian verses that have been attributed to him are of far greater merit. It has been thought that some of the famous quatrains of 'Umar Khayyām are really his; and were introduced into the collection of 'Umar by anthologists. This, however, has been a difficult question to determine. It is quite conceivable that in his moments of loneliness—and they must have been frequent—he should have taken to verse in his own mother-tongue; but on the whole his claim to eminence cannot be extended to the field of poetry.

CHAPTER III

PROBLEMS OF LOGIC

WHAT is the object of logic, and what is its relation to philosophy? This had become the subject of some dispute among the Greeks of the post-classical period. Aristotle himself was not clear on the point, and had been inclined to consider logic as a creative art (*téchne*); he could not very well classify it as one of the theoretical or practical sciences. The Stoics after him contended that logic was actually a part of philosophy; while the Peripatetics maintained that it was merely an instrument of thought. Alexander of Aphrodisias, between the second and third century, was the first to call it an organon (instrument) of the sciences; and it is after him that the logical works of Aristotle became known as the *Organon*. The Platonists, taking a middle course, said that it was both a part of philosophy and an instrument of the sciences.

Both views are reflected in the conception of the Islamic philosophers, but not regarded as being of any great importance. The subject had been entirely new to them, and its methods and applications seemed almost revolutionary. The deductive method of reasoning from general premisses which had now reached them, was seized upon with great enthusiasm and led them into fields as yet unexplored. They were therefore principally occupied with the use of logic in their reasoning, and did not worry overmuch about how to classify it. It had focused their attention on Aristotle as 'the owner of logic,' though some Christian and Muslim theologians took strong exception to it. The Islamic philosophers became acquainted almost simultaneously with the Arabic renderings of the Aristotelian *Organon* and various commentaries by Peripatetic, Neo-Platonic and

Stoic authors who had raised the question of the use and purpose of logic. They could not therefore avoid taking some part in the controversy, more especially since they had taken upon themselves the task of justifying the whole subject and defending it against its detractors. Kindī, of whose works not all have survived, seems silent on this matter; he speaks of the eight books which included the *Poetica* and the *Rhetorica* as the logicals (*al-Manṭiqīyyāt*).[1] Fārābī calls logic an art in his classification; and takes no part in the dispute, at least in any of his published writings. In the *Epistles* we find some reflection of the point at issue. There, probably under Stoic influence, logic is classified as one of the four species of 'true philosophy'; and is also spoken of as 'the scales of philosophy,' and as 'the tool of the philosopher,' which conforms to the Peripatetic conception.

Avicenna is fully aware of the problem but avoids taking sides. He insists in the *Shifā* that the entire dispute is irrelevant, and that 'there is no contradiction between considering it a part of philosophy and an instrument of it.' He adopts the term instrument (*āla*) which he knew came from Alexander, and refers to logic as 'the instrumental science.' But having considered it a science in one place, he calls it an art (*ṣinā'a*) in another; while in Persian following the *Epistles*, he names it 'the science of the scales' (*tarāzū*). He thus follows Boethius, called the last of the Romans and the first of the Scholastics, who maintains that logic is both a science and an instrument of science.

Aristotle had never used the term logic in its modern sense; nor is it quite clear who it was that first gave it that sense. It has been contended that the credit must go to the Stoics, and we know that the term already occurs in Chrysippus.[2] Cicero employs it, but only to mean dialectics. By the time of Alexander of Aphrodisias and Galen, it is in current use in the form of the Greek *logiké*. The Arabic term *manṭiq* we find in the fragments of the translation of the *Metaphysica* being used more than once

[1] Later the *Eisagoge* of Porphyry was added to make them nine books.
[2] *Stoic. Vet. Frag.*, II, 42.

as the equivalent of the Greek *dialektiké*[1] and also, in some passages, of *logiké*.[2] The rendering is that of Usṭāth who, as has already been observed, was one of the early pre-Ḥunain translators. It may be thought, therefore, that he was the man who chose the word that he supposed had never had that connotation in the Arabic language, only to find that even before him Ibn al-Muqaffa' had given it that same new sense in one of his literary works; and also in that short paraphrase of Aristotelian logic of which mention has already been made. Arab purists never approved of this neologism, and the subject of logic was never to the taste of the theologians whether Christian or Muslim. Cases are recorded where in their heated discussions with logicians, they poured ridicule on the choice of the word, even though linguistically it is perfectly justified.

Kindī's definition of logic has not come down to us in a clear form. Fārābī says 'the art of logic gives in general the principles whose purpose it is to help the intelligence forward, and to lead man to the path of correct [thought], and to the truth . . . the relation of the art of logic to the intelligence and the intelligibles is as the relation of the art of syntax to language and words.'[3] For Aristotle also logic was primarily a matter of right thinking and secondarily of correct speaking. The authors of the *Epistles* maintained that 'the sciences of logic are of two kinds, linguistic and philosophical; the linguistic is such as the art of syntax . . . and the logic of judgements is of different branches, among which is the art of reasoning, and of dialectics, and of sophistics.'[4] The logic of language, they thought, should be mastered before the logic of philosophy, for 'it is incumbent upon him who desires to theorize in philosophical logic, to be first trained in the science of syntax.'[5]

Avicenna's definitions are numerous and somewhat varied. In one place he says, 'logic is that science in which may be seen the

1 Naẓīf (*Metaph.* 987b32), translates *ṣinā 'at al-jadal.*

2 Cf. *Metaph.*, 1004b25, and 1005b22.

3 *Iḥṣā'* . . ., p. 53.

4 Edit. Zirgalī, Vol. 3, p. 404.

5 *Ibid.*, Vol. 1, p. 332.

state of knowing the unknown by the known; that which it is that is in truth, and that which it is that is near the truth, and that which it is that is false; and the different varieties of each.'[1] In another place he states that logic 'is for the intelligence a guarding instrument against error, in what we conceive and give assent to; and it is that which leads to true belief by giving the reasons and methods of arriving at it.'[2] In still another he remarks, 'thus logic is a science from which is learnt the modes of passing from matters determined in the human thought, to matters to be determined; and the state of these matters, and the number and varieties wherein the order and the form of the transposition lead to correctness, and the varieties wherein it is otherwise.'[3]

The logic of Avicenna has not yet been properly studied. Nor would the effort prove fruitful unless the logic of the Commentators of Aristotle had first been carefully examined. No such study of the original Greek has yet been made; for the purposes of the present inquiry it would be even more important to study the Arabic version, for only then could the contributions of Avicenna be placed in their historical setting, and their originality, if any, definitely determined. Even the most superficial acquaintance with Islamic logic reveals the fact that although Aristotelian in general outline, it goes much farther in scope and subject-matter. Many have suspected that the additions are derived from Stoic sources; but there were Peripatetic and Neo-Platonic influences as well. Furthermore, it remains to be seen whether such additions as are indisputably Stoic reached them directly or through the various commentators of whom there were so many in the Hellenistic age. One author makes mention of the 'fourth figure' in syllogisms,[4] which as has been shown[5] was not introduced by Galen, but by some unknown logician after the fifth century; and Avicenna, well aware of the Stoic attempt to reduce the Aristotelian categories, speaks of 'those

[1] *Dānish-Nāmeh*, p. 9. [2] *Najāt*, p. 3. [3] *Ishārāt*, p. 3.
[4] Qazwīnī: *Al-Risālat al-Shamsīyya*, p. 21.
[5] Lukasiewicz: *Aristotle's Syllogistic*, p. 38.

who took pains to make some of these enter into others, and to limit them to categories of fewer number; among them those who made the categories four.' In fact throughout the *Shifā* he differentiates between what he calls 'the first teaching (*al-ta'līm al-awwal*),' meaning the Aristotelian, and later teachings; and significantly adds that 'philosophy, where it is according to the Peripatetics (*al-Mashshā'īn*), and where according to the Stoics (*al-Rawāqīyyīn*), is not to be referred to with absolute synonymity.'[1]

But by far the most conclusive evidence is in the field of terminology. The vocabulary of Avicenna abounds in logical terms[2] for which there are no equivalents in the translations of the *Organon*, and which correspond very well with such Stoic terms as have survived. Although our knowledge of Stoic logic is very limited,[3] and all *a priori* attempts to equate Avicennian terms with those used by the Stoics are to be discouraged as dangerous, the correspondence is sometimes so close as to give some measure of certainty. Nevertheless, we have the testimony of Ibn Taimīya that 'Avicenna and his followers dissented from the ancients in a number of their logical statements and in various other things.'[4]

The Islamic *Fālasifa* did know of Zeno and Chrysippus and also Diogenes,[5] but it is difficult to say to what extent they were acquainted with their works. Fārābī has frequent references to Zeno the great, and Zeno the small, as he calls them. In one source-book there is mention of 'a group who are associated with the science of Aristotle, and they are those who are called and known as the men of the shaded place (*aṣḥāb al-maẓalla*), and they are the spirituals,'[6] which clearly points to the Stoics. Nevertheless, it is far more likely that Stoic logic reached Avicenna not directly but by way of Peripatetic and Neo-Platonic commentators. Among these were Galen, whose work on logic we know

1 *Shifā*, Paris, MS. Fol. 22.
2 Cf. *Lexicon of Logic*, mimeographed edition.
3 Cf. Mates: *Stoic Logic*.
4 *Kitāb al-Radd . . .*, p. 209.
5 Uṣaibi'a, Vol. 1, pp. 36, 87.
6 Qifṭī, p. 124.

to have been translated into Arabic and widely read; Alexander, for whom Avicenna expresses much appreciation and who in his refutation of the Stoics had discussed much of their logic; Ammonius, the noted disciple of Proclus and the author of various commentaries on Aristotelian logic; Porphyry, whose commentary was almost a textbook in its Arabic rendering and was sometimes called by its Greek name of *Eisagoge* (Introduction) or by the Arabic equivalent of *al-Madkhal*. This was considered a necessary introduction to logic and some supposed it actually a part of the *Organon*; and finally John Philoponus of Alexandria, commonly called the Grammarian. It is from these, besides the works of Aristotle, that Avicenna must have derived most of his knowledge of Greek logic.

Lukasiewicz was among the first to demonstrate that whereas the Aristotelian was a logic of classes, the Stoic was one of propositions. But towards the close of the Greek period in the history of logic, the two had already merged; and while the Arabs had the whole of the *Organon* before them, and may have had a translation of the Stoic works, this particular amalgam of the two which developed in the late Hellenistic age influenced them greatly. With this in mind it may be claimed that the logic of Avicenna really combines the two, not by a mechanical superimposition of one on the other, but via a critical assessment of the two doctrines, with a good measure of simplification and perfecting on his part. Simplification was desirable for one whose conception of the subject was practical: logic, as a tool for correct thinking, was to be made sharp and effective. In point of fact a distinctive feature of Avicenna's entire philosophy is that he shows himself perfectly ready to accept, to discard, to modify and to augment without the least hesitation. Avicenna does not go as far as Russell in dismissing all the Aristotelian categories, and even the word 'category,' as meaningless, but he does not mind stating that at least one of them means nothing to him; and on the other hand he asserts in his *Physics* that we need not necessarily postulate only ten genera of being, for other categories may be added, including one of motion. In the case of the hypothetical syllogism, which, as Alexander and John Philoponus testify, was first discussed by Theophrastus and Eudemus and later developed by the Stoics, Avicenna, ignoring the original sources, simplifies the matter almost out of all recognition.

Avicenna had discussed logic in some fifteen different works, but judging from what has survived, they differ somewhat in form and in content. In the *Shifā*, mistakenly translated by the Latins as *Sufficientia*, as well as in the abridged version called *Najāt* (Deliverance), he may be considered more Aristotelian in approach and to some extent in subject-matter. In later books such as *al-Ishārāt wa al-Tanbīhāt* (The Directives and Remarks), in his Persian *Dānish-Nāmeh* (Book of Knowledge), and in the fragment called *Manṭiq al-Mashriqīyyīn* (Logic of the Orientals), he is inclined to deviate from Aristotle. It should not be supposed that the deviation is very marked, but there is certainly an attempt to think over the problems independently. The *Logic of the Orientals* has become the subject of much controversy; both title and contents have been interpreted in various ways. The latest and the most plausible theory is that it formed part of a much larger book[1] which we know Avicenna had written, which was entitled *al-Ḥikmat al-Mashriqīyya* (The Philosophy of the Orientals) and in which he had expressed his own mature views towards the end of his life. It is contended that he called it 'Oriental' so as to contrast it with the servile Aristotelianism of some Christian philosophers in Baghdad who were to him 'Occidentals.' 'We do not worry,' he says, 'to show a departure . . . from those philosophers enamoured of the Peripatetics who imagine that God did not guide any except themselves.'[2]

This attitude is best expressed in what is supposed to be his last work on logic. 'That we may put down some statements on what men of investigation have disagreed upon . . . we do not worry

[1] Cf. Pines: *La Philosophie orientale . . . Arch. d'Histoire . . . du Moyen Âge* 1953.

[2] *Manṭiq*, p. 2.

about any departure that may appear on our part from what the expounders of the books of the Greeks have been occupied with, either out of oversight or lack of understanding . . . it became easy for us to comprehend what they said, when we first took up that subject. And it is not improbable that certain sciences may have reached us from elsewhere than the side of the Greeks . . . we then compared all these with that variety of science which the Greeks call logic—and it is not improbable that it may have a different name among the Orientals . . . and because those who occupy themselves with science are extremely proud of the Peripatetics . . . we disliked to dissent from and oppose the public . . . and we overlooked what they were struggling with . . . and if we venture to oppose them, it is in things in which we can no more show patience . . . they consider that looking deep into matters is a heresy, and that opposing what is widely accepted is a departure from the right path . . . and we did not compile this book except for ourselves, I mean for those who take the same position as ourselves. And as to the common people who engage in such things, we gave them in the book of the *Shifā* what is even too much for them and beyond their requirements.'[1] This passage is provocative. What is the source other than the Greek from which, he says, certain sciences may have reached us; and what is the name the Orientals gave to logic different from that of the Greeks? Is he referring to Indian thought, or Middle Persian writings, or what had developed in his own part of the world? In spite of innumerable theories, no satisfactory answer has yet been found. In any case the vague and fragmentary parts that have reached us of this work hardly fulfil the promise that he gives.

Having defined logic, Avicenna, like the Stoics, begins with a brief discussion of the theory of knowledge. All knowledge, according to Aristotle, starts from particulars, and every belief comes by way of a syllogism. For Fārābī 'the knowledge of a thing could be through the rational faculty, and it could be

[1] *Manṭiq*, pp. 2–4.

through the imaginative faculty, and it could be through the senses.'[1] For Avicenna 'all knowledge and cognition is either a concept (*taṣawwur*) or an assent (*taṣdīq*); and the concept is the first knowledge and is acquired through definition and what follows the same method, such as our conception of the quiddity of man. And assent is acquired through syllogism and what follows the same method, such as our assent that for everything there is a beginning. Thus definition and syllogism are twin tools with which are acquired the knowledgeables that are known and which through thought become known.'[2]

The origin of these two terms and their Greek equivalents in particular have 'baffled modern scholarship for over a century.'[3] Some have tried to attribute them to Sextus Empiricus.[4] They could just as well be attributed to Chrysippus.[5] Actually the terms of Avicenna and to some extent the concept, can be traced back to Arabic translations of the *Organon*.[6] But the Stoics, with their well-known interest in language, altered the terms and developed the thought, and it may be presumed, though there is no direct evidence, that it was through some commentator that it reached Avicenna. Among the *Falāsifa* it is first found in Fārābī, but in a highly suspect treatise which may be actually by his successor.[7] After Avicenna it becomes the introductory statement of almost every manual on logic whether in Arabic or Persian.

Again he says that all knowledge is either the concept of some particular notion that has meaning (*ma'na*)[8] or an assent to it. There could be a concept without an assent, and all assents and concepts are either acquired as a result of some investigation or they are *a priori*. It may be observed that he regards concepts and assents as the primary sources and correlates them with what he takes to be the fundamentals of logic, viz. definition and syllogism. But there are matters to which we give our assent

[1] *Madīnat* . . ., p. 51. [2] *Najāt*, p. 3. [3] Wolfson: *Moslem World*, 1943.
[4] *Ibid.* [5] *Stoic. Vet. Frag.*, II, 55, 56, 59. [6] Afnan, *op. cit.*
[7] '*Uyūn al-Masā'il.*
[8] Aristotelian *νοήμα θεώρημα* (what is perceived), *πρᾶγμα* (deed, thing) and Stoic *λεκτόν* (abstraction: what is capable of being spoken).

without the intermediary of syllogistic reasoning. There are sense data (*maḥsūsāt*) 'which are matters to which the sense causes assent,' and empirical data (*mujarrabāt*) 'which are matters to which the sense in association with syllogistic reasoning causes assent.' And there are transmitted data (*mutuwātirāt*) 'which are matters to which the transmission of news causes assent.' And there are the accepted data (*maqbūlāt*) 'which are matters to which the word of the person in whose truthfulness there is confidence causes assent; this is either because of a heavenly injunction in his favour, or because of an opinion and effective thought by which he has distinguished himself.' And there are imagined data (*wahmīyyāt*) 'which are opinions in which the faculty of the imagination necessitates a belief.' And there are generally widespread data (*dhā'ī'āt*) 'which are propositions and opinions, famous and praiseworthy, to which the evidence of everybody . . . or of the majority or the evidence of the learned or of most of them, causes assent.' And there are presumed data (*maẓnūnāt*). And there are imaginative data (*mukhayyalāt*) which are propositions not stated to obtain assent of any kind, but 'to imagine something to be something else.' And there are *a priori* data (*awwalīyyāt*) 'which are premisses and propositions originating in man by way of his intellectual faculty without any cause except its self to necessitate its assent.'[1] Moreover the current practice has been to call what leads to the required concept an expository discourse (*qawlun shāriḥ*);[2] definitions, descriptions and similar statements are of this kind, and to call what leads to the required assent a proof, and proofs are of three varieties, syllogism, induction and analogy.

Avicenna pays much attention throughout to definition, and considers it of fundamental importance; but before taking up that subject he realizes the necessity of specifying the terms and determining their meaning, because there is a certain relation between the vocable (*lafẓ*)[3] and its connotation; and states affect-

[1] *Najāt*, pp. 60 ff. [2] Cf. *Stoic. Vet. Frag.*, II, pp. 43, 62.
[3] φωνή, φάσις, λέξις.

ing the vocables may also affect what they designate. There are three ways, he points out, in which a vocable signifies the meaning for which it stands. One is by way of complete accord (*muṭābaqa*) between the two, another is by way of implication (*taḍammun*), and yet another is by way of concomitance (*iltizām*).[1]

The vocable could be singular (*mufrad*) or composite, and the composite (*murakkab*) may be a complete or an incomplete discourse. The vocable could also be particular or universal; and every universal could be essential or accidental. It may be noted that some of the terms used here are shared by Arabic grammar; and the problem thus arises; did Greek logic have any influence on the development of Arabic grammar, which was systematized and established rather late in the history of the language? This is a moot question on which opinion is divided. In our view there is very little evidence in favour of this theory, though some scholars have held to it tenaciously.

On predication, Avicenna says that every predicate may be either constitutive or concomitant or accidental. Aristotle had discussed the predicables in the *Topica* and had there specified that they were *definition*, *genus*, *property*, and *accident*, with *differentia* as a subdivision, thus making them five in all. Porphyry in his *Eisagoge*, 'losing sight of the principle on which the division was made,'[2] replaced definition by species and maintained that the predicables were *genus*, *species*, *differentia*, *property*, and *accident*. This was for him an unusual departure from Aristotle which proved rather confusing to his successors who had thought of him as a faithful interpreter of the Stagirite, though he eventually lost that position after the bitter attacks of Avicenna and his scornful reference to his works. The *Eisagoge* had been translated into Arabic, and this division of the predicables had been accepted by some logicians of Baghdad, though there occurs a curious classification into six: *genus*, *species*, *individual*, *differentia*, *property* and *accident*,[3] probably under Stoic

[1] *Ishārāt*, p. 4. [2] Cf. Joseph: *An Introd. to Logic.*
[3] *Risālat al-Jāmi'a*, Vol. 1, p. 262.

influence. Avicenna accepts the five predicables, but not Porphyry's definition in every case. 'Do not pay any attention,' he says, 'to what the author of the *Eisagoge* has to say on the descriptive definition of the *genus* by the species.' Avicenna is opposed to this because he himself distinguishes between *natural genus* and *logical genus*. *Natural genus* is equivalent to the actual essence of a thing in answer to the question 'What is it?,' such as animality; *logical genus* on the other hand is what is added to *natural genus* in order to give it universality, for logic is a subject that treats of universals. And in this connection he dubs Porphyry 'the master of bluff and misrepresentation,' whereas Alexander he had called 'the accomplished of the latter ones,' and Themistius, 'he who polished his phrases on the books of the first teacher [i.e. Aristotle].' Modern logicians share Avicenna's view on this point and take exception to Porphyry's definition of the *genus*. Again Porphyry had divided *accident* into separable and inseparable,[1] which modern logicians consider impermissible, because 'if a singular term be the subject, it is confused; if a general, self-contradictory';[2] and Avicenna says 'do not worry that [an accident] be inseparable (*mulāzim*) or separable (*mufāriq*).'[3] He then proceeds on his descriptive definitions. 'A genus may be descriptively defined as a universal predicated of things of different essences in answer to the question "what is it?"'[4] 'A differentia may be descriptively defined as a universal predicated of a thing in answer to the question "which thing is it?" in its substance. And species may be descriptively defined in either of two meanings: first as a universal predicated of things that do not differ except in number in answer to the question "what is it?" and . . . in the second meaning as a universal to which, as to others, the genus is given as predicate, an essential and primary predication. And property may be descriptively defined as a universal predicated of what is, under one essence only, an attribute that is not essential. And the general accident may

[1] χωριστόν—ἀχώριστον.
[2] Joseph: *op. cit.*, p. 108.
[3] *Najāt*, p. 10.
[4] Cf. *Top*, 102a31.

be descriptively defined as a universal predicated of what is under one essence, and also of others, an attribute that is not essential.'[1]

Just as Aristotelian metaphysics was to become sadly confused with Neo-Platonic thought through the translation of the so-called *Theology* of Aristotle, to the utter confusion of Islamic philosophers, so here we find Aristotelian logic becoming intermingled with that of his followers and also with Stoic logic either directly or through the perplexing disquisitions of the commentators. Galen, whose extant *Institutio Logica* has been vehemently denounced as spurious and equally vehemently proclaimed authentic, was among those who transmitted this combination. As to Chrysippus, of whom it was said 'if gods have logic, this must be Chrysippian,' there is no sufficient evidence that the *Falāsifa*, and Avicenna in particular, had direct knowledge of his work.

With regard to definition, which Avicenna discusses in a number of places and at great length, he states that it is not something that can be obtained through division, which we know to have been the method suggested by Plato. Nor is it possible to reach an adequate definition through demonstration; and even induction must be ruled out since it does not give conclusive knowledge and cannot therefore be of much help. Definition can only be attained through a combination of the above, based on the individuals (*ashkhāṣ*)[2] that are indivisible. In attempting a definition, philosophers do not seek differentiation even though that may follow. What they seek is the reality of a thing and its essence. For this reason there is really no definition for what has no existence: there could only be a statement explaining the name. Where definition is confined to the cause, it is called the principle of demonstration; and where it is confined to the caused or effect, it is then called the consequence of demonstration. The complete definition combines these two together with the genus. Like Aristotle, Avicenna defines a definition as 'a phrase signifying

[1] *Ishārāt*, p. 16. [2] ἄτομα.

the essence of a thing.'[1] And in Persian he repeats that the purpose of a definition is the recognition of the actual essence of that thing, and differentiation is something that follows by itself. It is to be remembered that the authors of the *Epistles* before him had stated that differentiation was an actual element and a part of every definition; and Averroës after him asserts that all definitions are composed of two natural parts, genus and differentia.

From definition Avicenna turns his attention to the second source of knowledge which is assent, obtainable through syllogistic reasoning. But actually he continually reverts to the subject of definition, particularly descriptive definition (*rasm*: a term used by the translators of the *Organon* as the equivalent of a number of Greek words used by Aristotle).[2] A proposition he defines as 'every discourse in which there is a relation between two things in such manner that a true or false judgement follows.'[3] It is known that the Stoics also considered a proposition to be either true or false;[4] they believed that Aristotle held that propositions about future contingencies were neither true nor false. Avicenna adds that 'as with interrogation, supplication, expectation, request, surprise and the like, the person who expresses them is not told that he is truthful or untruthful except accidentally.'[5]

Like the Stoics, Avicenna divides propositions into atomic and molecular; the latter being compounded out of the former by a conjunction or connective (*ribāṭ*).[6] The molecular is then divided into 'the categorical (*al-ḥamlīy*), the hypothetical conjunctive (*al sharṭiy al-muttaṣil*) and the hypothetical disjunctive (*al-sharṭīy al-munfaṣil*)'—a classification which has its Stoic counterpart.[7]

The hypothetical proposition was already known to Aristotle[8]

[1] Cf. *Top.*, 101b37; *Ishārāt*, p. 17.

[2] *τύπος, διαγράμματα, γράφω, σημεία.*

[3] *Najāt*, p. 12.

[4] *ἀξίωμα δέ ἐστιν ὅ ἐστιν ἀληθές ἤ Ψεῦδος.*

[5] *Ishārāt*, p. 22.

[6] *σύνδεσμος.*

[7] Arnim, II, p. 68. *τῶν δ' οὐχ ἁπλῶν ἀξιωμά τῶν συννημένον μέν . . . συμπεπλεγμένον δέ . . . διεζευγμένον δέ . . .*

[8] *ἐκ ὑποθέσεως* (*A. Pr.* 50a32) 'an sharīṭa.

though he does not seem to have explored it. Theophrastus is supposed to have studied it, but only to a limited extent. It is therefore impossible to state with any certainty the source from which it reached Avicenna. The similarity of his approach to that of the Stoics, however, is very close, and like them he devotes much attention to it. Yet he does not stop there and goes on to discuss a number of other propositions such as the singular, the particular, the indefinite, the limited or quantified, the modal, the absolute, and various others for not all of which it is possible to find an equivalent in Aristotelian logic or those Stoic writings that have reached us. One proposition which he definitely claims to be his own, is what he calls 'the existential' (*wujūdīyya*), and this he explains in detail in the *Shifā*. It arises from the fact that the copula does not exist in the Arabic language, and this was a complication of which Avicenna was well aware and to which he frequently refers. To remedy this linguistic obstacle, various equivalents had been used in different contexts, and among them was the verb 'to exist' (*wajada*). It was from this root and for this purpose that he formed his existential proposition. And Ibn Ṭumlus testifies to that and explains that it was called existential because it signifies existence without having anything in common with the idea of necessity or contingence. Avicenna, of course, was not the source of Boethius who centuries earlier had discussed these matters in his *De Syllogismis Categoricis* and *De Syllogismis Hypotheticis*.[1] These works which had an undoubted influence on mediaeval logic stem from Neo-Platonic and Stoic writings which Boethius had imbibed in Rome.

A review of the conditional proposition leads to the theory of consequence, a notion which, as the fundamental conception of formal logic, played an important role in all Arabic and Persian as well as Western mediaeval systems, and continues to occupy contemporary logicians.[2] Whether the doctrine can or cannot be traced farther back than the Stoic and Megarian school, as

[1] Cf. Durr: *The Propositional Logic of Boethius*.
[2] Cf. Carnap: *Logical Syntax*, p. 168.

described by Sextus Empiricus and Diogenes Laertius, it is the case that the Arabic terms for antecedent (*muqaddam*) and consequence (*tālī*) are not to be found in the translation of the *Organon*, and must therefore have entered the language through some other source. This could have been through Stoic writings directly, in which we find the Greek equivalents,[1] or through the works of some of the commentators of Aristotle. It is in Avicenna that the terms are first defined, and successors like Suhrawardī and Ibn Ṭumlūs only copy him. He states that just as the categorical has two parts, a subject and a predicate, the conditional also has two parts. In the hypothetical conjunctive proposition there are two and only two parts or clauses; one is the antecedent and the other the consequent. The antecedent is that to which the condition is bound, and the consequent is that which constitutes the answer. In the disjunctive, however, there could be one or many consequents to the antecedent. So that the difference between antecedent and consequent and subject and predicate is that subject and predicate could be replaced by a simple term, whereas antecedent and consequent could not because each is in itself a proposition.

Another set of terms for which there are no Aristotelian equivalents, and which must have therefore entered Arabic from some other—probably Stoic—source, are those used for a conclusive (*muntij*) and an inconclusive (*'aqīm*) proposition. But in his definition of a thing (*pragma*) which so occupied the Stoics and led to so much discussion, Avicenna follows 'the owner of logic,' as stated in the *De Interpretatione*. 'A thing (*shai'*) is either an existing entity; or a form derived from it existing in the imagination or in the mind . . . or a sound signifying the form . . . or a writing signifying the sound. . . .'[2]

These examples go to show that Avicenna is no servile imitator of any school, but thinks over every question independently and with an open mind. Another illustration of this attitude occurs in connection with his examination of absolute propositions.

[1] *τό ἡγούμενον—τό λῆγον.* [2] *Najāt*, p. 11.

'There are two views with regard to the absolute [proposition],' he says, 'the view of Theophrastus and Themistius and others; and that of Alexander and a number of the accomplished ones.' And after giving their viewpoint, he adds what he supposes may have been the original conception of Aristotle himself. And he finally concludes with the remark that 'we do not occupy ourselves with showing preference for either the Themistian or the Alexandrian viewpoint; we would rather consider judgements concerning the absolute in both manners.'[1]

There are three procedures for proving something. One is syllogism (*qiyās*), the second is induction (*istiqrā'*) and what accompanies it, and the third is analogy (*tamthīl*) and what accompanies it.[2] In agreement with Aristotle in the *Analytica Priora*, Avicenna says, 'a syllogism is a statement composed of statements from which, when made, another different statement by itself and not by accident, follows necessarily'; and syllogisms are perfect or imperfect. It is in his division of the kinds of syllogism that he differs from Aristotle. In all his works without exception (and therefore it could not be a late development in his system), he says that syllogisms are of two kinds, the *iqtirānīy* (by combination, by coupling) and the *istithnā'īy* (by exclusion, exceptive); and in one passage he claims that this division is 'according to what we verified ourselves.'[3] The origin of this division, if indeed it has any outside Avicenna's own mind, is not known. (Aristotle in the *Topica* had divided syllogisms into the demonstrative, the dialectical, and the sophistic. Galen divides syllogisms into the hypothetical, the categorical and the relative.)[4] It may well be a case of Avicennian simplification; but the terms that he has employed are difficult to translate correctly. The attempt of a modern author to equate them with the categorical and the hypothetical is not satisfactory. They are definitely not of Aristotelian origin. The term *iqtirān* does indeed occur in an Arabic translation of a fragment by Themistius

[1] *Najāt*, p. 23. [2] *Ishārāt*, p. 64.
[3] *Ibid.*, p. 65. [4] ὑποθετικοί, κατηγορικοί, κατά τό πρός τι.

without any explanation, however. Ghazālī says 'the categorical syllogism is sometimes called the *iqtirānīy* syllogism and sometimes the ostensive,'[1] but he seems confused himself. Avicenna states in Persian that 'an *iqtirānīy* syllogism is that in which two premisses are brought together, having one term in common and the other different; then there necessarily follows from them another proposition which is composed of those two terms which were not in common between them . . . "every body is formed," and "everything that is formed is created," hence it necessarily follows that "every body is created." '[2] All this is simple, and in Arabic he adds that '*iqtirānīy* syllogisms could be formed from pure categoricals, or from pure hypotheticals, or from the two combined.'[3] What is to be resolved is the origin of the name. This is of Stoic origin and is a literal translation of the Greek *συζυγία* (yoke) which had a vague and general sense in Aristotle, but which became a technical term with the Stoics.[4] The word as used by Aristotle in the *Organon* had been translated into Arabic as *izdiwāj*. On the other hand the Arab *iqtirān* had been used by the translators to render other Aristotelian terms in the *Sophistics* and the *De Interpretatione*.[5] The equivalence of the Avicennian *iqtirān* with the Stoic *συζυγία* becomes evident from the statement of various authors before and after him;[6] and on the Stoic side by some fragments that have survived.[7]

The *istithnā'īy* (by exclusion) syllogism is more difficult to identify by association with any particular Aristotelian or Stoic term. He explains that it 'is composed of two premises, one conditional and the other with an ecthesis (*waḍ'*)[8] or exclusion (*raf'*) of either of the two parts; and it could possibly be categorical or hypothetical; and it is this which is called the excluded

[1] *Mi'yār . . .*, p. 77. [2] *Dānish-Nāmeh*, p. 62. [3] *Ishārāt*, p. 66.

[4] Cf. Lukasiewicz, p. 63. [5] *συζυγία* (*Top.* 113a12) *izdiwāj*.
συλλογίζεσθαι (*Soph.* 169b29) *qarana iqtirānan*.
συγκεῖσθαι (*P. Herm.* 19b21) *maqrūn*.

[6] *Epistles*, edit. Zirgalī, I, p. 337; Ṭūsī, *Asās . . .*, p. 186; Tahānawī, II, p. 1229

[7] Cf. von Arnim, II, 166, 48. [8] *θέσις* (*Categ.* 4b21), *waḍ'*.
ἔκθεσις (*A. Pr.* 28a14) *al-waḍ'*.

(*al-mustathnāt*)'.[1] And again 'the *istithnā'īy* syllogism is different from the *iqtirānīy* in that one of the two extremes of what is wanted (*maṭlūb*),[2] is found in the *istithnā'īy* syllogism actually, and is not found in the *iqtirānīy* syllogism except potentially.'[3]

Aristotle had divided the syllogistic modes into three figures; and all throughout his logical works we have not seen Avicenna make any mention of the fourth figure. But the fact that it had been introduced into Islamic logic through some external source —possibly Galen—is shown by its use in Qazwīnī, as we have already noted, and also in Ṭūsī.[4]

The Stoics, we are told, distinguished between 'true' and 'the truth';[5] and the same distinction is found in Avicenna who calls the first *ṣādiq* and the second *ṣidq*. This corresponds with his differentiation between *ḥaqq* and *ḥaqīqa* which go back to Aristotle himself and are to be found in the translations of his *Organon*. Fārābī had said that 'the truth of a thing, is the existence particular to that thing.' Avicenna stated that 'the truth of a thing is that particularity of its existence which is proven of it'; and Suhrawardī, after repeating the definition of Avicenna, adds that 'truth is a mental consideration'; which corresponds with the Stoic doctrine that it was a simple and incorporeal notion (*lekton*).

An argument, according to the Stoics, was a statement composed of premisses and a conclusion. With their zeal for linguistic innovation, they had changed the terms of Aristotle into those of their own; but the Arabic equivalents of both the Aristotelian and Stoic remained the same; and we find them used by Avicenna also as *muqaddima* (premiss) and *natīja* (conclusion).[6] It is, however, in his enumeration of the different varieties of premisses that we find him going beyond anything said by Aristotle; and it is difficult to determine whether the varieties were his own or taken from some other source. He mentions as many as thirteen.

1 *Najāt*, p. 50. 2 *ζητούμενον*. 3 *Shifā*, Paris, MS., Fol. 160.

4 *Asās* . . ., p. 279. 5 *τό ἀληθές, ἡ ἀλέθεια.*

6 Peripatetic *πρότασις, συμπέρασμα* Stoic *λῆμμα, ἐπιφορά.*

V The doctrine of the *Quantification of the Predicate* is not of Aristotelian origin, and the Arabic term *sūr* standing for quantification is not to be found in the translations of the *Organon*. Kindī uses the term rather vaguely; the authors of the *Epistles* have more to say on the subject and distinguish two forms of predication: the general and the particular; it may be presumed that Fārābī too dealt with it, though it does not appear in any of the works so far published. In Avicenna it is discussed at length and all his successors follow him in stressing that there are two forms. Considering that this doctrine had already a long history in the post-classical period, before it was invented anew by Hamilton and Jevons; and that in the opinion of some modern logicians there can be no truth in it, it is interesting to speculate on the sources from which it entered Arabic and Persian logic. Avicenna says '*sūr* is the term which signifies the quantity of limitation, like *all* and *not one* and *some* and *not all*';[1] and a lexicographer explains that 'a proposition that comprises the *sūr* is called quantified (*musawwara*) and limited (*maḥṣūra*) and it is either general or particular.'[2]

Aristotle's distinctions of modality are four, viz. the possible, the contingent, the impossible and the necessary.[3] This is confirmed in the commentary of Ammonius, who is said to have been the first to use the term *tropos* in that sense. Modern scholars have argued with some justice that actually the contingent and the possible are practically indistinguishable in Aristotle. In any case we find Avicenna saying 'the modalities (*jihāt*) are three, necessary, which denotes permanence of existence, impossible, which denotes permanence of non-existence, and possible, which denotes neither permanence of existence nor of non-existence.'[4] This division into three rather than four is copied by his successors as far away as Andalusia. This might suggest that unlike Aristotle, Avicenna does not differentiate between the possible and the contingent; but in fact he does differentiate between the

[1] *Najāt*, p. 14.
[2] Tahānawī, 1, p. 658.
[3] *P. Herm*, 21a34–37; *An. Pri.*, 25a1.
[4] *Najāt*, p. 17.

two notions, contrary to what some have supposed. The confusion is only due to terminology. The Aristotelian term for contingency has been translated differently in different passages.[1] Avicenna, who had no access to the original Greek, seems to have preferred the term *mumkin* for both notions, specifying at the same time, in Persian[2] and at much greater length and clarity in Arabic, that it had a twofold connotation comprising possibility and contingency. He even coins Persian abstract terms for these concepts.

His definition of the contingent as 'that judgement which in the negative or the affirmative is not necessary,'[3] hardly differs from that of Aristotle.[4] But in his lengthy explanations he contrasts the ordinary and the special senses of the term *mumkin* and he distinguishes between what is binding (*wājib*)[5] and what is necessary (*ḍarūrī*). In fact the notions of possibility and contingency are of fundamental importance to him, and extend far beyond logic to the field of metaphysics, which is the pivot of his entire philosophy. Philo had defined the necessary as 'that which being true, is in its very nature not susceptible of falsehood.'

Avicenna ends his logical treatises in the traditional way with a discussion of the different fallacies (*mughāliṭāt*), and in close correspondence with the *Sophistics* of Aristotle. But even before arriving at that, he takes up the problem of the *Petitio Principii* (*al-muṣādara 'ala al-maṭlūb al-awwal*). It is generally thought that this problem first appears in the *Prior Analytics*, but the Arabic terms as used by Avicenna are slightly different from those of the actual translations, and may therefore have come to him by way of some commentary and not from the Aristotelian texts direct. There is a passing mention of it in the *Epistles*; Avicenna, however, devotes more attention to it, even though he is inclined to consider it a fallacy. In the *Shifā* he speaks of

[1] *τό δυνατον* (*P. Herm.* 21a35), *mumkin*.
τό ἐνδεχόμενον (*P. Herm.* 21a35), *muḥtamal*.
τό ἐνδεχόμενον (*A. Pr.* 32a19), *al-mumkin*.

[2] *Dānish-Nāmeh*, p. 44; *Najāt*, p. 17.

[3] *Najāt*, p. 25.

[4] *A. Pri.* 32a19.

[5] *τό δέον* (*Soph.* 165b35) *wājib*.

'the *petitio principii* that is included among the genus [of those things] that it has not been possible to prove'; while in the shorter works like the *Najāt*, he refers to the matter with an explanation and without specifying whether it is a correct method of reasoning. In the writings of his successors and certain lexicographers, it seems to be accepted as a valid way of reasoning.

The question whether Avicenna was a nominalist or realist is not easy to resolve, and his position not always very clear. But he maintains that 'a definition is either according to the name or according to the essence; and that which is according to the name is a detailed discourse signifying what is understood by the name for the person who uses it; and that which is according to the essence is a detailed discourse making known the essence through its quiddity';[1] thus he accepts the conceptions of both nominalism and realism, and may therefore be considered a conceptualist. This is confirmed by his statement in the *Shifā* that 'the logical science . . . its subject was the secondary intelligible meanings (*maʿānī*) that are based on the primary intelligible meanings'; and this conceptualism is the attitude of many modern logicians.

The Aristotelian *Organon* with its sometimes conflicting accretions in the form of treatises of Hellenistic origin had produced a hybrid mixture of extraordinary complexity and of diverse traditions, Megarian, Stoic, Peripatetic and Neo-Platonic. The genius of Avicenna consisted in his careful selection of the fundamental principles from what he called 'the first teaching'; in his discriminating acceptance of some of the later additions and modifications; and finally in his critical reconstruction of a system which he considered valid and adequate. Furthermore he can claim the credit of having set the direction of development —if there was to be any—for those who were to follow, along the path that he had opened. When the logical works of his successors are examined, it is seen that they had hardly anything to add. Even among the Andalusian philosophers who were

[1] *Manṭiq* . . ., p. 34.

highly critical of him, such as Averroës with his sterile Aristotelianism, or Ibn Ṭumlūs with his avowed preference for Fārābī, there is nothing worthy of note.

The only person to challenge his philosophy effectively, and attack his logic, and even try to change some of its terms, was Ghazālī. But the measure of his success, as far as logic was concerned, is reflected in the disparaging remarks of Ibn Ṭumlūs. The arguments of Ibn Taimīyya,[1] one of the most able and accomplished theologians, was directed against Greek logic in general. Nevertheless interest in the subject continued until it became an essential part of the curriculum in all seminaries. One person who attempted alterations and the development of what he called a logic of his own was Suhrawardī, the mystic author of the 'illuminative' philosophy, not with any notable results, however.

In the long vista of Arabic and Persian logic, early authors tended to give the place of honour to Fārābī, but until more of his works come to light we are in no position to judge his full contribution. After him Avicenna stands supreme. His influence dominates every single book on the subject in either of the two languages. The line extends directly to mediaeval times; and we find Albertus Magnus saying: 'Quae ex logicis doctrinis arabum in latinum transtulit Avendar israelita Philosophus et maxime de logica Avicennae.'

[1] Cf. *Kitāb al-Radd* . . .

CHAPTER IV

PROBLEMS OF METAPHYSICS

METAPHYSICS which has hardly yet recovered from the fierce onslaught of logical positivism in modern times, was of the essence of Islamic philosophy and the realm of its chief contribution to the history of ideas.

Two factors helped to place it in a position of eminence among the intellectual disciplines that reached the Islamic world from Greece, viz. the classical and the religious. Aristotle had justified it in the short opening phrase of his own *Metaphysica* on the basis that 'all men by nature desire to know.' Philosophy springing, in his view, from primitive wonder and moving towards its abolition through an understanding of the world, was an effort 'to inquire of what kind are the causes and the principles, the knowledge of which is Wisdom'; particularly of the first and most universal causes. And a single supreme science of metaphysics, devoted to the study of the real as such was possible, he maintained, and may be fruitfully pursued.

The impact upon revealed religion proved a more powerful factor. Transcendental elements had already found some place in classical philosophy, though the system remained fundamentally rationalistic. Through contact with the East, some religious influences were brought to bear upon it, as is reflected in the writings of the Stoics, the Neo-Platonists and other Hellenistic schools; but it continued separate and distinct. Now revealed religion set a rival and more formidable claim to knowledge. In the search after the ultimate realities, it asserted that faith in the human mind was vain, for the source of all knowledge was in God. Philo Judaeus attempted to reconcile classical philosophy with the tenets of his religion; and Christian thinkers made a bold and earnest endeavour in that direction. And when the rational speculations of the Greeks reached Islamic society, and came face to face with a triumphant religion at the height of its power, the matter became an urgent and important issue. It finally came to be thought that it was in the realm of metaphysics that the relation between reason and revelation could be best explored, and that the fundamentals of religion could find rational justification and proof. Whether they divided philosophy into four branches as found in the *Epistles*, to comprise mathematics, logic, the natural sciences and metaphysics; or into three as Avicenna does after Aristotle, to include the higher science (metaphysics), the middle science (mathematics), and the lower science (the phenomena of nature); it was metaphysics that concerned itself with the ultimate realities. Logic, today of the essence of philosophy, was for them only an instrument, a tool in the search after truth.

The arrangement of Aristotle's *Metaphysica* proved just as confusing to them as it is to modern scholars. Book *Lambda*, now considered an independent treatise and his only systematic essay in theology, became the basis of a distinct branch of study called the Science of the Divine (*al-ʿIlm al-Ilāhī*). Some confused it with the whole of metaphysics, others kept it separate; and their reactions to it were not all the same. Some, like the Brethren of Purity, thought that the rival disciplines could and should be reconciled; others, like the theologians, repudiated any such possibility; and still others, like the *Falāsifa*, propounded the belief that the fundamentals were different but complementary rather than totally negative to one another. In his evaluation of philosophy, Avicenna finds it necessary to assert that 'there is nothing in it that comprises matters contrary to the *sharʿ* (religious law). Those who put forth this claim . . . are going astray of their own accord.'[1] This Science of the Divine which, in spite of some confusing statements here and there, he, just like Aristotle, considered only a part, though perhaps the more essential part of metaphysics, is then divided into five separate

[1] *Tisʿa Rasāʾil*, p. 80.

sections. Metaphysics was to gain added importance because whereas Averroës found his proof for the existence of God in physics, Avicenna founded his arguments upon both physics and metaphysics.

For Kindī metaphysics was 'the science of that which does not move,' and 'the science of the First Truth which is the cause of all truth.' Fārābī divided metaphysics into three parts: The first dealing with beings in general and the states through which they pass; the second dealing with the principles of demonstration used in the theoretical sciences; and the third dealing with beings that are not corporeal in themselves, nor to be found in bodies; and about these he asks whether they exist, whether they are many or limited in number, and whether they all have the same degree of perfection. And finally this examination culminates in a demonstration that one Being could not possibly have acquired its existence from any other, 'the True that granted everything possessing truth its truth . . . who verily is God.'[1]

For Avicenna the first impression received by the soul, and the first acquisition of certain knowledge, is the distinct notion of *being*; and as such it constitutes the first and the true object of metaphysics. Not just any particular being in space or in time, but 'absolute being inasmuch as it is absolute.' This thought which had been already suggested by Aristotle[2] became for him a central theme to be developed far beyond anything envisaged by the Stagirite himself. Thus if it be said that the central element of Platonic metaphysics is the theory of Ideas, and that of the Aristotelian is the doctrine of potentiality and actuality, that of Avicennian metaphysics is the study of being as being. With that as a starting-point we may seek the knowledge of things that are separate from matter. This is philosophy in its true sense; and it can prove useful in correcting the principles of the other sciences. It begins with the subject of an existing being (*mawjūd*); and it is called the first philosophy because it leads to the knowledge of the first in existence.

[1] *Iḥṣa'* . . ., p. 60. [2] *Metaph.*, 1003a21.

In his approach to the inquiry Avicenna's background is a combination of religious orthodoxy as represented by the Mutakallemūn, rational explanation of dogma as propounded by the school of Mu'tazila, and syncretistic tendencies as favoured by the followers of the Ismā'īlī heterodoxy. Not that he adhered to any of these groups himself, in fact he had very little sympathy for any of them; but he certainly thought their views worth considering. His philosophical outlook was determined by Platonic and by Aristotelian thought with additions from Neo-Platonic and Stoic as well as late Peripatetic sources. Again he never followed any of these schools consistently, but traces of their doctrines can be found in almost all that he wrote.

*　　*　　*　　*

Metaphysics was for Aristotle a matter of problems or difficulties (*aporiai*). In like manner Avicenna turns from a description of the subject and its chief purpose to certain preliminary questions (*masā'il*) that he feels should be first elucidated and solved. It is only then that its relation to religion can be properly assessed and determined. Avicenna chose to explore what Russell calls the No Man's Land dividing science from theology, the strip—narrow and unmarked—whereon they meet. This may have shown unjustified optimism on his part, yet he continued confident and persistent.

All existing beings can be seen 'in a manner of division into substance and accident.' In Book E of the *Metaphysica*, Aristotle had pointed out that accidental or incidental being, and being as truth, were irrelevant to metaphysics. Avicenna could not disagree with the first statement, but the second was different. When using the resources of the whole subject to prove the existence of God, one of whose attributes was 'the truth,' he could not very well agree on that point. He therefore devoted some attention to the differentiation between 'the truth' and 'true,' a logical distinction to which he gave an ontological significance. The categories other than substance were mere concomitants. Classification into them was like division according to differentia. And the classification into potentiality and actuality, the one and the multiple, the eternal and the created, the complete and the incomplete, the cause and the effect, is like division according to accident.

The existence of substance and its distinction from the other categories was self-evident to Aristotle, and Avicenna accepts the substance-accident division which so much was to occupy his successors and the Scholastics after them. Like Aristotle he maintains that 'all essence that is not present in a subject is substance; and all essence that is constituted in a subject is accident.' Substance can be material or immaterial; and in the hierarchy of existence it is *immaterial substance* that has supremacy over all; then comes *form*, then *body* composed as it is of form and matter put together; and finally *matter* itself. Substance could be in different states. Where it is part of a body, it could be its form, or it could be its matter; and if it is entirely apart and separate, it could have a relation of authority over the body through movement and it is then called 'the soul'; and it could be entirely free of matter in every way and it is then called 'an intellect.' This leads to the opposition between matter and form so familiar in Aristotle.

Matter is that which is presupposed by change—in position, in quality, in size, and in coming into being and passing away. But is there such a thing as matter? Avicenna tries to assure himself of its existence. A body is not a body because it has actually three dimensions. It is not necessary to have points and lines to make a body. In the case of the sphere there are no such intersections. As to the plane surface, it does not enter into the definition of a body as body, but of body as finite. And the fact of its being finite does not enter into the essence of it but is just a concomitant. It is possible to conceive the essence of a body and its reality, and have it confirmed in the mind, without its being thought of as finite. It can also be known through demonstration and observation. A body is supposed to have three dimensions and no more. It is first supposed to have length, and if so then breadth, and if so then depth. This notion of it is its *material form*, and it is for the physicists to occupy themselves with it. The delimited dimensions are not its form, they fall under the category of quantity, and that is a subject for mathematicians. They are concomitants and not constituents and they may change with the change in form. Then there is the substance which constitutes its essence. This is constituted in something and is present in a subject which in relation to form is an accident. 'We therefore say that the dimensions and the material form must necessarily have a subject or prime matter (*hayūla*) in which to be constituted.'[1] This is the substance that accepts union with material form to become one complete body with constituents and concomitants.

Yet in the scale of existence form is superior to matter. It is more real. Bodily matter cannot divest itself of material form and so remain separate. Its very existence is that of one disposed to receive, just as that of an accident is an existence disposed to be received. Form is what gives unity to a portion of matter, and form is dependent upon disposition. Under Platonic rather than Aristotelian influence Avicenna may be thought to give to form a superior reality which is somewhat degraded when united with matter. Thus in his view intelligible reality is superior to sensible reality. The connection of form with matter does not fall under the category of relation, because we can imagine form without matter and matter without form. Could one be the cause of the other? Matter cannot be the cause of form, since it has only the power to receive form. What is *in potentia* cannot become the cause of what is *in actu*. Furthermore, if matter were the cause of form, it ought to be anterior to it in essence, and we know that in the scale of existence it is not. Hence there is no possibility of its being the cause. Could it then be the effect of form? Here there is a distinction to be made between separate form and a particular material form. Matter may lose a particular form only

[1] *Najāt*, p. 329.

to receive another. The cause of matter is form in conjunction with a separate agent whom he, together with Fārābī, calls the Giver of Forms (*Wāhib al-Ṣuwar*) known to the Scholastics as *Dator formarum*. This agent is the *active intelligence* and in the last resort God Himself. Here then they both depart from Aristotle and under Neo-Platonic influence draw nearer to religious belief. For the Stagirite reality did not belong either to form or to matter; it resided in the union of the two.

The doctrine of matter and form is connected with the distinction between potentiality and actuality. We cannot explain change without it. Actuality is prior to potentiality. God is actual and so is form. Matter is potential, but not of the potentiality of non-being (*'adam*). This leads to the theory of causes. All the Islamic *Falāsifa* accepted the four causes: the material, the formal, the efficient and the final cause. 'Cause is said of the agent . . . and cause is said of the matter . . . and cause is said of the form . . . and cause is said of the end . . . and each of these is either proximate . . . or distant . . . it is either *in potentia* or it is *in actu*. It is either individual . . . or it is general . . . it is either in essence . . . or it is by accident.'[1] The material and the formal cause Avicenna is inclined to subdivide each into two. The material he divides into matter of the compound, and matter of the subject. And the formal he divides into form of the compound, and form of the primary matter. This has led some to believe that for him there are six causes. In fact he states in the *Shifā* that 'the causes are four.' As for Aristotle, all the four causes are required to produce an effect; and the effect follows necessarily from the causes, contrary to the views of the theologians. This deterministic attitude is one of the essential features of the Avicennian system. The final cause is the most important, for 'the chief agent and the chief mover in every thing is the end; the physician acts for the restoration of health.' The agent and what is disposed to receive are prior to the effect, but the form never precedes in time at all.

There was some conflict between the religious and the Aris-

[1] *Najāt*, p. 83.

totelian views regarding the priority of potentiality and actuality. The theologians insisted that potentiality was prior in every respect and not only in time; and Aristotle claimed that actuality came first. Many of the ancients, Avicenna says, were inclined to the belief that matter existed before form, and that the supreme agent gave it that form. This is the conception of religious law-givers, that God took over matter and gave it the best constituent form. And there were those who said that in pre-eternity these material things used to move by nature in a disorderly manner, and that the Almighty changed their nature and put them into a fixed order. And others contended that the eternal was the great darkness or the chaos of which Anaxagoras had spoken. All that was because they insisted that as in a seed, potentiality was prior to actuality. It is true that in certain corruptible things potentiality comes before actuality with a priority in time. But in universal and eternal matters that are not corruptible, even if they are particular, in them what is potential is not prior at all, because potentiality does not stand by itself. It must be constituted together with a substance that must be actual. The eternal beings, for instance, are always actual. The reality of what is actual comes before the reality of what is potential. And Avicenna concludes, just as Aristotle had done in this connection, that 'what is *in actu* is the Good in itself, and what is *in potentia* is the evil, or from it comes evil.'[1]

The problem of the one and the multiple had to be considered because 'the One is closely connected with the being who is the subject of this science.' Oneness is asserted of what is indivisible, whether it be in genus or in species or in accident or in relation or in subject or in definition. There is a manner in which the One in number could actually have multiplicity in it; in that case it would be one in composition and in combination; or it could potentially have multiplicity, in that case it is continuous and it is one in continuity; or it could be one as an absolute number. The multiple is the number opposed to one, and it is what con-

[1] *Shifā, Ilāhīyyāt.*

tains one, though by definition is not one. It may be a multiple in an absolute sense, or in relation to something else. Then comes the curious statement that 'the smallest number is two.'[1] It is reflected in the assertion of many Islamic philosophers that 'one is not a number'; and we find an ancient lexicographer saying 'and so one would not be a number.'[2] There could be two sources for this notion. There is first Plotinus who in the *Fifth Ennead* puts it down that 'the One is not one of the units which make up the number Two.'[3] There is also a gross mistranslation of a passage in Aristotle's *Metaphysica*[4] where the translator who knew no Greek and was translating from Syriac, makes the statement that 'one is not a number.' Although this was later corrected by another translator, the error for some reason persisted. However that may be, it became current in Islamic philosophy, and we find it continuously repeated. Unity, Avicenna says, is not the essence of anything. It is only an attribute that is necessary for its essence. Unity is not a constituent. Essence is one thing; and then it is qualified as being one and existing. Unity is the concomitant of a substance; it is subsequent to matter, or it is predicated of accidents.

As in his logic, Avicenna devotes a section of his metaphysics to the principles of definition and its relation to that which is being defined. He finds a special significance in definition and gives it an application much wider than the purely formal one. It is well to remember that though he is essentially a metaphysician, and logic does not occupy him excessively, he constantly uses logical distinctions and the whole resources of what was for him only an instrument and a tool in establishing the basis of his arguments and in constructing the vital points of his metaphysics. And he complains that 'most of those who philosophize learn logic but do not use it, they ultimately revert to their intuitions.' He is also inclined to think in terms of thesis, anti-

[1] *Najāt*, p. 365. [2] Jurjānī, p. 152

[3] Cf. Dean Inge: *Philos. of Plotinus*, Vol. 2, p. 108.

[4] *Metaph.*, 1052b23–24, Arabic trans. edit., Bouyges.

thesis and synthesis. Carra de Vaux, writing some fifty years ago, drew attention to this and tried to show its similarity to the Kantian method of thought. The tendency is of course Aristotelian. It might also be thought that the form which philosophy had taken in Islamic lands had something to do with it. Thinking in terms of contraries as reflected in substance and accident, matter and form, potentiality and actuality, became a distinctive feature, almost a tradition that has persisted in the East down to modern times. It may be supposed that the inclination was strengthened by the polarity between philosophy and religion, which was a constant thought in the minds of Islamic thinkers. The accusation—so often repeated—that Avicenna was apt to compromise in his attempt to bring about a *rapprochement* with the principles of religious thought, loses its point when we find Gomperz describing Aristotle as the great compromiser.

* * * *

With some preliminary problems surveyed, attention may now be directed to the fundamentals of Avicenna's thesis. It was stated above that for him the concept of being is the first acquisition of the human mind. The knowledge of the concept of being is arrived at both subjectively and objectively. Even if we suppose ourselves to be in a state where we are completely unconscious of our body, we are still aware of the fact that we *are* and we exist. This is shown by the illustration of the man suspended in the air, to be described in the next chapter on Psychology. Objectively we gain the impression of *being* through sense-perception and physical contact with the things around us. Being is not a *genus*, Avicenna insists, and cannot therefore be divided into different species. But there are two elements to it; and these may be separate from one another or unified. One is *essence* and the other *existence*. This is so when we are trying to analyse being. But when we observe beings, we ask are they necesary or possible; and if necessary, are they so of their own account or as a result of some outside agency? And we come to the logical conclusion that beings may take three forms. They could be *necessary*, *possible* or *impossible*. But between what is necessary of itself and what is possible of itself and necessary through the action of some separate agent, there is an intervening process. And that is what is commonly called *creation*. Is this process conscious and direct? It takes place *necessarily*, through successive stages of emanation proceeding from the supremely Necessary Being who is God. Let us now turn to the texts for further explanation.

The concept of being comprises both essence and existence. There is the reality of a thing which is the truth that is in it. And there is its essence which is that by which 'it is what it is.'[1] And there is its actual existence. Thus for a triangle there is a reality that is triangle, and for whiteness a reality that is whiteness. This may be called their particular existence, since what is meant by a thing is usually associated with the notion of existence, though in fact they are entirely separate. The idea of an existent being accompanies a thing, because it either exists in the concrete or in the imagination and the mind, otherwise it would not be a thing. Could a thing be absolutely non-existent? If by that is meant existing in the concrete, then it may be allowed. A thing could be conceived by the mind and yet not exist among external things. But there cannot be a thing that the mind or the imagination cannot conceive. Information is always of what can be realized mentally; and of what is absolutely non-existent, no information can be given, neither in the form of an assertion nor of a negation. Should we suppose that there is some information, then the non-existent would have an attribute; and if there is an attribute, there must be that to which it is attributed. And that would mean that the non-existent exists, which is absurd. 'Everything has a particular reality (*ḥaqīqa*) which is its essence (*māhīyya*); and it is known that the reality of everything which is particular to it, is other than the existence (*wujūd*) that goes with its assertion.'[2]

[1] *τό τί ἦν εἶναι*. Cf. Afnan: *Lexicon*.

[2] *Shifā*, *Ilāhīyyāt*.

Thus Avicenna transforms a logical distinction which Aristotle had drawn between essence and existence into an ontological distinction of great import. Was this an original contribution on his part? Some have declared it the first of the two outstanding contributions that he made in the field of metaphysics. Others have found traces of his distinction in Aristotle,[1] in Plotinus[2] and in Fārābī.[3] Avicenna himself nowhere claims to have been the first to make this distinction. But all throughout the East, and in Scholastic Europe as well, it has been associated with his name. The fact is that even if it did occur to others before him—and the significance of their statements has been stretched sometimes to prove that it did—none of them followed up the idea and applied it in the manner that he did. He drew conclusions from it that can hardly be attributed to any of his predecessors. And yet in none of his works do we find the subject treated as fully as might be desired. Perhaps in the *Ishārāt*—a late and reflective composition—it is expressed best. Significantly, however, it is in discussing logic that he raises the matter, and he is quite conscious that it is essentially a logical distinction.

Take the subject-predicate statement. To attribute a certain quality to a subject does not necessarily imply that the significance of the quality is the same as that of the subject. If we say that figure is predicated of a triangle, that does not mean that the reality of the triangle is the same as that of the figure itself. An attribute may be (1) *essentially constitutive* (*al-dhātīy al-muqawwim*), i.e. necessary for the subject to be what it is. It enters the quiddity of a thing and is part of it, such as in the case of figure in relation to triangle, and body in relation to man. It is part of its definition, without which the thing cannot be conceived. It has nothing to do with the notion of existence. We can define and imagine man irrespective of the fact whether he exists in the concrete or not. Everything that has a quiddity can be believed to be existing in itself or imagined in the mind by having its part present with it. And if it has a reality other than the fact that it exists in one

[1] *Anal. Post.*, 92b10. [2] *Enneads*, VI. [3] *'Uyūn al-Masā'il.*

or other of these two forms, and that is not constituted by it, then existence becomes a notion that is *added* to its reality as a concomitant or otherwise. And the causes of its existence also are other than the causes of its quiddity. Thus humanity is in itself a certain reality and quiddity. Not that its existence, in the concrete or in the mind, is a constitutive of it. It is just a correlative. If it were a constitutive, it would be impossible to form a proper idea of its meaning without its constituent parts. We could not obtain for the notion of humanity an 'existence in the mind'; and one would doubt if it actually exists in itself. No such difficulty occurs in the case of man, not because of our comprehension of the concept 'man,' but as a result of the sensible perception that we have of his parts.

These considerations have been compared with a passage in Aristotle[1] where he raises similar questions. If, he asks, definition can prove what a thing is, can it also prove that it exists? And how could it prove essence and existence at the same time and by the same reasoning, since definition like demonstration makes known just one single thing at a time? What man is, is one thing; and the fact that he exists is another. This confirms our previous statement that the logical distinction was not new, and already existed in Aristotle, but that Avicenna had the insight to apply it in the construction of a system that he was to make entirely his own. In philosophy as in many other things, the quest after originality is an idle pursuit. Ideas grow out of other ideas, they are suggested by random thoughts, and can be developed out of all recognition.

An attribute may also be (2) *accidental concomitant non-constitutive*. In that case 'it is what accompanies quiddity without being a part of it,' such as in a triangle where the angles are equal to two right angles. Here again he gives an example which Aristotle had given in the *Metaphysica*. Or it may be (3) a *non-concomitant accidental*. The predicates that are neither constitutive nor concomitant are all those that can separate themselves from the

[1] *Anal. Post.*, 92b8–11.

subject, rapidly or slowly, easily or with difficulty, such as man being described as young or old, in a sitting or standing posture.

But what exactly is meant by essence for which Avicenna also sometimes uses the word reality (*ḥaqīqa*) and at other times self (*dhāt*)? Essence is what is asserted by an answer to the question 'what is it'?[1] It should not be confused with the essential attributes of a thing which are more general. Logicians have failed to make the proper distinction. A thing may have many attributes, all of which are essential, yet it is what it is not by one but by the sum-total of all the essential attributes. He who asks the question seeks the quiddity of the thing which is found by adding up all the constituents. And there is a difference between what is expressed in answer to the question 'what is it?' and what is included in the answer by implication, and the particular manner in which it is said. What the questioner wants to know is the essence of the thing, and the meaning that is conveyed by its name, not its existence nor whether the name accords with it. The answer may take three forms. It may be (1) in an absolutely particular manner, as in the way a definition points out the quiddity of the name; thus 'a reasonable animal' denotes man. Or the answer may be (2) according to the common factor found in different things. Or again it may be (3) according to the particular and the common factors together.

Thus Avicenna's comprehension of essence does not differ much from that of Aristotle as found in Book Z of the *Metaphysica*. What was necessary and important for his chief argument was to stress its distinction from the notion of existence. Modern philosophers may think that the idea of essence is 'purely linguistic,' and that 'a word may have an essence, but a thing cannot,' yet at that early stage the conception was real and helpful.

And what of the notion of existence? It is commonly supposed, Avicenna says, that the existent is what the senses perceive, and that it is impossible to accept the existence of what cannot be sensed in its substance: that that which is not identified by its

[1] *Mā huwa*; *τό τί ἐστιν*.

place or position like a body, or with respect to that in which it is found, like the states of a body, has no share of existence. Only a little thought, however, is necessary to prove that this is not the case. Man inasmuch as he possesses a unique reality or rather inasmuch as his fundamental reality does not alter with numbers, is not something that the senses can perceive, but 'pure intelligible.' And the same is the case for all universals. 'All true being is true according to its essential reality. And it is agreed that He is One and cannot be pointed out. How then could what through Him attains all the truth of its existence.'

A thing may be caused in relation to its quiddity and reality, or it may be caused in its existence. For example the reality of a triangle is bound up with the plane surface and the line which is the side, and they constitute it in so far as it is a triangle. And it also has the reality of triangularity, and it might be thought that these two were its material and formal cause. But its existence depends on some other cause also besides these, that does not constitute its triangularity and is not part of its definition, and this is the efficient or final cause; and the final cause is 'an efficient cause for the efficient cause.'

In seeking to know whether a thing, such as a triangle represented by lines and a plane surface, exists in the concrete, it should be noted that the originating factor which brings about the existence of a thing that already has constitutive causes to its quiddity, may be the cause of some of these, such as in the case of form, or it may be what brings all of them into existence and unifies them into a whole. And the final cause on account of which the thing is, is a cause by means of its quiddity. For the idea which it represents belongs to the causality of the efficient cause, and it is the effect of it in its existence. The efficient cause is a reason for the existence of the final cause, if the latter is one of the ends that actually take place. It is not the cause of its causality nor of the idea that it represents. It is thus seen that for Avicenna the efficient cause is the most decisive. Neither form nor matter nor the end could find precedence over the agent. And he immediately goes on to say: 'If it is the First Cause, it is the cause of all existence, and of the cause of the reality of every existent thing in existence.'[1]

And again, it is quite possible that the quiddity of a thing should be the cause of one of the attributes, or that one of the attributes be the cause of another; but it is not possible that the attribute denoting existence should be due to a quiddity that is not conditional on existence; or should be due to some other attribute. The reason for that is that the cause comes first, and there is nothing prior to existence itself. In other words existence is different from the other attributes in that quiddity exists as a result of existence, whereas the other attributes exist because of quiddity.

* * * *

From an analysis of *being* into *essence* and *existence*, we turn to the different forms that being could take. It could be *necessary*, *possible* or *impossible*. Being is not a genus and these are not its species. Subjectively they are the different forms in which being is mentally conceived, objectively they represent the different ways in which they are related to one another. All things that we sensibly apprehend may be thought to be necessary. But are they necessary by themselves? They possess no power to make themselves so. They are possible beings in themselves that have been made necessary. And this could be effected only through the power of some intervening force that would have to be a necessary being independently and by itself. Hence the possible beings that were made necessary were caused; and the agent that made them so was the cause; and being the prime agent he is the First Cause. Again the question arises whether this classification of being according to the forms that it takes was or was not an original contribution in the field of metaphysics. Opposed to those who have declared it the second original contribution of

[1] *Ishārāt*, p. 140.

Avicenna, are those scholars who insist that there are traces of this idea in Fārābī, moreover the whole idea may have been suggested by the claim of the theologians who basing themselves on the doctrine of creation *ex nihilo*, placed the world and indeed all creation in the category of the possible. Again, it is a distinction already anticipated in Aristotelian logic to which Avicenna gave an ontological sense and which in his own special way he applied to new and fruitful fields.

In a proposition there are three essential parts, the subject, the predicate, and that which denotes the relation between the two. According to another division, and this is not Aristotelian, there is a matter (*mādda*) and a mode (*jihat*) to every proposition; and each of these may be necessary, possible or impossible. The *necessary matter* represents a state of the predicate in its relation to the subject, where it becomes necessary without any doubt, and at all times. The truth will be always in the affirmative and the negative will be out of consideration, such as the state of 'the animal' in man. The *impossible matter* represents a state of the predicate where the truth is always in the negative, contrary to the first, and the affirmative is not to be considered, such as the state of 'the stone' in man. And the *possible matter* is a state of the predicate where the truth whether in the affirmative or negative is not permanent and for all time, such as the state of 'the writer' in man. It may also be said that the *possible* is that on which there has been no judgement passed in the past and in the present, but there may be one in future. With regard to the modes, the *necessary* denotes 'continuation of existence'; the *impossible* 'continuation of non-existence'; and the *possible* indicates neither the one nor the other. 'The difference between mode and matter,' he adds, 'is that mode is a term fully expressed indicating one of these notions. And matter is a state of the proposition in itself, not expressed, and the two may not agree.'[1] In other words in one and the same judgement, the mode and the matter might differ. For instance in the statement 'Zaid could

[1] *Najāt*, p. 24.

possibly be an animal,' the matter is necessary and the mode possible.

The *impossible* need not detain us, since 'existence is better known than non-existence.' The way in which Avicenna's predecessors—and he may be referring to the theologians here—attempted to define the *necessary* and the *possible* was most unsatisfactory. 'If they want to define the possible, they take in its definition either the necessary or the impossible . . . and if they want to define the necessary, they take in its definition either the possible or the impossible.' They are apt to argue in a circle. The common people understand by possible what is not impossible, without determining whether it is necessary or not; and by the not possible what is impossible. And everything for them is either possible or impossible with no third situation. But specialists found a notion of what is neither necessary nor impossible. Here he introduces what we take to be the idea of contingency, though some scholars insist that there is no notion of contingency in Avicennian thought. He calls it possibility in the special sense, distinct from the common idea of it.

Necessity is divided into the absolute and the conditional. Absolute necessity is such as in the statement 'God exists.' The conditional might be dependent upon whether the existence of the thing continues, as when we say: 'Man is necessarily a talking animal,' we mean so long as he lives. Or the condition might be the continuance of the subject being qualified by what was stated with it, such as 'every thing that moves changes,' which does not mean absolutely, nor as long as it exists, but so long as the movable continues to move. These divisions and subdivisions which he is so fond of making, might be thought evident in some cases and superfluous in others, but he attached importance to them in building up his argument.

With the logical basis established, there remains its transposition to the plane of metaphysics, and its application for the purpose in view. Definition is essential. 'The *necessary being* is that being which when supposed to be not existing, an impossibility occurs from it. And a *possible being* is that which when supposed to be not existing or existing, an impossibility does not occur from it.' Here again there are distinctions to be made. A necessary being may or may not be necessary in itself. When it is necessary 'in essence' the supposition of its non-existence becomes an impossibility; but when not necessary in essence, it is something that only when put with another besides itself, becomes necessary. For instance the number four is not necessary in essence, it becomes necessary only when two and two are put together. Combustion is not necessary in essence, it becomes necessary only when fire and some inflammable material are brought into contact with one another. In like manner a possible being may be possible in the sense that in its existence or non-existence there is no element of impossibility; or in the sense that it is something potential and may develop into some sort of being; or still, it may stand for all things that are in their 'proper existence.' This last sense was the one held by the theologians. Furthermore, a thing cannot be a necessary being in essence, and together with something else simultaneously. For in the latter case, if that other thing is removed, it would cease to be a necessary being. So it may be said that 'everything that is a necessary being through association with something else, is itself a possible being in essence.' Obviously this is because the necessity of its existence is bound up with and follows from some association or relation with another thing. And association and relation cannot have the same consideration as 'the essence of the thing itself.' Consideration of the essence alone may be applicable to the necessity of a being's existence, to the possibility of it, or to the impossibility of it. The last case must be ruled out, since that thing the existence of which is impossible in its essence, cannot exist in association with another thing either. There remain only the first two cases.

It was said that all necessary being through association with what is other than itself, becomes in essence a possible being. The inverse also is true, and 'all possible being in essence, once it attains existence, becomes a necessary being in association with another.' The reason for that is that it either actually attains existence or does not. If it fails to do so it would be an impossible being. On the other hand, if it does actually attain existence, then that existence must be either necessary or not. If it is true, then it is considered a possible being with an equal chance of existence and non-existence. But it was originally in that state and it came into existence. It may therefore be concluded that the fact that it has come into existence proves that 'its emergence into existence was a necessity.' And again, the existence of a possible being is either through its essence or as a result of some particular cause. If it is through its essence, then that would be a necessary not a possible being. If it is through some cause, then it cannot exist without that cause, but together with it. And so what is a possible being in essence, would be a necessary being in association with what is other than itself.

We have followed Avicenna's reasoning in order to show the manner in which he draws the distinction between the necessary and the possible being and the relation between the two. It might be thought that the differentiation with its logical origin and form is more linguistic than real, but he has his arguments for what makes a necessary being really necessary. Nor is the religious application far to seek. God is the *Necessary Being*. All creations are *possible beings* brought into existence through a process and for a reason that was absolutely necessary; and through association with what is a necessary being, they became themselves necessary. Furthermore, when the distinction between essence and existence is applied to necessary and possible beings, it is found that it is only in possible beings that they are different. In God as the Necessary Being they are one and the same. Actuality and potentiality are closely related to the distinction between necessary and possible. Actuality may be equated with the necessary being and potentiality with the possible. 'We call the possibility of being the potentiality of being, and we call the bearer of the potentiality of being which possesses the power of the existence of the thing, a subject and prime matter.'[1] And as such, 'the necessary being is the Truth in essence always; and the possible being is true in virtue of something besides itself.' That which is a necessary being in essence 'is pure truth because the reality of everything is the particularity of its existence.'[2] Furthermore, as actuality, the Necessary Being is pure Good; and has no cause like possible beings. Its existence is not conditional upon anything other than itself. It does not stand in relation to any other thing, nor is it changeable, or multiple, or in association with anything other than its own essence.

* * * *

Between the Necessary Being and all possible beings there was a stage and a process involved. That is what is called creation. Here Avicenna is on delicate ground, and comes face to face with one of the most challenging and uncompromising problems in the conflict between religion and philosophy.

The concept of creation *ex nihilo* is not Greek, and Aristotle did not produce any theory about this. Yet as a fundamental principle of religion it could not be lightly dismissed. Was there a possibility of reconciling the claim that the world was eternal, and the doctrine that it was created by God through His own wish and will out of total non-existence? Fārābī had thought that he could take an intermediate position by doubting that Aristotle really meant that the world was eternal; and by adopting the theory propounded in the so-called *Theology* of Aristotle, actually parts of the *Enneads* of Plotinus. There creation was explained in Neo-Platonic fashion as successive stages of emanation proceeding from God. Avicenna, who was to take the same view with some minor modifications, had to reason it out for himself. With his rational temperament he was deeply attached to Aristotle; but he was reluctant to depart from such an essential principle in his Faith. He had already assured himself that there is such a thing as matter. Was this matter to be considered

[1] *Najāt*, p. 358. [2] *Ibid.*, p. 373.

eternal (*qadīm*) as Aristotle had taught, or created (*muḥdath*) as the theologians, justifiably from their point of view, insisted? Here, he thought, there are some distinctions to be made. A thing may be eternal according to essence, or it may be eternal with respect to time. According to the former it is 'that whose essence has no origin from which it exists'; and with respect to the latter 'it is that for whose age there was no beginning.' And the word 'created' also has two distinct meanings that should not be confounded. In one sense 'it is that for whose essence there was an origin by which it exists'; and in the other 'it is that for the age of which there was a beginning, and there was a time when it did not exist. A prior-period (*qablīyya*) during which it was non-existent, and that prior period was terminated.'[1] Hence there is a notion of time involved in the whole matter. Let us follow this argument. Everything that had for its existence a temporal beginning aside from a creative beginning, must have been preceded by time and matter; and previous to that was altogether non-existent. Its non-existence could not have been together with its existence. It must have been earlier, which means that there was a period prior to its existence which has expired and is no more. And what constitutes that period is 'either a quiddity to itself' which in this case is time, 'or a quiddity to something other than itself, which is its time.'[2] In both cases it is a proof of the existence of time.

Subscribing to the Aristotelian conception of the eternity of matter, it may be shown that all temporal creation is invariably preceded by it. To be created everything must needs have been a possible being in itself; and it has been stated that the possibility of being is the potentiality of being. It does not depend on the ability or inability of the agent to create. The two things are entirely distinct, and the agent cannot create unless the thing is in itself possible. Now the notion of the possibility of being can exist only in relation to what is possible to it. It is not a substance in itself, it is a notion present in a subject and an accident to it.

[1] *Najāt*, p. 218. [2] *Ibid.*, p. 219.

And that subject which is in a potential state is what we call primary matter. 'And so every created thing is preceded by matter.'[1]

If matter is eternal then creation can no more be *ex nihilo*. But what exactly is meant by creation? 'Creation means nothing except existence after non-existence.' The non-existence of the thing is not a condition, it is just an attribute and an accident. And after coming into existence, it becomes either a necessary or a not-necessary being. So a thing in so far as its existence is said to have been from non-existence, need not have a cause in itself. Contrary to what people suppose, 'the cause is for the existence only.' If it so happens that it was previously a non-existent thing, it becomes a creation in itself, otherwise it should not be called a creation. So the agent whom the people call the Agent is not given that name for the reasons that they proffer. He is not an agent only because he is the cause, but due to the fact that he is 'the cause and a necessary being at the same time.' The two are interrelated. But does cause always precede the effect? It should be realized that 'the essential causes of a thing that bring about the actual existence of the essence of that thing, must be together with it and not precede it in existence.' In other words cause and effect in this case are simultaneous. This is the meaning of what philosophers call bringing into original existence (*ibdā'*).[2] And he uses the term preferred by the *Falāsifa* to what the theologians called creation (*ḥudūth*). In the case of this originating act which implies 'bringing something to be (*ta'yīs*) after an absolute non-beingness (*laisa*),' there is no priority in time whatever between cause and effect. There is only priority in essence; so that 'every effect comes *to be* after *not-being* with a posteriority in essence.' While the notion of creation to which the religious-minded were committed implied that the process is conditioned by a priority in time.

But if there is no priority in time, why and how could there

[1] *Shifā. Ilāhīyyāt.*

[2] For distinctions between *ibdā'*; *khalq*; *takwīn*, cf. Afnan: *Lexicon.*

be a priority in essence? Like all beings, a cause also may be either necessary in its essence or necessary through some other thing than that. In the latter case once it attains necessity, another may proceed from it. Should that come to pass, the effect would be in essence possible, and the cause in essence either necessary or possible. If it should be necessary, then its existence would be more true (*aḥaqq*) than the existence of the possible. And if it is possible, then the effect is not necessary in itself, but becomes so through it. In all cases the cause would be prior in essence, and it would be also more true than the effect. In full agreement with the Stagirite, Avicenna holds that the chain of causation cannot be traced indefinitely. All the Islamic philosophers had insisted on and emphasized that point. There must needs be a first cause, who is the cause of all causes, and can only be God. He is the efficient cause—a point which the theologians liked to stress. But contrary to their declarations, God is also the final cause. Aristotle had said practically the same thing, if not in the same words. In fact He is the efficient cause by being the final cause as well. Moreover, just as it is impossible to retrace the original cause indefinitely, in like manner it is not possible to follow the end indefinitely. God is thus the cause of all causes and the end of all ends. He is the final cause in the sense that He is something that always is to be.

There is no point in what 'the infirm among the Mutakallumūn' say. According to their view there are two different states to the thing on which the agent, who grants existence after non-existence, has acted. There is first a previous non-existence, and second an existence in the present. Surely the agent could have had no influence upon it during its state of non-existence; and his influence began only after it was brought into existence. The fact that it was non-existent in its essence could not have been due to the influence of the agent. Now if it be imagined that the influence coming from the agent, and which constitutes the bringing into existence of what did not exist, did not take place because the thing existed eternally, then in that case the agent would be even more omnipotent because his action would have been eternally in progress.

And again, they claim that the act is not legitimate and proper except after the non-existence of that which has been acted upon.[1] Although it was shown that non-existence could not be from the agent, only existence is. The thing which it is claimed that a creator brings into existence, may be described as his creation and useful for his own being, either in its state of non-existence or existence, or in both states. Evidently there could be no creator to what was still in the state of non-existence. There is a creator only for what exists. In which case the creator would be the creator of the existent. Hence for Avicenna as for Plato and Aristotle, God's act of creation meant the giving of form to pre-existent matter. He was an artificer rather than a creator *ex nihilo*, a conception for which the religious-minded never forgave him.

God gives form to pre-existent matter through the agency of the *active intelligence* which is the Giver of Forms. Theologians may teach that God as the efficient cause is in the act of continually creating accidents that subsist only through His action. Yet it is only when a new disposition makes matter ready to receive a new form that the old one disappears and God through the active intelligence grants a new form. Thus the Almighty is omnipotent but He does not create *ex nihilo*.

These considerations are meant to prepare the way for the proof of the existence of God which for Avicenna is the consummation of all metaphysical speculation. To be better appreciated, they should be viewed with relation to Greek thought on the one hand, and orthodox religious doctrine on the other. His most renowned proof grew out of the distinction between essence and existence, and the threefold classification of being. There is no doubt, he repeats, that there is existence; and that every existing being could be either necessary or possible. If it is necessary, it would be what we seek; if it is possible, it would be for

[1] Cf. *Najāt*, pp. 347–8.

us to show that it originated from a being that must be necessary. There cannot be for an essentially possible being, essentially possible causes without end at one time. The chain of causation cannot be retraced indefinitely. So long as it is a possible being unable to produce itself, there must be some original being that was able to give it existence. And that original being could not be within it, because it is itself a possible being, in whole or in part, that owes its existence to something else. It must therefore be separate. And the original being must be the cause of its own existence and able to produce itself. It must therefore be a necessary being, otherwise it could not have these qualifications and capacities. The chain of causation ends in him, and that indicates his existence; and the conditions of his being cannot but make him a necessary being. If he were not necessary, how then could he be the cause of his own existence and able to proceed from himself?

And again, supposing all beings were possible. They would either have to be created or uncreated. If they be uncreated, then the cause of their permanent existence must be either in their essence or in something else. If in their essence, they would be necessary beings, if in something else then possible beings. If they be created, then there must be a cause for their creation and a cause for their permanence; and the cause of both may be the same. Then the same argument holds good with regard to the cause of their permanence. Again the chain of causation cannot be retraced indefinitely; and the cause of their permanence will end in a necessary being that gives permanence to created beings. It may be argued that Avicenna starts with certain assumptions that may or may not be warranted. These are the religious claims that were bound to influence him and which he could not ignore. The theologians maintained that the world and all therein was in the category of the possible (*jā'iz*). He accepts that, and upon it as a basis constructs his argument that the existence of possible being necessitates the existence of a necessary being, who is the first cause and the originator of all.

He did not reject the Aristotelian proof of God as the *Unmoved Mover*. In his own Physics he developed the same thought with certain modifications that were to infuriate the more faithful Aristotelian that Averroës was. There are three causes to movement: nature (*ṭab*ʿ), will (*irāda*) and force (*qasr*). Natural movement is from an unsuitable state to a suitable state. Hence it is not itself a cause unless it combined with something *in actu*. Will in order to be the cause of movement must be permanent and all-embracing, and at the same time be an active will in the nature of authority and command that can originate movement. Force can be ultimately reduced to the nature and will of the mover. And even in the case of attraction and repulsion and such-like, it originates in the mover. Hence the necessity which Avicenna so much emphasized in the case of existence, applies equally in the case of movement and points to the existence of a necessary First Mover. Furthermore it is through the *will* of the Mover—so essential according to the religious view—that all existing things move.

* * * *

With the existence of the Necessary Being established, and the meaning of creation explained, it remains to be seen how the act takes place, and the world proceeds from God.

Brief reference was made to the way in which Fārābī under Neo-Platonic influence approached the problem. Avicenna follows along practically the same lines though more resourcefully and comprehensively. He had concurred with Aristotle's view that the world was eternal, and agreed with the theologians that it was in the realm of the possible, and hence owed its existence to some cause. Was there a contradiction involved? None whatever. Creation presupposes possibility, but possibility is not a substance and cannot exist separately and independently. The notion of possibility as an accident can only reside in a subject, and that subject is matter. And we saw how the existence of matter may be shown to be eternal. Therefore possibility and creation are co-eternal with matter. Or again, since the priority of the Necessary Being over the world of possible beings was not a priority in time, as the theologians maintained, but like cause over effect, a priority in essence and rank, then God and the world are co-eternal.

Here a problem is posed. If it be accepted as a principle that from one nothing can proceed except one, and God is One, how does the world with all its multiplicity proceed from Him? Here the Neo-Platonic theory of emanation (*faiḍ*) proved helpful. It was in itself a congenial conception that came to be adopted by Islamic mystics, and after that generally accepted. From the Necessary Being who is one, and not a body nor in a body; and not divisible nor to be defined, there proceeds through emanation the first caused (*al-ma'lūl al-awwal*) which is also one. It is a pure intelligence, because of being a form that is not in matter. It is thus the first of the separate intelligences. But how exactly does this act of emanation take place? Thinking or contemplation, for the separate substances, is equivalent to creation and produces the same results. The idea precedes the actual thing. The Necessary Being by an act of pure reflection creates the *first intelligence* which like Him is one and simple. He ponders His own essence, and from that there results this act of creation. The capacity to think and as a consequence create is not special to the Necessary Being, it is equally true of and shared by the intelligences. And the first intelligence by reflection upon itself, produces the first cause. But there is a difference to be noted. The first intelligence, because it is itself created, is possible in its essence, and necessary only in association with the Necessary Being. In so far as it is necessary, when it reflects upon its essence, the soul of the particular sphere[1] proceeds from it. And in so far as it is possible, when it reflects upon its essence, the body of the particular sphere proceeds from it. It is only in this manner that multiplicity comes to take place. And it is this twofold feature of the first intelligence that is the cause of it. It in no wise emanates from the Necessary

[1] Cf. the nine spheres already enumerated under Fārābī.

Being himself directly. Hence the first intelligence that possesses necessity as a result of its emanation from the Necessary Being, and possibility as a result of its proper essence, is one and multiple at the same time. In a similar manner and by a similar process, a second intelligence emanates from it with the same qualities. The soul of the first sphere that emanates from the first intelligence, is the form of the celestial sphere and the cause of its perfection. And the body of it is due to the potentiality that resides in that intelligence. Thus three things emanate from the first intelligence: (1) the second intelligence, (2) the soul of the first sphere which is its form, and (3) the body of it which is its matter. A similar triad proceed from the second intelligence, i.e. a third intelligence, and the form and body of another sphere. The process continues in succession until 'it ends in the intelligence from which our souls emanate, and it is the intelligence of the terrestrial world, and we call it the *active intelligence* (*al-'aql al-fa''āl*).' But why does not the process continue indefinitely creating new and more intelligences and spheres? This is because the world is finite; and the series of emanations stop where the world requires no more intelligences, and where the last presides over the generation and corruption of the elements. Though 'according to the belief of the first teacher (i.e. Aristotle), they were about fifty and more, and their last was the active intelligence,' there were only ten intelligences in addition to the first cause. And what is the object of these successive emanations from the Necessary Being? The purpose is not governed by blind necessity, but by a conscious necessity meant to establish order and the good of the world. And what is the exact relation between these intelligences? They are not all of the same species,[1] but their succession is governed by necessity and determined by their essence, not by time. In fact we should not think in terms of time, 'whose accidentality and attachment to movement was proved to you.' Every intelligence has its sphere independently with its matter and form which is the soul of it. But they differ in rank and order, and one is more

[1] *Najāt*, p. 455.

to be preferred (*afḍal*) than the other. Nor are they 'according to their significance entirely the same.' Even in substantial things, the element of time is to be belittled. 'The genesis of a thing is from another thing, not the sense of being after a thing, but that in the second there is an element of the first included in its substance . . . and it is the part corresponding to its potentiality . . . in fact one is not prior in essence to the other, the priority being only by accident, and in consideration of its individuality not its species.'[1]

The function of the soul of a sphere, in which Plotinus and Leibnitz among others believed, was to constitute the form and the entelechy or perfection of every sphere. Not a separate substance, for in that case it would be an intelligence and not a soul. It is not able to cause motion at all except by way of provoking desire. It is not affected by the movement of the body and would not be associated with the faculty of the imagination of that body. If it were separate in essence and in action, it would be the soul of everything and not only of that body. In other words the creative power is in the intelligence which is separate, and not in the soul which as the proximate cause brings about movement. Its conceptions and will are in constant renewal, having the capacity for it in each individual case. The distant cause remains the intelligence, though the immediate one is the soul. It is in alteration, changeable, and not separate from matter. And its relation to the sphere is similar to the relation of the animal soul which we have to ourselves. Thus the proximate cause of the motion of the heavenly spheres is neither nature nor intelligence, but the soul.

Finally, it may be asked if different bodies are made of a common matter, and individual species take the same form, on what basis does individuation take place? This is in consequence of the matter which under the influence of outside agencies develops a disposition and potentiality to receive the form that it merits. When marked by a determined quantity it becomes appropriate to take a particular form.

[1] *Shifā, Illāhiyyāt.*

CHAPTER V

PROBLEMS OF PSYCHOLOGY

AVICENNA'S definition of the soul does not differ from that of Aristotle, and like him he conceives of psychology in terms of faculties. The soul as a 'single genus' may be divided into three species. There is (1) the *vegetable* which is 'the first entelechy (perfection or actuality) of a natural body possessing organs in so far as it reproduces, and grows and is nourished.' Then (2) there is the *animal* which is 'the first entelechy of a natural body possessing organs in so far as it perceives individual things and moves by volition.' Then (3) there is the *human* which is 'the first entelechy of a natural body possessing organs in so far as it commits acts of rational choice and deduction through opinion; and in so far as it perceives universal matters.'[1] The genesis of the soul is attributed to heavenly powers and it is preconditioned by a harmonious blending of the elements, though its psychical functions are distinct from and above the simple mixture.

The animal soul has two faculties, the *motive* and the *perceptive*. The motive is again of two kinds, either it gives an impulse or it is active. Where it gives an impulse it is the faculty of *appetence* and may be subdivided into desire and anger; and where it is active it provides the power of *movement*. The perceptive faculty may also be divided into two, one perceives externally, and the other internally. The *external* are 'the five or eight senses.' If the sense of touch is only one, they are five; if it is supposed to comprise the four pairs of contraries—hot and cold, dry and moist, hard and soft, smooth and rough—then they can be counted as eight. Sight is a faculty located in the concave nerve which perceives the image of the forms of coloured bodies imprinted on the

[1] *Najāt*, p. 258.

vitreous humour; and the forms are transmitted through transparent media to polished surfaces. Avicenna refutes at length the Platonic theory of sight as proposed in the *Timaeus*, and accepts the Aristotelian explanation. Hearing, a faculty located in the nerves distributed over the surface of the ear-hole, perceives through the vibration of the air that produces the sound. The waves touch the nerve and hearing takes place. Smell, located in the two protuberances of the front part of the brain, perceives odour conveyed by inhaled air, either mixed with the vapour in the air or imprinted on it through qualitative change produced by an odorous body. Taste, located in the nerves distributed over the tongue, perceives the taste dissolved from bodies and mingling with the saliva, thus producing a qualitative change on the tongue. Touch, distributed over the entire skin and flesh of the body, perceives what touches the nerves and what affects them, thus causing change in their constitution or structure. But what exactly is sensation? Aristotle's predecessors had treated it as essentially a passive process in which the sense-organs are qualitatively changed by the object. He himself had thought of it as the 'realization of potentiality,' without holding to the notion as a purely mental activity. Avicenna, like other Islamic philosophers, may be said to agree, at least as far as the mechanism is concerned, with the belief in the passive process. 'All the sensibles convey their images to the organs of sensation and are imprinted on them, and are then perceived by the sensory faculty.'[1]

Of the *internal* senses, some are faculties that perceive the form of sensed objects, and others perceive their meaning or purpose. The term 'internal senses' is probably of Stoic origin, though the faculties included under it are found in Aristotle. Some of these faculties can both perceive and act, others only perceive; some possess primary perception and others secondary perception. What is first perceived by the sense and then by the internal faculties is the form of the sensed object, and what is perceived by the internal faculties only is the meaning or intended purpose

[1] *Najāt*, p. 261.

of the object. One of the animal internal senses is the faculty of fantasy, i.e. *sensus communis*, located in the forepart of the front ventricle of the brain. Next comes the faculty of *representation*, located in the rear part of the front ventricle of the brain, which preserves what the *sensus communis* has received from the five senses. The belief that the internal senses were located in the brain was of Galenic origin. Aristotle had maintained that the heart was the seat of *sensus communis* and therefore of imagination and memory; and in this he had been followed by many of the Islamic *Falāsifa* including Fārābī. Ghāzālī subscribed to it also. In Aristotle *phantasia* has a variety of functions, but Avicenna treats each as a separate faculty. Other faculties in the animal are the 'sensitive imagination' which is called 'rational imagination' in relation to the human soul; the *estimative* faculty which perceives the non-sensible meaning or intentions; and the *retentive* and *recollective* faculty which retains what the estimative perceives.

The human or, as it is commonly called, the rational soul, has a practical and a theoretical faculty, both of which are rather equivocally called intelligence. The practical is the principle of movement of the body urging to action: deliberate and purposive. It has a certain correspondence with the animal faculties of appetence, imagination and estimation. It is the source of human behaviour and closely connected with moral considerations. The practical intelligence must control the irrational tendencies in man, and by not allowing them to get the upper hand dispose him to the consideration of knowledge from above by the theoretical intelligence. Its function includes also attention to everyday matters and to 'human arts.' The theoretical faculty serves the purpose of receiving the impressions of the universal forms abstracted from matter. If the forms be already separate in themselves, it simply receives them; if not, it makes them immaterial by abstraction, leaving no trace of material attachments in them. These functions the theoretical intelligence performs in stages. There is first the stage of absolute, or material, potentiality as in an infant; second, that of relative, or possible, potentiality when only the instrument for the reception of actuality has been achieved, after which comes the stage of the perfection of the original potentiality, or *habitus*. Sometimes, Avicenna says, the second stage is termed *habitus* and the third the perfection of potentiality.

It may thus be said that the relation of the theoretical faculty to the abstract immaterial forms is sometimes in the nature of absolute potentiality, which belongs to the soul that has not yet realized any portion of the perfection due to it potentially. At this stage it is called the 'material intelligence,' present in every individual of the human species, and so called because of its resemblance to primary matter. Or it is in the nature of possible potentiality, when only the primary intelligibles which are the source and instrument of the secondary intelligibles have been acquired by the 'material potentiality.' When only this amount of actualization has been achieved, it is called *intellectus in habitu* (*al-'aql bil-malaka*). In relation to the first it may also be called the actual intelligence, because the first cannot actually think at all. It is called *intellectus in actu* because it thinks whenever it wills without any further process of perception. Lastly, its relation to the forms may be in the nature of absolute actuality, when they are present to it and it actually and knowingly contemplates them. At this stage it becomes the *intellectus acquisitus* (*al-'aql al-mustafād*), because the forms are acquired from without. With it the animal genus and its human species are prefected, and the faculty of man becomes similar to the first principles of all existence. The much disputed origin of this classification is not Aristotelian, and must have been influenced by Alexander's commentary on the *De Anima*. It is found in a slightly different form in Fārābī, to whom Avicenna is often indebted.

As to the way in which the rational soul acquires knowledge, it may be pointed out that whether through the intermediary of someone else or through one's own self, the degree of receptivity differs with each individual. Some people come very near to having immediate perception because of their more powerful potential intellects. Where a person can acquire knowledge from within himself, the capacity is called *intuition.* It enables him to make contact with the *active intelligence* without much effort or instruction, until it seems as though he knows everything. This is the highest stage of the disposition; and this state of the material intelligence should be called the 'Divine Spirit.' It is of the same genus as *intellectus in habitu*, but far superior; and not all people share it. It is possible that some of the actions attributed to the 'Divine Intelligence' should, because of their power and lofty nature, overflow into the imagination and be imitated by it in the form of sensible symbols and concrete words. There are two ways in which intelligible truths may be acquired. Sometimes it is done through intuition which is an act of the mind, and 'quick apprehension is the power of intuition.'[1] And sometimes it is through instruction. And since the first principles of instruction are obtained through intuition, it may be said that ultimately all things are reduced to intuitions passed on by those who have had them to their pupils. Intuitive people vary in their capacities; the lowest are those wholly devoid of intuition; and the highest are those who seem to have an intuition regarding all or most problems, and in the shortest time. Thus a man may be of such purity of soul and so closely in contact with the rational principles that he becomes 'ablaze' with intuition, i.e. with receptivity for inspiration from the active intelligence in all things, so that the forms that are in the active intelligence are imprinted on his soul either all at once or very nearly so. And he does not accept them on authority, but in their logical sequence and order. For beliefs based on authority possess no rational certainty. 'This is a kind of prophetic inspiration, rather the highest faculty of it; and should preferably be called Divine Power; and it represents the highest state of the faculties of man.'[2] Although the idea of

[1] Cf. *ἥ δ' ἀγχίνοια ἐστιν εὐστοχία τις* (*A. Post*, 89b11), *al-dhukā' fa huwa ḥusn ḥadsin mā.*

[2] *Najāt*, p. 274.

intuition is of Aristotelian origin, where it has more the sense of sagacity and quick-wittedness, its application to the man endowed with prophetic insight has of course no Greek source. It is most probably Avicenna's own personal conception, and is in keeping with his views regarding the powers of a prophet and his mission in life, as will be seen.

There is, however, a regular hierarchy among the faculties of man. The acquired intellect, which is the ultimate goal, is found to govern them all. The *intellectus in habitu* serves the *intellectus in actu* and is in turn served by the material intellect. The practical intellect serves all of them and is in turn served by the faculty of estimation; and estimation is served by an anterior and a posterior faculty. The posterior conserves what is brought to it by estimation; and the anterior is the sum total of animal faculties. The faculty of representation is served by the appetitive which obeys it, and by the imagination which accepts its combined or separate images. In turn, the imagination is served by *phantasia*, which is itself served by the five senses. The appetitive is served by desire and anger; and these last by the motive faculty. This concludes the list of what constitute the different animal faculties which are served in their entirety by the vegetable faculties, of which the reproductive is the first in rank. Growth serves the reproductive, and the nutritive serves them both. The four 'natural' faculties of digestion, retention, assimilation and excretion are subservient to all these.

Taking up the question of perception, it is pointed out that there is a difference between perception by sense, by imagination, by estimation and by the mind. 'It appears that all perception is but the apprehension of the form of the perceived object.' If it is of some material thing, it consists in perceiving the form abstracted to some extent from the matter. Except that the kinds of separation or abstraction are different and its grades varied; because the material form is subject to certain states and conditions that do not belong to it as form, and the abstraction is sometimes complete and at other times partial. Sensation cannot disentangle form completely and divorce it from material accidents, nor can it retain the form in the absence of matter. Thus the presence of matter is needed if the form is to remain presented to it. But the faculty of representation or imagination purifies the abstracted form to a higher degree. The faculty of estimation goes a little further, for it receives the meanings which are immaterial, although by accident they happen to be in matter. For instance shape, colour and position cannot be found except in bodily matter, but good and evil are in themselves immaterial entities and it is by accident that they are found in matter. In the case of estimation the abstraction is relatively more complete than in the previous two forms of perception. It is the intellectual faculty that perceives the forms as completely abstracted from matter as possible. 'In this way differ perception through the power of sense, perception through the power of the imagination, perception through the power of estimation, and perception through the power of the intellect.'[1] This differentiation between the different forms of perception can also be traced to Alexander of Aphrodisias, with the usual modifications that Avicenna is apt to introduce.

Furthermore the particular is perceived only by what is material and the universal by what is immaterial and separate. Thus the perception of particular forms occurs by means of a bodily organ. The external senses perceive them in a way not completely divested of matter, because these forms are perceptible only if their matter is present, and a body cannot be present to what is incorporeal. A thing in space cannot be present or absent to something that is non-spatial. The faculty of imagination also needs a physical organ, because it cannot perceive without the forms being imprinted on a body in such a manner that both it and the body share the same imprint. This is proved by the case of images, which unless they have a definite position, cannot become images at all. Additions and combinations take place only in the conceptual realm. The same is true of the estimative faculty

[1] *Najāt*, p. 279.

which is also dependent on a bodily organ as it perceives its objects only in particular images.

* * * *

So far Avicenna is concerned with the powers and faculties of the vegetable, animal and human souls, their distinctions from, and their relations to, one another. From that he proceeds to the nature of the soul, before, however, taking up the question whether such a thing as a soul exists at all.

The substance in which the intelligibles reside is not a body in itself, nor is it constituted by a body. In a manner it is a faculty found in the body, and a form imprinted upon it. If the place of the intelligibles were in a body then the place of the forms would be in divisible or indivisible parts of that body. It is not possible to suppose that the form is imprinted on some indivisible part. The position of a point cannot be distinguished from the whole line, and what is imprinted on a point is imprinted on a part of the line. Points are not combined into a line by being put together, and have no particular and distinct position in a line, as Aristotle had shown. If, however, the form is imprinted on divisible matter then with the division of the matter it would be divided also, and the only alternatives are that it would be divided into similar or dissimilar parts. Should they be exactly similar their totality could not be different from them except in quantity or numbers. And in that case the intelligible form would acquire some sort of figure or number. It would be no more an intellectual but a representational form. And since a part cannot be the whole, the form cannot be divided into exactly similar parts. On the other hand the division of form into dissimilar parts can only be a division into genera and differentiae, and from this impossibilities follow. For since every part of matter is potentially divisible *ad infinitum*, the genera and differentiae of a given form would also be infinite, which is not possible. Furthermore, when the intelligible form is imprinted in matter, genus and differentia do not have the coherence that they possess in a definition, and their position will depend on some external element. And again not every intelligible can be divided into simpler intelligibles, for there are those which are of the simplest, constituting the principles for others; and they have neither genus nor differentia, nor are they divisible in quantity or in meaning, and their parts, therefore, cannot be dissimilar. 'It is thus evident that the place in which the intelligibles reside is a substance, not a body, nor a faculty in a body liable to division and the impossibilities it involves.'

To take another argument, it is the rational faculty that abstracts the intelligibles from all the different categories such as quantity, place and position. And the abstraction is made in the mind; so when it comes to exist as a form in the intellect, it has no quantity, place or position to be indicated or divided or subjected to similar processes, and this shows that it cannot be in a body. Again, if a simple indivisible form were to exist in a divisible matter, its relation will be either with every part of that matter or with some parts or with none at all. If with none, then the whole cannot have any relation either. If some parts have a relation and others have not, then those that have not cannot enter as factors into the form. If all the parts have a relation with the form, then they are no more parts, but each is a complete intelligible in itself, and the intelligible as it actually is at a certain moment of time. Should each have different relations with the form or with the different parts of the form, this would mean that it is divisible, which cannot be maintained. From this may be seen that the forms imprinted in matter are just the exterior forms of particular divisible entities, every part of which has an actual or potential relation with the other. Moreover what is by definition composed of different parts, has in its completeness a unity of its own that is indivisible? How then can this unity as such be imprinted in what is divisible? Finally, it is established that the supposed intelligibles which are for the reasonable faculty to conceive actually and in succession, are potentially unlimited; and what has the capacity to be unlimited cannot reside in a body, nor be the faculty of a body. This has been proved, Avicenna says, in Aristotle's *Physics*. 'It is not possible therefore, that the entity which is capable of conceiving intelligibles be constituted in a body at all, nor its action be in a body or through a body.'[1] These arguments, which have their source not only in Aristotle but in various commentators to his *De Anima*,[2] such as John Philoponus and Themistius, are here restated with Avicenna's ability to reinterpret the views of his predecessors in his own way.

Furthermore, the activity of the rational faculty is not performed by means of a physical organ; nothing intervenes between that faculty and its own self, nor between it and its special organ or the fact of its intellection. It is purely rationally that it knows its own self, and that which is called its organ, and its act of intellection. Let us suppose that it was otherwise. In that case the rational faculty could know itself either through the form of that organ, or through some numerically different form, or through some entirely different form. The second and third alternatives are obviously not possible. There remains only the possibility that it should know its own organ only and continuously, which it does not. This is a proof, Avicenna says, that it is not possible for the percipient to perceive an organ which it uses as its own in its perception. And this is the reason why, contrary to Aristotle, he maintains that 'sensation senses something external, and does not sense itself, nor its organ, nor its act of sensation; and in like manner imagination does not imagine itself, nor its act, nor its organ.'[3] Another proof is that those faculties that perceive through bodily organs weaken and ultimately corrupt those organs through the constant use of them, as in the case of the sense-organs and the effect of excessive light on human sight and thunderous noise on the hearing. Whereas in the case of the rational faculty the contrary is true. Through continued intellection and thought and the consideration of complex matters, it gains in power and versatility. And if it sometimes gets tired

[1] *Najāt*, p. 292. [2] Cf. Rahman: *Avicenna's Psychology*, p. 101.
[3] *Najāt*, p. 293.

—an interesting point—'it is because the intellect seeks the help of the imagination which employs an organ liable to fatigue and so does not serve the mind.'[1] Furthermore, the members of the human body after reaching maturity, which is usually before or at the age of forty, gradually begin to lose their strength; whereas in most cases the rational faculty grows in capacity after that age. If it were one of the bodily faculties it ought to follow the same course as the others, and this in itself shows that it is not. As to the objection that the soul forgets its intelligibles and ceases activity in case of illness of the body and with old age, it should be remembered that the soul has a twofold activity, one in relation to the body in the form of governance and control, and another in relation to itself and its principles in the form of intellection. These two activities are opposed to one another and mutually obstructive, so that if the soul becomes occupied with one, it turns away from the other—it is very difficult for it to combine the two. Its occupation with respect to the body is sensation, imagination, appetite, anger, fear, sorrow, pain. It is commonly known that thought of the intelligibles makes one forget all these and that sensation in turn inhibits the soul from intellection. Once the soul is engrossed with the sensibles, it is kept away from the intelligible without the organ of intellection or the faculty itself being in any way impaired. Hence in cases of illness the activities of the mind do not stop entirely, they are only diverted to something else. Not only does this dual activity of the soul produce this situation, but occupation with even one of them produces exactly the same effect—fear keeps away hunger, appetite hinders anger, and anger makes one forget fear. The cause of all this is the complete preoccupation of the soul with just one thing. All this goes to show that the soul is not imprinted in the body, nor constituted by it. The exact relation of the soul to the body is determined by its particular disposition to occupy itself with the governance and control of that body; and this results from an inherent inclination of its own.

[1] *Najāt*, p. 295.

The rational soul is assisted by the animal faculties in various ways. For instance, sensation brings to it particulars from which four processes result. By the first process, the soul separates individual universals from the particulars by abstracting their concepts from the matter and material attachments and concomitants; and by considering the common factors between them; and the differences; and the essentials; and the accidentals. From these the soul obtains the fundamental concepts by using the imagination and the estimative faculty. By the second process, the soul seeks the relation between these individual universals such as negation and affirmation. Where the combination depending on negation and affirmation is self-evident, it readily accepts it; where it is not, it waits till it finds the middle term of the syllogistic reasoning. By the third process it acquires empirical premisses. This process consists in finding through sense-experience a necessary predicate for a subject whether in the negative or affirmative; or consequences affirmatively or negatively conjoin with or disjoined from the antecedents, the whole relation being recognized as necessary and true in all cases. By the fourth process, the human soul acquires what has been generally accepted, through an unbroken chain of transmission, as a basis for concept and assent. All this goes to show that the soul is independent of the body and has activities of its own.

* * * *

But what exactly is the nature of the soul? Is it a unity, or is it characterized by multiplicity, and what happens to it after the death of the body?

Human souls are all of the same species and significance. If they existed before the body, they must have been either single or multiple entities. It is impossible that they should have been either; it is therefore impossible that they should have existed before the body. In the supposed case of multiplicity, the difference among the souls could be according to their quiddity and form, or according to their relation to the elements, or according to the time in which they became attached to the body, or still more according to the causes which determined their material existence. Their differences could not be according to quiddity and form, because their form is necessarily one. They must therefore differ according to the recipient of the form. That is to say, according to the individual body to which that particular form and quiddity became attached. Since the souls are pure and simple quiddities, there could be no essential or numerical differentiation between them. If they are absolutely separate entities, and the enumerated categories do not apply to them in any way, the souls cannot be different and of diverse kinds. And when there is no diversity, there can be no multiplicity. On the other hand, it is impossible that all human souls should have just one single essence in common. For when two bodies come into existence, two souls also come to be. In that case these two are either the parts of one and the same soul—and that would mean that what does not possess magnitude and extension is potentially divisible, which is absurd—or a soul which is numerically one could be in two bodies at the same time, which is equally absurd. It thus stands that 'a soul comes into existence whenever a body suitable to it comes into existence.' And this body will be 'the domain and the instrument of the soul.' There is at the same time created in it a natural yearning to associate itself completely with that particular body—to use it, to control it, and to be attracted by it. This bond unites it to that body and keeps it away from all others different in nature. And when those peculiar dispositions which constitute the principle of its individualization are present in combination, it is combined and transformed into an individual 'although that state and that relationship may remain obscure to us.' The soul thus achieves the principles on which its perfection is based, through the instrumentality of the body. Its subsequent development, however, remains bound to its own nature and is not conditioned by the body after it has completely left it. Once they have forsaken their bodies, souls survive each as a separate entity, duly shaped by the different material elements in which they had resided, and the different times of their coming into existence, and also the different forms and figures of their bodies.

Here Avicenna is characteristically influenced by a host of classical and Hellenistic philosophers, as well as by some of the assertions of religious dogma, without, however, agreeing with any of them on all points. He holds with Aristotle that the soul is the form and the quiddity of the body which controls and gives it its particular character; but contrary to him asserts that it is a separate substance capable of existing independently of the body; and that after separation it has an activity of its own regardless of its previous connections. In fact ever since the translation of the *Phaedo* into Arabic—a highly prized dialogue—and the *De Anima* of Aristotle, problems of the soul, its nature and existence, had become the subject of much study among the Islamic philosophers owing to its religious implications. Because of this preoccupation the commentaries of Neo-Platonic authors who had tried to reconcile Plato and Aristotle on the subject of the soul were also translated, as well as the works of Alexander, whose writings on logic had been so much favoured by Avicenna. It has been claimed that the earliest statements on the substantiality of the soul are found in his commentary on the *De Anima* of Aristotle. This had been accepted by most subsequent philosophers; and Avicenna seems to attribute substantiality not only to the human soul, but to the vegetative and animal souls as well. Though it should be noted that substance here is not strictly that of Aristotle's conception. The attempt to draw parallels between the assertions of Avicenna and those of Plotinus has produced some interesting results showing clearly the relation of one to the other; and a more thorough study of the correspondence may prove even more revealing. Avicenna had carefully studied the so-called *Theology* of Aristotle with its excerpts from the *Enneads*, and had even written a commentary on it.[1] The idea of

[1] Edit. Badawī: *Arisṭu 'ind al-'Arab.*

the soul yearning for the body once it has itself come into existence as a separate entity is definitely of Plotinian origin.

Now that he has disposed of the faculties of the vegetative, animal and human souls and has demonstrated the nature of the human soul and its relation to the body, Avicenna turns to what is perhaps the more interesting and important part of his psychology, viz. his arguments in proof of the existence of the soul. The *Ishārāt* contains an illustration, already introduced in the *Shifā*, which later became famous among mediaeval scholastics.

Turn to yourself, Avicenna says, and ponder. When you are in good health, or rather in a normal state, such that you can comprehend matters properly, are you ever forgetful of your own existence, and do you ever cease to assert your own self? This could not happen to an alert observer; and even to the man in his sleep and to the drunkard in his intoxication the consciousness of his inner self is never absent from his mind even though he may not be aware of his whereabouts. And if you imagine yourself to have been born from the very beginning with a healthy mind and disposition and then imagine that you are suspended in space for an instant, in such a way that you do not see the parts of your body and the members of it do not touch one another, you will find that you are unaware of everything about yourself except the fact that you are—that you exist. With what do you perceive your self in such a state, or before or after it? And what is the percipient in you? Is it your senses, or your mind, or some faculty in addition to your senses and corresponding to them? If it be your mind and a faculty besides your senses, is it through some intermediary or directly? You will be in no need of an intermediary at such a time, and there is none. Therefore you perceive yourself without needing of any other faculty or medium; and the perception takes place through your senses or some internal sense. Let us look further. Do you deduce from all this that the perceived in you is what the sight perceives from your flesh? That could not be, because if you were to lose that flesh and have another, you would still be what you are. Or is it what the sense of touch perceives? That could not be so either, except for the external members of your body. 'It thus becomes clear that what you then perceive is not one of your members like a heart or a brain; for how could this be when their existence is hidden from you unless they are exposed by dissection? Nor is what you perceive an assemblage of things in so far as it is an assemblage. . . . So what you perceive is something other than these things which you do not perceive while you are perceiving your self, and which you do not find necessary to make you what you are. Thus that self which you perceive does not belong to the order of things that you perceive through the senses in any way whatever, or through what resembles the senses.'[1]

Avicenna continues. 'Perhaps you will say, indeed I prove [the existence of] my self through the medium of my action. In that case you will have to have an act to prove . . . or a movement or some other thing. In the supposition of suspension in space we isolate you from all that. But as a general principle, if you prove your act as absolutely an act, you must prove from it an agent absolutely and not particularly, who is your self definitely. If you prove that it is an act of yours and you do not prove yourself through it, and if it is part of what is understood from your act in so far as it is your act, it would then have been proved in the understanding, before it or at least with it but not through it. Your self is thus not proved through it.'[2]

This illuminating demonstration of the suspended man was quoted and copied by many Eastern and Western philosophers after Avicenna with occasional variations. It has been stated that it is of Neo-Platonic origin, yet the passages that have been cited from Plotinus, though related, are extremely remote from the vivid presentation we have here. That it inspired the *cogito ergo sum* of Descartes, scholars are no more in doubt; but it should be remembered that there is a reference to the suspended man in St. Augustine also. In fact, if thought is a form of activity, the statement of Avicenna which, however, he does not pursue, to

[1] *Ishārāt*, p. 120. [2] *Ibid.*, p. 120.

the effect that 'I prove my self by means of my act' is more comprehensive than that of the French philosopher.

Moreover, take the case of an animal. It moves by means of something other than its corporeal body or the organic combination of it, as may well be observed. This may sometimes be actually an obstacle to movement. And an animal perceives by something other than that corporeal construction or the combination of its parts, which is sometimes an obstacle to perception. The principle of the faculty of perception, of motion, and of protection in the general temperament of an animal is something else which you might call with justification the soul. This is the substance that pervades and rules the parts of the human body as well. 'This substance is unique in you, it is rather yourself in fact. And it has ramifications and faculties spread in your organs. And when you feel something through one of your organs, or you imagine, or you desire, or you are in anger, the connection existing between that substance and these branches casts a disposition in it so that it creates through repetition a certain inclination, or rather a habit and nature, which master this controlling substance in the same manner as natural dispositions do.'[1]

And is the soul immortal? The soul does not die with the body nor does it suffer corruption in any way. This is because everything that is corrupted with the corruption of something else, must be attached to it in some way. And the attachment or relationship must be one of coexistence, or of posteriority, or of priority—a priority that is in essence and not in time. If the relation of the soul to the body be one of coexistence and the attachment be in essence and not accidentally, then each is essentially correlated to the other, and neither of them would be an independent substance, whereas in fact we know that they are independent. And if the attachment be accidental and not in essence, then the corruption of one annuls the accidental relationship and does not corrupt the essence. If the attachment of the soul to the body is such that it is posterior to it in existence, then

[1] *Ishārāt*, p. 121.

the body would be the cause of the soul and one of the four causes would apply. It could not possibly be the efficient cause of the soul for it acts only through its faculties. If it were to act through its essence, all bodies would act in exactly the same way. Nor could the body possibly be the receptive and material cause of the soul, for it has been shown that the soul is in no way imprinted in the body, and the latter does not take the form of the former whether in simplicity or composition. Nor indeed could the body possibly be the formal or the final cause of the soul. It is the reverse that is more comprehensible and likely. It may therefore be concluded that the attachment of the soul to the body does not correspond to the attachment of an effect to some essential cause. Admittedly the body and the temperament could stand as an accessory cause to the soul, for when the matter of a body suitable to be the instrument and the domain of the soul comes into being, the separate causes bring a particular soul into being. And that is how the soul is said to originate from them, because the bringing into being for no special reason one soul and not another is impossible. And at the same time it prevents numerical multiplicity which, as was shown, cannot be ascribed to the soul. Furthermore, whenever a new entity comes into being it is necessary that it should be preceded by matter fully disposed to receive it or to become related to it. And if it were possible that an individual soul should come into being, without a corresponding instrument through which to act and attain perfection, its existence would be purposeless, and in nature there is nothing without a purpose. Nothing that necessarily comes into being together with the coming into existence of another thing need become corrupted with the corruption of the other. The former does not logically entail the latter. It would do so only if the essence of the first were constituted by and in the second, which does not apply here.

There are cases where things originating from other things survive the latter's corruption provided their essences are not constituted in them, and especially if what brings them into existence is different from what only prepares their coming into being together with itself, which here means the body. And the soul, as has been repeatedly said, does not come from the body, nor is it due to a faculty of it. It is an entirely different substance. If, then, it owes its being to some other thing, and it is only the time of its realization that it owes to the body, it is not inseparably bound up with it in its very existence, and the body is not its cause except by accident. Therefore it may not be said that the attachment between the two is such as to necessitate that the body should be prior to the soul and possess an essential causal priority.

There remains the third possibility, namely, that the attachment of the soul to the body should be one of priority in existence. In that case it could be temporal or essential. The soul could not be attached to the body in time because it preceded it. And if it were attached to it in essence, then the body could neither exist nor die independently of it. If the body died, it would have to be through the destruction of the soul, whereas in fact it dies through causes peculiar to itself and its composition. Thus for their existence the soul and the body are in no way interdependent on one another, as a result of an essential priority. This goes to show that ultimately all forms of attachment between the soul and the body prove to be false; and the soul in its being can be in true relationship only with other principles that do not suffer change or corruption.

There is another reason for the immortality of the soul. Every thing that is liable to corruption through some cause, possesses in itself the potentiality of corruption and, before that occurs, the actuality of persistence. It is impossible to suppose that in one and the same thing there could be both corruption and persistence, and the liability to one cannot be due to the other, because the two concepts are contrary to one another. And their relations also differ, one being correlated with the notion of corruption and the other with that of persistence. The two may exist jointly in composite things and in simple things that are constituted in the composite, but in simple things whose essence is separate, they cannot. It may further be said that in an absolute sense the two notions cannot exist together in something possessing a unitary essence, because the potentiality of persistence is something to be found in the very substance of the thing. To be sure the actuality of persistence is not the same as the potentiality of persistence, the one being a fact that happens to a body possessing the other. Hence that potentiality belongs to something to which actual existence is only accidental and not of its essence. From this it follows that its being is composed of two factors, (1) one the possession of which gives it its actual existence, which is the form. And (2) one which attained this actual existence though in itself it had only the potentiality of it, which is the matter. It may thus be concluded that if the soul is absolutely simple and in no way divisible into matter and form, it will not admit of corruption.

But what if the soul is composite? To answer that we have to go back to the substance which is its matter. 'We say: either that matter will continue to be divisible and so the same analysis will go on being applied to it and we shall then have a regress *ad infinitum*, which is absurd; or this substance and base will never cease to exist. But if so, then our present discourse is devoted to this factor . . . and not to the composite thing which is composed of this factor and some other. So it is clear that everything which is simple . . . cannot in itself possess both the actuality of persistence and the potentiality of corruption.'[1] If it has the potentiality of corruption it is impossible that it should possess the actuality of persistence also; and if it has the actuality to exist and persist, it cannot have the potentiality of corruption. Hence the substance of the soul does not contain the potentiality of corruption. As to those beings that suffer corruption, it is the composite in them that is corruptible. Furthermore the potentiality to corruption and persistence is not to be found in something that gives unity to a composite, but in the matter which potentially admits of both contraries. And so the corruptible

[1] *Najāt*, p. 188, trans. of Rahman, *Avicenna's Psychology*, p. 62.

composite has neither the potentiality to persist nor to suffer corruption, nor both together, while the matter either has persistence without its being due to the potentiality that can give it the capacity to persist, as some suppose, or it has persistence through that potentiality, but does not have the potentiality of corruption, which is something that it acquires.

There remains the case of the simple entities that are constituted in matter. With them the potentiality of corruption is something that is found in their matter and not in their actual substance. And the condition that everything that has come to be should suffer some form of corruption on account of the finitude of the potentialities of persistence and corruption in it, applies only to those things whose being is composed of matter and form. In their matter there would be the potentiality that their forms may persist in them, and at the same time the potentiality that these forms may cease to persist in them. From all this it becomes evident that the soul does not suffer corruption at all.

These arguments in proof of the immortality of the soul are not of Aristotelian origin. They are to be found in a fragmentary and perhaps elementary form in Neo-Platonic writings that had been rendered into Arabic, and were therefore available to Avicenna. As with the theory of emanation, Islamic psychology found Neo-Platonic conceptions with regard to the soul and its nature highly congenial particularly in what may be called its spiritual aspects. In his interesting work[1] Dr Rahman has pointed out that the idea that destruction is the fate of composite substances only, and that the soul being by nature simple and incorporeal is not liable to corruption, is to be found in Plotinus, as also is the view that the soul is not imprinted on the body as form is in matter. But that does not mean that Avicenna deserts Aristotle completely. On the contrary embedded in his own distinctive line of thought, there is a happy combination of the best of both Aristotle and Plotinus. Nor is the influence of Hellenistic commentators altogether absent.

[1] *Avicenna's Psychology*, Oxford, 1952.

Avicenna could not entertain the idea of the transmigration of the soul. Contrary to Plato and in agreement with Aristotle, he rejected what to any Muslim was an abhorrent notion. It has been made clear, he says, that souls come into being—and they are in endless number—only when bodies are prepared to receive them; and it is this readiness of the body that necessitates their emanation from the separate causes. Obviously this cannot happen by accident or chance. If we were to suppose that the soul exists already and it just happens that a body comes into existence at the same time and the two somehow combine, without the need of a temperament and suitability in the body requiring a particular soul to govern and control it, there would be no essential cause for multiformity, only an accidental one; and it has been learnt that essential causes are prior to accidental ones. If that is the case then every body requires a special soul to itself, suitable to its elements; and this applies to all and not only to some bodies. Now if it be supposed that one soul can migrate into several bodies each of which requires for its existence, and therefore already has, a separate soul, there would then be two souls in one and the same body at the same time, which is absurd. And again, it has been maintained that the relationship between the soul and the body is not such that the soul is imprinted in the body, but that it controls and governs it in such a way that it is conscious of the body and the body is in turn influenced by it. This prevents the possibility of a second soul having exactly the same relationship to it. And consequently transmigration cannot take place in any manner.

For Avicenna as for Aristotle, the soul is a single unity and not as Plato had taught a compound of three 'kinds.' The soul is one entity with many faculties. If these faculties did not unite into a greater whole, and sensation and anger and each of the others had a principle of its own, different actions might proceed from the same faculty or different faculties might become confused with one another. Of course these faculties interact and influence each other, but they do not change with the other's change, for the activity of each is special to the function that it performs. The faculty of anger does not perceive and that of perception does not become angry. What happens is that all the faculties bring what they receive to one unifying and controlling centre. This unitary thing could be a man's body or his soul. If it were his body it would either be the totality of his organs or some of them. It could not be the totality for obviously his hands and feet could have nothing to do with it; nor could it be just two, one sensing and the other becoming angry, because there would then be no one thing that sensed and consequently became angry. Nor indeed could it be one single organ which, according to those who hold this view, would be the basis of both functions. What becomes angry is that thing to which sense-perception transmits its sensation; and it must have a faculty of combining both sensations, perception and anger. That thing cannot be the totality of our bodily organs, nor two of them, nor just one. The uniting substance can only be the soul or the body inasmuch as it possesses a soul, which really means the same thing as the soul, the principle of all the faculties. This soul should necessarily be attached to the first organ in which life begins, and so it is impossible that an organ should be alive without a psychical faculty attached to it. And the first thing joined to the body cannot be some thing posterior to this. Hence the organ to which this psychical faculty has to be attached must be the heart. 'This opinion of the philosopher' (i.e. Aristotle), Avicenna says, 'is contrary to that of the divine Plato.'

But there are vegetative faculties in the plants, and plants do not possess the perceptive and rational faculties. And there are the vegetative and the perceptive in the animals, and animals do not possess the rational faculty. This shows that each of these is a separate faculty by itself having no connection with the others. What then of the all-embracing unity of the soul? It must be understood that among elemental bodies their absolute contrariness prevents them from receiving life. The more they are able to break that contrariness and approach the mean, which has no opposite, the nearer they approach a resemblance to the heavenly bodies and to that extent they deserve to receive an animating force from the originating separate principle. The nearer they get to the mean, the more capable of life they become. And when they reach the limit beyond which it is impossible to approach the mean any nearer and to reduce the contrary extremes any further, they receive a substance which in some ways is similar to the separate substance, just as the heavenly substances had received it and become attached to it. Once the elemental bodies have received this substance, what was said to originate in them only through the external substance may be now said to originate through both.

Here emerges the idea of self-consciousness and the existence of a personal ego through which the unity of experience can be explained. Here Avicenna, like some of Aristotle's Hellenistic commentators, goes beyond what was envisaged by the Stagirite. A passage in John Philoponus throws some light on what seems to have been the subject of much argument. 'We, however, say about this that Aristotle's view is wrong. . . . He wants to attribute to individual senses the knowledge both of their objects and of their own acts. Alexander . . . attributes to the five senses the knowledge of their objects only, and to the *sensus communis* the knowledge of objects and the knowledge of their acts as well. Plutarch holds that it is a function of the rational soul to know the acts of the senses. . . . But the more recent interpreters . . . say that it is the function of the attentive part of the rational soul to know the acts of the senses. For according to them, the rational soul has not only five faculties—intellect, reason, opinion, will and choice—but besides these, also a sixth faculty which they add to the rational soul and which they call the attentive faculty. . . . We agree . . . in saying that there is no sixth sense which possesses self-consciousness . . . it is false to attribute self-consciousness to sensation itself. Sensation having perceived colour must at all events reflect upon itself. . . . If it thus reflects upon itself it belongs to the kind of separate activity, and . . .

also to a separate substance, and is therefore incorporeal and eternal.'[1] It has been pointed out in this connection that the Stoics were the first to use the word 'ego' in a technical sense.

There remains to be considered the element that gives actuality to a potential human intellect. The theoretical faculty in man emerges from a potential to an actual state through the illuminating action of a substance that has this effect upon it. A thing does not change from potentiality to actuality all by itself but through something that produces that result, and the actuality conferred consists of the forms of the intelligibles. Here then is something that from its own substance grants to the human soul and imprints upon it the forms of the intelligibles. The essence of this thing undoubtedly possesses these forms, and is therefore an intellect in itself. If it were a potential intellect it would mean a regression *ad infinitum*, which is absurd. The regression must halt at some thing which is in essence an intellect, and which is the cause of all potential intellects becoming actual intellects, and which alone is sufficient to bring this about. This thing is called, in relation to the potential intellects that pass through it into actuality, an active intellect (*al-'aql al-fa''āl*). In like manner the material intellect is called in relation to it a passive intellect; and the imagination also is called in relation to it another passive intellect. The intellect that comes between the active and the passive is called the acquired intellect. The relation of the active intellect to our souls which are potentially intellect, and to the intelligibles which are potential intelligibles, is as the relation of the sun to our eyes which are potential percipients, and to the colours which are potentially perceptible. For when light falls on the potential objects of sight, they become actually perceptible and the eye becomes an actual percipient. In a similar fashion there is some power that emanates from this active intellect and extends to the objects of imagination which are potential intelligibles to make them actually so, and transforms the potential into an actual intellect. And just as the sun is by itself an object

[1] Cf. Rahman: *Avicenna's Psychology*, p. 111.

of sight and the agency which makes what is a potential object of sight actually so, in just the same way this substance is in itself intelligible and an agency which transforms all potential intelligibles into actual ones. But one thing that is in itself intelligible is an intellect in essence, for it is the form separated from matter, especially when it is in itself abstract and not present through the action of something else. This thing is the active intelligence, and it is actually eternally intelligible as well as intelligent in itself.

Here then is an important distinction between the intellect, the intelligible, and the act of intellection. In this Avicenna rejects the Peripatetic idea that the intellect and the object of its intellection are identical, and adopts the Neo-Platonic doctrine of emanation, which was to become prevalent among all Islamic thinkers after him. Again, somewhat similar statements may be found by Hellenistic commentators and by Fārābī, but none correspond exactly to what Avicenna envisages even where the terms used are the same. The significance and the function he gives them are quite different if not altogether original. For him they had to conform to the general system which he was attempting to build.

But what of dreams in Avicenna's system? In his view as in that of Aristotle, dreams are the work of the imagination. During sleep a man's imaginative faculty is more active than when he is awake because it is not overwhelmed by the external senses. In two conditions the soul diverts the imagination from the performance of its proper function. One is when it is itself occupied with the external senses and devotes the image-forming power to their use rather than to that of the imaginative faculty which as a result becomes involved in other than its proper function. And the *sensus communis* also cannot come to its aid since it is busy with the external senses. The other condition is that of the soul when employing the imagination in its intellectual activities, either to construct together with the *sensus communis* concrete forms or to discourage it from imagining things that do not conform with actual objects; and as a result weakening its powers of representation. When, however, it becomes disengaged from such preoccupations and impediments as in sleep, or during the illness of the body, when the soul ceases to employ the mind and make fine distinctions, the imagination finds an opportunity to grow in intensity and to engage the image-forming power and make use of it. The combination of the two powers adds still more to their activity, and the image thereby produced falls on the *sensus communis*, and the object is seen as though it were externally existent.

* * * *

The foregoing account is based on what Avicenna wrote on psychology in the *Shifā*, the *Najāt* and the *Ishārāt*. Notice might also be taken of a very short treatise on the subject, because it is certainly one of the earliest things he ever wrote, and may quite possibly be the very earliest. It is addressed to the Prince of Bukhārā, Nūḥ ibn Manṣūr, whom he had been invited to treat for an illness, when himself just a young physician of promise. It opens in the diffident language of a youthful aspirant seeking recognition and patronage; then develops into a clear exposition of his conception of the soul and its faculties. It is remarkable for the fact that in all that he wrote on psychology afterwards, he had, in spite of some additions, very little to change. His conception was based principally on the *De Anima* of Aristotle, though it included matters not to be found there. Later he did alter his views on two points. In the early work,[1] common sense and memory are considered as one and the same faculty, whereas in the *Shifā* and the *Najāt* they are entirely distinct. Moreover, he was at first inclined to attribute the power of recollection to animals, then later changed to the belief that 'memory may be found in all animals, but recollection, i.e. a conscious

1 Edit. Landauer, *Z.D.M.G.*, 1875; and Van Dyke, Cairo, 1325 A.H.

effort to reproduce what has gone out of memory, belongs I think only to man.'[1]

To animals he attributes an estimative faculty (*wahm* and sometimes *ẓann*) which the Latin Scholastics translated as *aestimatio*. This is the power by which the sheep senses that a wolf is to be avoided as an object of fear. Averroës and Ghazālī both asserted that this was a non-Aristotelian faculty invented by Avicenna himself; and the former took strong exception to it. And yet the fact that he already discusses it in this very early book written when hardly twenty years of age, makes it unlikely that they are right. For it may be supposed that he was then too young for original contributions in the field of what was a purely theoretical psychology; and that it must have come from some other source. Attempts to ascertain the correct Greek equivalents of the terms *wahm* and *ẓann* have caused sharp controversy, because the available materials have not yet been studied.[2] It has been claimed,[3] and with some good arguments, that actually all the 'internal senses' of which Avicenna speaks are differentiations or rather specifications of the Aristotelian *phantasia*, and that the so-called estimative faculty is one form of imagination or 'an operation subsidiary to imagination.' This may well be so when it is remembered that in more than one place in his philosophical system, Avicenna has taken an Aristotelian idea and divided it into subsidiary parts, giving each a significance not envisaged by the Stagirite himself. Averroës and Ghazālī may therefore have been right in thinking that the estimative faculty was a non-Aristotelian innovation of Avicenna; and Dr Rahman may be justified in believing that it is a subdivision of *phantasia*. But then

[1] *Shifā*. Cf. Rahman: *op. cit.*, p. 3.

[2] *φαντασία* Cf. (*Soph.* 165b25) *wahm*.
δόξα (*P. Herm.* 21a33) *al-tawahhum*.
ὑπόληψις (*Top.* 151a16) *wahm*.
διανοητός (*A. Pr.* 47b23) *mutuwahhim*.
δόξα (*Categ.* 4a23) *al-ẓann*.
ὑπόληψις (*A. Proc.* 64a10) *ẓann*

[3] Cf. Rahman, *op. cit.*, p. 83.

it would not need a Greek equivalent, which it has been shown to have, and which the translators used long before him. In any case, Avicenna was capable of taking an idea, or a suggestion, or just a term, and making it entirely his own. He was no servile commentator, like Averroës, and gave himself every liberty.

According to Avicenna, the estimative faculty plays its part in the grades of abstraction. Intellect was the recipient of universal forms, and sensation the recipient of individual forms as present in matter. Knowledge comes by means of bridging the gap between the material forms of sensible objects and the abstract forms of intelligibles. This is done through the faculties of imagination and estimation. In the acquisition of knowledge, the first stage is sensation. Sensation perceives forms embedded in matter. It could not possibly take place without the presence of matter. It arrives at knowledge of an object by perceiving its form, and this it can do only when the form is present in the matter of that object. In the next stage comes imagination, which can act without the presence of the physical object itself. The images that it forms are, consequently, not material images even though they may be fashioned after the pattern of material objects. Imagination knows an object not as matter or as present in matter, but in the image of the material attachments that it has acquired. The next process is taken up by the estimative faculty which perceives such notions as pleasure and pain, which sees goodness and badness in the individual objects that have been first sensed and then imagined. It comprehends meaning and intention in objects; and thereby carries the abstraction one stage further. In the final act reason comes to know things that have either been abstracted into pure form or that it abstracts itself completely and takes in their ultimate universality. This was Avicenna's attempt to explain knowledge when coming from sensation and when abstracted and universalized by the intellect, the difference between the two, and the means by which one led to the other—questions to which Aristotelian theory gave, in his view, no satisfactory answer.

The principle of individuation by matter entailed some difficulties. In the world of pure intelligences, Avicenna argued, form is the essential thing; and consequently differentiation is entirely on the basis of form and quiddity which determine species. In our material world, on the other hand, just the opposite is true. In this world of generation and corruption, it is quite evident that the species man, with the particular form that he possesses, is represented by more than one individual. And the same may be said of other species. The individual differences, therefore, could not come from the form, they must come from the matter which thereby permits that multiplicity of forms impossible among pure intelligences. But—and here comes the difficulty—if different individuals, as well as different bodies, have the same matter in common between them, and also have the same form in common, then why can they be so different from one another, and what is it that gives them their particular individuality? It has been shown that the basis of all beings in our world is matter; and that the Active Intelligence, as the Giver of Forms, bestows upon this matter a form to produce the different species. Now if the matter and the form be the same, how and why do they individualize? This problem arises in both the ontological as well as the psychological field—individualization among different species of being in general, and among individuals of the human species. The principle is matter, Avicenna says in agreement with Aristotle; but matter with a particular and predetermined disposition, in a certain predetermined state which make it 'merit' (*yastaḥiq*) one form to the exclusion of another. This, however, is only an explanation of the existence of different species, not of separate specimens of any species. It was important to know why individual persons differed among themselves, since religion asserted that their souls survived individually, and maintained their individual human identity.

Aristotle had denied intellectual memory.[1] Intelligibles, he had said, are never remembered in themselves as such. Avicenna

[1] *De Mem.*, 450a10–14.

asserts the same view in various places,[1] but supports it by means of the Neo-Platonic theory of the emanation of intelligibles directly from the Active Intelligence. His conception, which was to have a great influence on the mediaeval scholastics, was that there are two retentive faculties in the human soul. The first, as the representative faculty, stored images; the second, as the faculty of conservation, stored meanings or intentions. There is no special faculty for the retention of intelligibles as such. And when the soul wishes to contemplate the intelligibles, what happens is that it reunites itself with the Active Intelligence; and from it the intelligibles start to emanate again as they had done before.[2]

We may close this chapter with his celebrated Ode on the Soul as done into English by the late Prof. E. G. Browne of Cambridge.[3]

It descended upon thee from out of the regions above,
That exalted, ineffable, glorious, heavenly Dove.
'Twas concealed from the eyes of all those who its nature
  would ken,
Yet it wears not a veil, and is ever apparent to men.
Unwilling it sought thee and joined thee, and yet, though it
  grieve,
It is like to be still more unwilling thy body to leave.
It resisted and struggled, and would not be tamèd in haste,
Yet it joined thee, and slowly grew used to this desolate waste,
Till, forgotten at length, as I ween, were its haunts and its troth
In the heavenly gardens and groves, which to leave it was
  loath.

Until, when it entered the D of its downward Descent,
And to earth, to the C of its centre, unwillingly went,
The eye(I) of Infirmity smote it, and lo, it was hurled
Midst the sign-posts and ruined abodes of this desolate world.

[1] *Ishārāt*, p. 137. [2] *Ibid.*, p. 179. [3] *Lit. Hist. of Persia*, Vol. 2, pp. 110–11.

It weeps, when it thinks of its home and the peace it possessed,
With tears welling forth from its eyes without pausing or rest,
And with plaintive mourning it broodeth like one bereft
O'er such trace of its home as the fourfold winds have left.
Thick nets detain it, and strong is the cage whereby
It is held from seeking the lofty and spacious sky.
Until, when the hour of its homeward flight draws near,
And 'tis time for it to return to its ampler sphere,
It carols with joy, for the veil is raised, and it spies
Such things as cannot be witnessed by waking eyes.
On a lofty height doth it warble its songs of praise.
(For even the lowliest being doth knowledge raise.)
And so it returneth, aware of all hidden things
In the universe, while no stain to its garment clings.

Now why from its perch on high was it cast like this
To the lowest Nadir's gloomy and drear abyss?
Was it God who cast it forth for some purpose wise,
Concealed from the keenest seeker's inquiring eyes?
Then is its descent a discipline wise but stern,
That the things that it hath not heard it thus may learn,
So 'tis she whom Fate doth plunder, until her star
Setteth at length in a place from its rising far,
Like a gleam of lightning which over the meadows shone,
And, as though it ne'er had been, in a moment is gone.

*　*　*　*

CHAPTER VI

PROBLEMS OF RELIGION

NOWHERE in Islamic philosophy are the problems of reason and revelation better contrasted, and an agreement in essentials more consistently attempted, than in the system of Avicenna. Nothing remaining from the pen of Kindī, and nothing from the more extensive writings of Fārābī that we possess, requires us to qualify that statement. Of Avicenna's successors, Ghazālī's chief concern was to emphasize the limitations of reason, to insist on the necessity for dogma, and to call men to the higher regions of religious experience. As to Averroës, even when applying himself directly to the issue in question[1] he had nothing new to contribute, and confined himself to a re-statement of the position as he found it.

Avicenna's devotion to the principles of rational thought always predominated; but that need not cast doubt on his protestations of religious faith even though his faith is different from the orthodox. He may have refused to submit to tradition and unquestioned dogma, but he realized that the mind does not succeed in proving the truth of things in every case. He may never have failed to attack the theologians when he thought they were in error, yet he was deeply animated by the desire to see both disciplines brought into harmony. He may not have succeeded completely, yet he captured and expressed the spirit of his age.

God, for Aristotle, was an ever-living being whose influence radiates throughout the universe; and who, though himself

[1] Cf. Gauthier: *La Théorie d'Ibn Rochd sure les Rapports de la Religion et de la Philosophie.*

unmoved, moved everything by inspiring love and desire in them. This Being whose existence he proves, among others, by what amounts to a form of the ontological argument, namely, that where there is a better there must needs also be a best, is form and actuality, life and mind. But his activity is only mental, and his knowledge 'involves no transition from premises to conclusion.' It is direct and intuitive, he has only himself as the object of his thought. God has no knowledge of the universe around us; nor of the evil that there may be in it. His influence is not direct, and does not flow from his knowledge. It would indeed detract from his perfection were he to be interested in this world of ours. Those who have tried to attribute to Aristotle a theistic view of the universe have failed to win general agreement.

The Neo-Platonic conception coloured much of Islamic thought. For Plotinus God was the One, the First, and (according to Plato) the Good. As the One he is the first cause; and as the Good, the final cause. He is transcendent as well as immanent in the world of the soul. The One is 'beyond substance,' and, *pace* Aristotle, he is 'beyond activity, beyond intellect and intellection.'

Finally, there was the religious belief in God as the all-knowing, all-powerful, all-controlling Creator of heaven and earth, to which Avicenna was anxious to conform and be faithful as far as he possibly could; not as a matter of policy or convenience as some have thought, but out of sincere desire. And between these hardly reconcilable views, and many others of which he was aware, he set out to develop his own conception of the Deity.

God, he says, 'is not a body, nor the matter of a body, nor the form of one; nor an intelligible matter for an intelligible form, nor an intelligible form in an intelligible matter. He is not divisible, neither in quantity, nor in principle, nor in definition. he is One.' Hence as a transcendental being God is, in accordance with the tenets of his Faith, strictly one. He is complete in himself, and no state in him is to be 'awaited.' He is a Necessary Being in essence as well as in all other respects. He could not be a necessary being in one sense and a possible being in another. He could not be both at the same time, because that would involve contradiction. And if he is necessary in every way, and everything that is possible has already become necessary in him, there remains nothing incomplete or lacking in him to be awaited —neither will, nor nature, nor knowledge, nor any of his attributes. Furthermore, he who is a necessary being in his essence, is pure Good and pure Perfection. The Good is what every being keenly desires in order to perfect its existence; it is a condition of perfection, and evil does not exist in essence. 'Existence is a goodness, and the perfection of existence is the goodness of existence.' Thus a being that does not suffer any evil in the form of the absence of a substance, or of any undesirable state of it, is pure Good. This could not apply to what is in essence a possible being. Good in the sense of useful and profitable is only with the object of attaining perfection in things. God as a source of help becomes a source of Good and free of all defect or evil.[1]

God as a necessary being in essence is pure truth, since the reality of every thing is the particularity of its existence which can be proved to belong to it; and there is nothing more true than him. By the very fact that he is in essence necessary he becomes a species apart and particular to himself; and therefore he has none like him, no associate and no contrary. And as a species in himself he is One because he is complete in his existence, because his definition applies only to himself, because he is indivisible and because in the scale of existence his position is that of the necessity of existence which he does not share with any other. God is 'in essence an intelligence, he intellects and he is intelligible.' It is as a separate and abstracted entity that he is an intelligence; it is in consideration of the fact that he is aware that his essence has a separate entity that he 'intellects'; and he is intelligible because everything that is in essence separate from matter and all the accidents, is intelligible in essence. God possesses the purest of beauty and light, for 'there can be no beauty

[1] Cf. *Najāt*, p. 229.

or light more than in a state where the quiddity is pure intellectuality, pure goodness, unblemished by any form of defect.' Every suitable beauty and perceptible good is desired and loved; it is perceived through the senses or the imagination or the mind and the intellectual perception is the highest of them all. So the Necessary Being who possesses the utmost beauty, perfection and light and who 'intellects' himself with full intellection, considering that the subject and the object of intellection are in reality one and the same in this case, 'his essence would be to himself the greatest lover and beloved' and the greatest source of pleasure.

As compared with the sensual, intellectual perception is much the stronger, and it is superior as regards the objects that it perceives and the manner of doing so and the purpose which it has in view. There is in fact no experience to be compared to it. This brings us to the nature of God's knowledge of things. God does not think of things from perception of those things directly; his intellection is not of changeable things with their constant changes in so far as they are individually changeable in time; he cannot think of them as sometimes existent and at other times non-existent, for in that case they would not be intellected but sensed or imagined and that would be a defect for him. The Necessary Being 'intellects every thing in a general way' and yet he is not ignorant of any particular thing. Not the smallest atom in the heavens or on earth is hidden from him 'and this is one of the miracles the imagination of which requires a subtle nature.' Thus Avicenna departs from Aristotle in asserting that God does have knowledge of the world, though that knowledge is only 'in a general way.' Then he feels constrained to quote a Qur'anic passage and to assert that He is at the same time aware, to the extent of a single atom, of all that happens in heaven and earth. Avicenna realizes the difficulty of his position and therefore proceeds to explain further.[1]

When the Necessary Being intellects his essence and the fact

[1] Cf. *Najāt*, pp. 243–7.

that he is the principle of every existing being, he intellects the origin of the existent things that have proceeded from him. And there is no single thing the existence of which did not become in some way necessary through him. It is the action and interaction of these causes that bring about particular events and matters. He who is the first cause knows full well the various causes and their application and working, and therefore knows necessarily the effects that they produce and the time involved between them and their recurrence. This is because he could not know the original causes and yet be unaware of their results. Hence God would be conscious of individual matters inasmuch as they are in principle general matters in their circumstances and nature, even though they may have occurred to a single person at a particular time and under special conditions. As an illustration, if you know the heavenly movements you can tell in a general way every eclipse or conjunction of the stars. Yet your knowledge would be limited by your ability to make the proper calculations and by the fact that you are yourself a momentary being. In the case of God his time, his knowledge and consequently his judgement are eternal and all-embracing. For you it is necessary to know a whole series of causes and effects in the movement of the heavenly bodies in order to know the circumstances of just one eclipse; but God knows everything because he is the principle of everything. He knows the causes and therefore the effects, the movements and therefore the results, and this leads to the knowledge of the world and 'the keys of what is hidden' from us.

God contemplates his essence as well as the order of the Good pervading all things. And by doing so, that order emanates from him to all existent things. We love and seek the good, but only for a purpose. God entertains no such purpose; and he possesses this form of pure intellectual will with no specific aim in view. Life for us is perfected through perception and action—two different forces in themselves. God only needs to think of things, and that becomes the cause and the starting-point of his acts and the origin of all that comes to be. The intelligible form that moves us, and becomes the source of the concrete form that we reproduce in art, is, when emanating from him, in itself sufficient to produce results without any intermediary. Moreover, in essence, the will of God does not differ from his knowledge. 'The knowledge that he has is exactly the will that he has.' And the power that he has, is due to the fact that his essence intellects every single thing, and that intellection becomes the principle of all things. It is a principle in itself, and is not derived from any thing nor dependent on the existence of any thing. In emanating existence, this will is not bound up with any specific consideration; it is out of sheer bounty (*jūd*).[1] In fact God's will is itself a bounty.

This leads to what became the subject of heated discussion among theologians of all shades of opinion, viz. the attributes of God. The first attribute of the Necessary Being is that he *is* and is *existent*. The other attributes have this specified existence with some additional quality affirmed or denied, without implying in any way multiplicity in essence. When it is said that he is an essence or an immaterial substance, it means that he is not in a subject. When said that he is One, this means that his existence does not allow division in quantity, or in definition, or in association with other than himself. When it is said that he is an intellect, he is intelligible, and is bent on intellection, the implication is that his existence is beyond the possibility of mixing with matter or with anything related to it. When it is said that he is the first, it is in relation to all other things; and 'powerful' denotes that the existence of all things proceeds from him. When it is said that he is a living God, the meaning is that his being, as pure intellect, perceives and acts continuously. When it is said that he is sought as a refuge, and supplicated in times of trouble, the reason is that he is the principle of the order of the Good. When it is said that he is bountiful, it is meant that he seeks nothing for himself. God, moreover, is pre-eternal (*azalīy*) as well as post-

[1] Cf. *Ishārāt*, p. 159.

eternal (*abadīy*). As a pure substance, he is simple; and, unlike all possible beings, his essence and his existence are one. He is love, he loves and he is beloved. He rejoices in all that emanates from him, and he is the most happy of beings. He has no quiddity, for every being that has quiddity besides existence is caused. These emanate from him, and he himself is pure existence.[1] Since he has no quiddity, he has no genus, for genus defines the nature of what is. And if he has no genus, he has no differentia, and hence has no definition. Nor do any of the categories of being apply to him. He cannot therefore be demonstrated; he demonstrates all things.

What of God's providence (*'ināyat*) of which we are all in need, and the evidences of which we see all around us? God, knowing himself and the existence of an order of the Good; being the source of all good and perfection in so far as it is possible; and desirous of the working of such an order, contemplates it in its highest conceivable form, and as a result of that contemplation it emanates from him to this world. This may be called divine providence.[2] And in another place Avicenna says that providence is the all-encompassing knowledge of God about things, and how they should be that they may attain the best order. This knowledge of the proper order of existence becomes the source from which good emanates to everything.[3] Hence his notion of providence is very general and rather abstract. It was probably for this reason that the Christian scholastics of the thirteenth century accused him of having denied divine providence completely. Actually his conception is in full accord with the principles of his metaphysics. It was seen how reflection or contemplation on the part of God makes what is possible in essence necessary for all possible beings. Here, then, as in the question of the attributes of God, Avicenna attempts a reconciliation between purely intellectual conceptions and the more concrete ideas of tradition and religious dogma. The attributes to which theologians attached such importance were numerous,

[1] *Shifā, Ilāhīyyāt.* [2] Cf. *Shifā, Ilāhīyāt.* [3] Cf. *Ishārāt*, p. 185.

and God's intervention through divine providence explained many a perplexity. Avicenna would not deny any of them, but in his characteristic manner gave them a purely rational interpretation.

* * * *

Creation is one of the acts of God most emphatically stressed by religion. How is that consummated? It takes two forms. One is through the process of emanation which is inherent in the Necessary Being; and by means of which the different spheres including our sub-lunary world come into existence. The other more active form of creation, which is specified by distinct terms, is more direct. In all cases it requires that God should be living and powerful and should possess a knowledge and a will of his own. These are all united in him and act in unison, not separately. His knowledge is his will, and his life is his power. With these he brings together the necessary causes; and through the action and interaction of the efficient cause and the material or receptive cause, creation takes place. The efficient cause may be a necessitating will or nature or instrument; and the material cause may be a particular disposition that did not exist previously. What is essential is that the two elements must be present. There must be an agent and there must be matter. The absence of one or the other renders an act of creation impossible of consummation. In other words, creation is not altogether *ex nihilo*, as dogma asserts. The matter that constitutes the material cause must be there. Moreover, creation does not depend merely on the wish and will of God at one specified moment and not at another. It necessarily takes place in consequence of His will and nature. There is necessity involved in the act, contrary to the views of the theologians to whom in any case the theory of emanation was also unacceptable. Thus God could not have will and wished not to create the world. The world could not have failed to proceed from Him.

Aristotle had no theory of divine providence nor of divine

creation. In fact he had argued against the creation of the world. But the translators of his works had used in their Arabic renderings a number of religious terms for creation which gradually came to acquire somewhat different connotations. They also came to mean one thing to the theologians and another to the *Falāsifa*, and the latter did not always define them in the same way. There was the case of *ibdā'* which appears in some verbal forms for the equivalent of various Greek words in the Arabic translation of the *Theology* and therefore of Plotinian texts. Then there was *khalq*,[1] then *ḥadth* or *iḥdāth*,[2] then *kawn* or *takwīn*.[3] These were not always used in a specific sense, and Avicenna differentiated between them and considered that '*ibdā'* is special to the intelligence . . . *khalq* to the natural beings . . . and *takwīn* to the corruptible among them.'[4] The purest and the most original act of God may be called an *ibdā'* because it is 'when from one thing existence is granted to another—an existence belonging to it only—without an intermediary, be it matter or instrument or time . . . so that *ibdā'* is of a higher order than *takwīn* or *iḥdāth*.'[5] Kindī and Fārābī had not given it the same connotation; and though it may have been used by some Ismā'īlī authors, it was after Avicenna that it became established in its specific sense. Before that it was a purely religious word of Qur'anic origin.

There were also some doctrinal questions involved in the problem of creation; as for instance: does God know what he creates; and after creation does he continue to keep some sort of relation with his creatures; and who or what determines the time of creation? Avicenna did not take the traditional view on these matters and thereby incurred the displeasure of the theologians. The time of creation was the most important issue. The Mu'tazelite school of theologians said that the world was created

[1] *ποιεῖν* (*Rhet.* 1393a30) *khalq*.
[2] *ποίησις* (*Top.* 124a30) *ḥadth*.
[3] *γένεσις* (*Top.* 124a30) *kawn*.
γένεσις (*Categ.* 9b35) *takwīn*.
[4] Cf. *Risālat al-Nairūzīyya*. [5] *Ishārāt*, p. 153.

at what was the most suitable time; and the Ash'arites said that the time was determined by God's own will only. Avicenna argues at length[1] to show that there can be no time more suitable than another for creation. How could one distinguish when pre-existence, which was a period of non-existence, began and when it ended; and in what way does one time differ from another? Creation must be due to God's nature, or some accident besides his will. There is no question of compulsion or chance. Must we suppose that these are changeable and they actually changed when the suitable time for creation arrived? God creates either for the very act of creation or for some purpose or profit. There could be no purpose or profit when the existence or non-existence of a thing in no way affects him and would be the same for him. If it is for creation itself, and it took place at a fixed time, are we to suppose that the moment for doing so just pleased him, or the time for it suddenly arrived, or that it was only at that moment that he felt puissant enough to do so? No, between God and his creation there is no priority in time.

Moreover, if God be considered the agent or artificer who acted, designed or brought into being what did not exist before, it may be supposed that once the act has taken place, there is no more need for the agent or artificer. Should he disappear, his creation will continue to exist. Architects often die leaving their buildings intact after them. In any case, God's disappearance could do no harm to the world nor injury to anyone. The way to answer this is to find out what exactly is meant by designing or bringing into effect. If the first beings are the intelligences, after which come the souls, and then the bodies, they are all distinct from the Necessary Being in that they came to be after not being. On another interpretation beings may be necessary in themselves and in their essence, or possible in themselves and in essence, but necessary through some something else. This latter class may be continuously necessary, or for a period of time. In either case they are necessary through some other agency and not in their

[1] *Ishārāt*, pp. 147 ff.; *Najāt*, pp. 411 ff.

essence. Surely those that are continuously necessary are the more general, and those necessary for only a certain period, just particular cases. Hence the relation or attachment (*ta'alluq*) of the Necessary Being with those that are caused (*ma'lūl*) or that have been acted upon (*maf'ūl*) is predominantly continuous—only in special circumstances is it temporary. And that being so, it has to extend beyond the period of creation in order that it may continue to be, though a possible being in essence, a necessary being through the agency of what is always and for ever a necessary being in essence.[1]

* * * *

The prophet and his role in society was a subject that Avicenna could not overlook in a system which though philosophical had to consider religious questions as well. Greek thought had nothing to contribute in this field; and the traditional teachings he could not accept in their entirety. Fārābī, as was seen, devoted some attention to the question, perhaps because the theologians had elaborated a rather complicated theory about it. His successor in turn developed one of his own which seemed to satisfy his rational inclinations, though the more religious took strong exception to it. What kind of a man is a prophet; in what way does he differ from others; and what is his mission in life? Man lives in a society, Avicenna argues;[2] no one is happy entirely alone. And in a human society men are bound to have constant association with one another. These relations must be governed and directed so that justice may prevail. To dispense justice there must needs be laws and to lay down laws there must be a lawgiver. To be a lawgiver, a man must rise to become the leader of men, and devote his life and efforts to the problems of society. And to be chosen for that mission he must possess merits that others either do not have at all or have to a lesser extent than he. By these merits he must win the submission and support of his

[1] Cf. *Ishārāt*, pp. 149–50.
[2] Cf. *Shifā, Ilāhīyyāt*; *Najāt*, p. 303; *Tis'a Rasā'il*.

fellow-men. Having gained these, he can attend to their needs and apply the 'order of the Good' provided for them by God. Obviously this leader could not but be a human being like all the rest; except that he is chosen, authorized and inspired by God who makes his holy spirit descend upon him.

Already in his psychology Avicenna had pointed out the lucidity of mind and unusual intellectual faculties that a prophet must possess. By an extraordinary capacity for intuition, the prophet acquires knowledge 'from within himself,' and by that same power he comes into contact with the Active Intelligence. This is the highest stage which man can reach. It is then that the material intelligence may be called the Divine Spirit; and it would then belong to the genus of *intellectus in habitu*. Furthermore, his faculty of imagination would be so strong as to reach the point of perfection. And presumably it is for this reason that he can use such vivid imagery and speak so effectively in metaphors and allegories. All others must seek 'the middle term of a syllogism' in their logical reasoning. He who is endowed with the prophetic gift need not do so. The intense purity of his soul and his firm link with the Active Intelligence make him 'ablaze with intuition.' The forms of the Active Intelligence become imprinted on his soul, and this is prophetic inspiration (*ilhām*) which becomes transformed into revelation (*waḥy*). He is thus a superior representative of the human species in his capacities; the most noble in character, and distinguished by godliness. To these is added what he receives through contact with the Active Intelligence. Hence contrary to the general opinion, God did not have an absolutely free choice, and could not appoint any man and make him the instrument of his divine dispensation. The qualities of a prophet were perfectly human and in no way supernatural, yet his unequalled excellences were sufficient to make him a necessary and not a free choice. 'The matter that receives an entelechy or perfection like his, occurs in very rare temperaments.'[1]

[1] Cf. *Shifā, Ilāhīyyāt, Najāt*, p. 303, and *Fī Ithbāt al-Nubuwwāt, Tis 'a Rasā'il.*

It is, however, the importance of his mission that makes it 'necessary in God's own wisdom' to send him forth as a messenger and prophet. This mission is political and social as well as religious. The Islamic conception of prophethood combined these three elements; and the *Falāsifa*, mainly under the influence of Plato's *Republic* and *Laws* and Aristotle's *Politics*, chose to stress the political and social aspects so prominently featured in Fārābī. The religious teachings of the prophet are composed of these essentials that men should accept and those practices that they must follow. He must teach that there is a Creator who is one and powerful and whom man must obey because He has provided rewards and punishment for all human acts. The prophet must not enter into abstruse disquisitions on the nature of God because the vast majority do not understand such things. They are apt 'to rush into the street' and argue and quarrel and be kept away from their proper duties. He must speak in allegories and symbols, and of things that people value highly. His descriptions of the hereafter must be full of imagery depicting eternal bliss or torment. There is, however, a danger that his teachings be neglected or completely lost sight of in later ages. To make them a permanent influence, he must lay down religious practices. Of these are prayers and fasting and a pilgrimage to the home of the prophet. This last makes men think of him, and by doing so think of God who chose him. It is to the common man that he must address his exhortations—the person who is most in need of his help and guidance.

* * * *

One of the practices that a prophet should enjoin people to observe is prayer. But what is prayer?[1] In contrast to his natural, animal and personal acts, man has a rational soul with activities of its own that are far more elevated and noble. Among these are contemplation and reflection and the thought of Him who has fashioned the world and all that is found therein. These make

[1] Cf. *Fi Māhīyyat al-Ṣalāt*, edit. Mehren; *Shifā*; *Najāt*.

the soul turn to realms beyond the life it leads on earth, and, like the angels who perceive without the need of senses and who understand without speech, ponder and speculate. They make it seek knowledge and perception and this timeless quest leads to worship. When man knows God through reasoning, and perceives him through his mind, and finds his grace through understanding—and be it noted that the recognition that Avicenna stresses is all intellectual—he is bound to think of the reality of creation. This moves him and makes him anxious and eager, and the emotional response drives him to worship the being he has come to accept as the 'Absolute Truth' and appeal to his unfailing loving-kindness. Prayer is an act of knowledge as well as an act of gratitude to the Necessary Being. It takes two forms, one is the outward and the ritualistic, the other is the inward and the 'real.' The outward is the one required by the religious law. It includes reading and kneeling and prostrating and has its usefulness because 'not all people can scale the heights of the mind.' But it is the inward prayer that is the most real and elevating. It means beholding 'the Truth' with a pure heart and a self cleansed of earthly desires. Supplication to God is not through the members of the body, nor by means of the human tongue. They who exercise inward prayers, behold God through the mind; and they who partake of true worship do so through the love of God. Hence, according to Avicenna's view, there is a twofold process in prayer. It begins as a purely intellectual recognition and wonder which provokes an emotional response; and that in turn inclines, if not forces, a man to turn towards God.

The love of God extends throughout nature. It is a force that pervades all beings,[1] even the simple inanimate substances. It takes different forms, and chooses different means to express itself, but the impulse is the same, whether it be sensuous love or the love of heavenly beings. Every living thing possesses an inherent love of the Absolute Good which in turn shines forth and illumines it. Death does not sever the bonds of love, for

[1] Cf. *Fī Māhīyyat al-'Ishq*, edit. Ates.

death is nothing but the separation of the immaterial soul from its material attachments.[1] It is ignorance of what there is in store that makes us so fearful of death. And just as there is a life of the will and a natural life, so also there is a death of the will and a natural death. We need not sorrow because there is death. If men were immortal, the world would have no room to hold them. And if the consequences of such a possibility be considered, it would soon be realized that death is an act of divine wisdom.

If death is a release that men should never mourn, what about the doctrine of the Resurrection insisted upon by religious dogma? Here Avicenna is obviously unhappy and feels constrained to point out that there are things which the religious law lays down, others which we can prove by reasoning and demonstration. In lengthy expositions[2] he completely disregards the resurrection of the body and dwells on the return (*ma'ād*) of the soul after its separation from the body. And in this he is very much influenced by Plotinian ideas passed on to the Islamic world through the so-called *Theology* of Aristotle. The perfection of the rational soul is achieved in attaining full intellectual knowledge, in receiving the imprint of the form of the universal order of the intelligible, and in partaking of the Good that emanates from God. It is in these that it finds eternal existence, not in the pleasures of a fleeting life on earth. The soul must perceive the essence of perfection by deducing the unknown from the known, and by striving towards it with constant effort and action. What it has suffered or will suffer as a result of what the body has done or sustained will not torment it for ever, but will gradually disappear until it has gained the happiness that is its due. And just as beings originated first as intelligences, then as souls and then as bodies, so on its return the soul leaves the body behind and goes to join the intelligences and through them the source of all emanations, who is God. Hence to speak of the resurrection of the body is only figurative. It is in fact the release and the resurrection of

[1] Cf. *Fī Daf' al-Ghamm min al-Maut*, edit. Mehren.

[2] *Shifā, Ilāhīyyāt; Najāt; Tis'a Rasā'il.*

the soul that takes place. It is the soul and not the body that is immortal.

The manner in which Avicenna treats the doctrine of the Resurrection is still better illustrated by the interpretations that he places on some of the verses of the Qur'ān.[1] He does not claim to be a fundamentalist, and does not feel bound by the literal meaning of certain of the passages. It is, we believe, with sincerity and in perfect good faith that he accepts the Scriptures of his religion; but he considers the language symbolic and metaphorical, meant to make the ideas more vivid. If it is full of imagery, that is in order that it should appeal to the ordinary man who is unable to appreciate the true significance of all that he reads. Otherwise, to accept the Scriptures literally and in their entirety is an affront to the intelligence, which for him was something that is in essence divine. He finds it idle to indulge in the formal exegesis associated with the different schools of theology. He seeks philosophical meanings, and he incorporates them into his system; and does not hesitate to quote Greek philosophers in support of his interpretations. His interpretation of one of the most impressive and elevating passages in the Qur'ān,[2] where God is spoken of as 'the light of the heavens and earth,' is a most revealing example of his religious writings; and shows clearly the attitude he chose to take. Only a Muslim can appreciate its boldness. It is, however, significant that the authors of the Epistles were among the very few—if there were any—who had taken that attitude before him; and that not many after him had the courage to do the same. He goes still farther and asserts that if there is a world of the senses, a world of the imagination, and a world of the mind; then that of the senses deserves to be considered 'the world of the graves'; and the world of the mind is the true 'abode and that is paradise.'[3]

Avicenna was not a moralist and all he has to say on ethics is derived from Aristotle,[4] but he dwells at some length on the

[1] Cf. *Tis'a Rasā'il.*
[2] *Sūra* 24, verse 35.
[3] *Tis'a Rasā'il.*
[4] Cf. *Fī 'Ilm al-Akhlāq*; *Risālat al-'Ahd.*

problem of evil. Evil takes various forms. It may be a defect coming from ignorance or from the disfigurement of the body; it may be something that causes pain or sorrow as the result of some act; it may be just the lack of what brings happiness and provides for the good. In essence it is the absence of something—a negative and not a positive element. It is not every form of negation, but the non-existence of what has been provided by nature for the perfection of things. Hence it is not something definite and determined in itself, otherwise there would be what might be called universal evil. As an accident it is the concomitant of matter and may come from outside and be an external factor, or from inside and be an internal factor. If clouds gather and prevent the sun from shining on a plant which as a result fails to reach fruition, the evil has come from outside. And if the plant has failed to respond to warmth and growth, the evil has come from the plant itself and as a result of some defect in it. 'All the causes of evil are to be found in this sub-lunary world . . . the evil that is in the sense of privation is an evil either with relation to some necessary or useful matter . . . or an evil with relation to something that is at least possible [of attainment].'[1] In the first case of course it is a greater evil. Its interaction with the good is not wholly devoid of usefulness and may be sometimes even profitable.

To the question why God did not make the pure good always prevail unaffected by the presence of evil, the answer is that such a situation would not be suitable for our *genre* of being. It could possibly be conceived of absolute being emanating from God and occupied with matters pertaining to the intelligence and the soul but not of the world as it is. If we were to suppose the absence of those privations which we have called evil, the consequences would constitute a still greater evil. Our judgement of evil is always relative and in terms of human action it is with reference to something. For the vindictive man vindictiveness is a perfection; should this quality in any way diminish in him,

[1] *Najāt*, p. 286.

he would consider it an evil that has befallen him; and it is of course at the same time an evil for those who suffer from his vindictiveness. Burning is for fire a perfection, and for those who may lose something as a result of it, an evil. God may be said to desire the good as the essence of everything and evil as an accident,[1] since it necessarily occurs. In this sense of the word there is much evil in the world, but it cannot be said that it is overwhelmingly more than the good. When we measure the two we still find reason to be grateful that there is more good in the world than evil. Here again we find Avicenna following Aristotle who believed that there is no evil principle in the world and that there is no evil apart from particular things. It is not a necessary feature of the universe but a by-product that seems to occur unfailingly.

What are angels and where do they reside? 'An angel is a pure substance endowed with life and reason, intellectual, immortal.'[2] With this definition Avicenna goes on to explain that angels are intermediaries between the Creator and terrestrial bodies. Some have intelligences, others have souls, and still others have bodies. The highest in rank are the spiritual angels that are pure and free of matter; they are called intelligences. Then come the spiritual angels that are called souls, and 'these are the active angels.'[3] And the third are the angels represented by the heavenly bodies. These last differ in grades, and beginning with the most noble of them, come down to those that are only one grade above corruptible bodies composed of matter and form. The spiritual angels that are intelligences and stand highest, are called by the philosophers active intelligences, and correspond to those that in the language of religion are spoken of as the angels nearest and closest to God.[4] Of the third class, Avicenna remarks, 'It is said that the celestial spheres are living, reasonable, do not die; and the living, reasonable, immortal, is called an angel; then the celestial spheres are called angels.'[5] The angels that act as

[1] Cf. *Najāt*, p. 474. [2] *Risālat al-Ḥudūd.* [3] *Najāt*, p. 229.
[4] *al-malā'ika al-muqarrabūn.* [5] *Fī Ithbāt al-Nubuwwāt.*

intermediaries between God and His prophets, are those that possess souls, that act as the souls of the celestial spheres. They are the bearers of inspiration. They speak in the sense that they make themselves heard, but not in the language of men and animals. The prophet sees and hears them, but not with his ordinary senses.

What is happiness, and what may be called good-fortune? The common people suppose that the most intense of pleasures are the sensuous, but that is not difficult to disprove. We see the man bent on avenging a wrong done to him, deny himself of all such forms of pleasures, and finding far more satisfaction in the accomplishment of his aim. And the same may be said of those who choose to renounce the world and become ascetics; they often gain a pleasure beyond anything we can imagine. The man who wishes to become a leader deems it necessary to forgo many forms of pleasure, without the least regret, in order to attain the greater pleasure of realizing his ambition. These and many other similar examples go to show that the 'inward pleasures' are far more powerful than the sensuous. They produce a satisfaction deeper and more lasting. That being the case, what should be said of intellectual pleasures that are more elevated than both the sensuous and the inward? But what exactly is pleasure? 'Pleasure is a perception and an attainment in the quest for that which to the perceiver is a perfection and a good in itself.'[1] And in like manner 'pain is a perception . . . which to the perceiver is a harm and an evil.'[2] But good and evil are relative, they differ according to the criteria with which they are judged. The human emotions have one conception of good and evil, and the mind has another, and they do not always agree.

Aristotle had discussed pleasure and pain at great length,[3] and had analysed the views of his predecessors, none of which he could accept in their entirety. And when his works were rendered into Arabic, the subject became a favourite topic of discussion among the *Falāsifa*, producing some very curious theories,

[1] *Ishārāt*, p. 191. [2] *Ibid.* [3] *Nicom. Ethic*, Book X.

though the majority followed along Aristotelian lines. In Persian one of the most interesting and detailed arguments is found in a work of Nāṣir Khosrow[1] who strongly disagrees with Rāzī's definition of pleasure as nothing but a return to the normal state, which is not altogether what Aristotle had said, though somewhat related. For Avicenna what is more important is the relation of the different forms of pleasure to one another, and the comparative value of each. He arrives at the conclusion that the highest and purest form is the intellectual pleasure available to those who can rise above the vulgar notions and practices of the rest. Under Plotinian influence he emphasizes the two elements of pleasure, viz. perfection and the perception of it as such. These can be attained far more effectively and fruitfully in the intellectual sphere, and with more elevating results. There is of course nothing new in his appreciation of the pleasures of contemplation. The Greeks, and Aristotle in particular, had stressed them long before him. What he tried to point out without expressly affirming it, was the contrast of this conception with the doctrinal ideas of pleasure and pain, the most sensuous forms of which were promised for the righteous and for the wicked in the world to come. He seemed to have had a natural aversion to this doctrine, and sometimes openly challenged its validity. His detractors hit back by saying that this was because he knew exactly where he was destined to end and he feared the punishments in store for him.

* * * *

Scholars have been undecided as to whether to call Avicenna a rational mystic or a mystic rationalist. There may be little in his early works to show an inclination towards mysticism; his hectic life could not have been particularly conducive to such a discipline; and the stories about his association with celebrated mystics are not authentic. And yet he devotes the closing pages

[1] *Zād el-Musāferīn.*

of one of his latest books, viz. the *Ishārāt*, to what is avowedly mystic thought. There are besides a number of short treatises, not all of which have been published, containing mystic tales and allegories. The dates of these have not yet been determined, but it is safe to assume that they are all rather late works; and that his interest in the mystics and their way of life did not develop early in him. Yet he had never denied what may be called divine truths and spiritual values. He had admitted and justified such things as inspiration, revelation, and the power of prayers. It is not therefore surprising that he should have gradually come to see the significance of the mystic path. Fārābī had done the same before him, and there is much that is similar in their attitudes towards it; except that they were of entirely different temperaments themselves. Unlike his predecessor, Avicenna was a high-spirited, active and ambitious man; and perhaps for that reason his is an intellectualized form of mysticism that never became a fundamental part of his philosophical system. The importance that some have attempted to give to this aspect of his thought is hardly justified. He writes with appreciation and sympathy about the mystics, but in a very objective tone, not pretending to be one of them.

The sources of Avicennian mysticism are twofold. There is the indigenous element and the Neo-Platonic. The theory that the chief features of the Islamic form of this discipline are all of Neo-Platonic origin has been discarded. Mysticism is a native growth in many parts of the world; and there is no doubt that what is known as Ṣūfism was in its essentials a distinctive contribution of the Persian mind. Nevertheless foreign influences from both the East and the West coloured many of its doctrines. Some ideas and practices can be traced to India, while others are indubitably of Neo-Platonic, Gnostic and perhaps Hermetic provenance. Exactly how they found their way into Ṣūfism is not clear, though oddly enough the writings of the *Falāsifa* may have had something to do with it. Avicenna does not seem particularly attracted to the devotional aspects of Ṣūfism; and he incurred the displeasure, and, in some cases, even the violent condemnation of Persian Ṣūfis. As a philosopher he was drawn inescapably to some of its principal conceptions, and the interpretations which it offered for problems that he had found difficult to explain. Often in his psychology he speaks of certain relations of the soul as being mysterious and baffling to the human mind. It is in such cases that he turns to mysticism, hoping to find some help. This explains why there is so much of Plotinian thought in his account of the soul, whether in relation to God, or during the period of its sojourn in the human body. The intellectualized form of Neo-Platonic mysticism seemed congenial and more to his liking, though the indigenous element is rarely absent.

He who has been initiated into the mystic order, Avicenna tells us, has states and stages particular to him and the life that he leads. He is the man who bears the name of *'ārif*, the knower (and whom here we might call the gnostic without in any way associating him with Gnostics, though there may be some relation between the two names). Mystics while still inhabiting their earthly bodies, have a way of escaping from them in order that, separated and free, they may take the path to 'the world of sanctity.' There are certain things that are hidden within them, and others that they show publicly. The things that they demonstrate to everyone are denounced by those who disapprove of them, and highly praised by those who know and understand; and 'we shall relate them to you.'[1] These introductory remarks summarize in some ways Avicenna's whole attitude to Ṣūfīsm. Interest, appreciation and acknowledgement they contain, but no commitment. Ṣūfīs are different from ascetics and pietists, he likes to point out. He who renounces the goods of the world and all the benefits that they offer, is called an ascetic (*zāhid*); he who devotes his whole time to religious practices such as prayers, fasting and nocturnal vigils, is considered a pietist and a worshipper (*'ābid*); and he who concentrates his thoughts on the Almighty

[1] Cf. *Ishārāt*, p. 198.

so that the light of God may dawn upon his inner self, is given the special name of knower (*'ārif*) or gnostic. These qualities are sometimes held separately; and there are cases where they are found in combination. And yet among others besides the gnostics ascetism takes the form of a business transaction. It is as though it buys the goods of the next world with those of this world. Whereas with the gnostic, renunciation is abstention from anything that may distract his inner self from its intimacy with the Truth, a rising above everything other than the Truth.

In a similar manner pietism or worship is with other than the gnostic a commercial transaction. It is as though the pietist labours in this world for a payment that he will receive in the next world, in the form of rewards that he has been promised. But for the gnostic it is a discipline for his energy and an exercise for the estimative and imaginative faculties of his soul. He thereby turns them away from the near regions of pride to the distant realms of divine truth. There they will abide in peace with the intimate (*sirr*) of the inner self, when Truth turns its effulgence upon them with nothing to mar the light. It is then that the intimate of the inner self becomes enamoured of the brilliant dawn; and that love and devotion become an established habit; so that whenever it wishes to penetrate into the light of truth without doubts or fears to obstruct, it will be encouraged by that light until it finds itself wholly and completely in the path of sanctity (*quds*).[1]

In this passage in which we have tried to be as faithful to the original as possible, two points are noticeable. One is the scorn with which Avicenna speaks of ascetics and pietists, the other is the respect that he entertains for the gnostic and his graphic description of mystic experience. When the ways of his life are remembered, it is not surprising that he had no use for ascetism or pietism, but can it be said that he must have had some mystic experience himself? Certain scholars have been positive about it, though we do not find sufficient evidence for that. The passage

[1] *Ishārāt*, p. 199.

does, however, prove an intimate knowledge of all that the mystics strive for and ultimately claim to have attained.

Man does not live alone; he is in social contact with his fellow-men; there is agreement and disagreement between him and the others, a constant exchange of things and ideas; he cannot do everything for himself, nor can he think everything by himself. There must be a law to regulate these relations, and that necessitates a lawgiver who must prove by signs and symbols that he has been appointed by God. He has also to promise reward and punishment, for obvious reasons. These have to come from God; and that makes people try to know Him and worship Him. They are taught how to do so; they are enjoined to say their prayers so often because repetition helps them to remember God in their daily lives, which in turn assists in the maintenance of justice necessary for the survival of the human species. The gnostics, on the other hand, have the advantage of deriving from these forms of worship a profit peculiar to themselves when they turn their faces completely towards God. In the regulation of this all-encompassing order we can see God's wisdom, loving-kindness and bounty at work. In contrast to the practical requirements of the ordinary man, the gnostic seeks the truth only for its own sake. There is nothing that he would prefer to knowing God and worshipping Him; not because of hope or fear, but due to the fact that God deserves to be worshipped, and the position of worshipper is a noble relationship towards Him. It is then that the truth is no more the goal, but an intermediary leading to Him who is the ultimate goal sought by all. And yet he who gives an intermediary position to truth is to be pitied in a way. It means that he has not yet attained full satisfaction and joy. He stands to the real gnostic as a young boy in comparison to the man of mature experience.

The first stage in the progressive development of the mystic is what they call 'the will' (*al-irāda*). It is that with which he strengthens his resolve to demonstrate his convictions. With it he gains the ardent desire to bind himself with the bonds of faith;

to attach himself to that unfailing source of determination, and thus bring peace to his soul. It is then that the intimate of his inner self moves towards the realms of sanctity that it may profit from the bliss of attaining that goal. So long as he is in that stage, he is a 'seeker' (*murīd*). But he needs other things in addition. He must have spiritual discipline and exercise (*riyāḍa*). The purpose of these is threefold. First to enable him to turn away and disregard all things save the Truth. Second, to enable him to overcome the self that rules the passions, and make a satisfied and confident soul rule supreme. In such a case the imaginative and estimative faculties cease to be occupied with matters that are base and low, and become concentrated solely on what is sanctified. And third, it is to render the 'intimate' more gentle and capable of yielding his undivided attention and complete devotion. The first form of discipline leads to real ascetism. The second form includes various exercises, such as the practice of worship associated with thought; the use of melodies to serve the faculties of the soul, to which may be added the words that are chanted; the sermon of a preacher when it is intelligent, eloquently expressed and delivered in an impressive tone. The third form requires subtle thought, and pure and chaste love directed by the beauty of the beloved, not by the force of passion.[1]

So far the man of the mystic path has gone through states and stages of preparation. He has used his will and strengthened his resolve; with discipline and exercise he has passed the different stages of self-purification. And when that has advanced sufficiently, and a certain limit has been reached, furtive glimpses of the light of God begin to be revealed to him—visions 'delicious to behold.' Like lightning they appear and they are gone. These are the occasions they themselves call 'moments' (*awqāt*). And these moments are preceded and also followed by periods of ecstasy (*wajd*)—one period leading to the moment, and the other following the mystic experience. And if he perseveres in the exercises, the moments will become more frequent, and therefore

[1] Cf. *Ishārāt*, p. 202.

the ecstasies. Until the time comes when, with no more exercises necessary, he is overwhelmed by the frequency with which the moments come to him. It is then that by merely fixing his eyes on something, and every time that he does so, he is carried away to the realms of sanctity by the evocation of a happy memory. It might be said that he sees the Creative Truth in everything; his labours have borne fruit; he has reached the highest degree and attained the goal. He is now in contact (*ittiṣāl*) with God. The long periods of quietude (*sakīna*) have ended; and his companions can notice that he is no more at rest. And yet he can proceed still farther. Exercise can carry him to the stage where his 'moments' would be thought to be periods of 'quietude'; his ecstatic escapes would become habitual; and the lightning glimpses would be transformed into flames of light. He gains an acquaintance that will remain permanently with him and whose constant companionship affords him profit and satisfaction. Should that acquaintance ever desert him thenceforth, he would be left sad and perplexed.[1]

In the account on which this last passage is based, Avicenna unexpectedly changes his terminology. He has been describing throughout the journey of the gnostic (*'ārif*) along the mystic path in his quest for knowledge or gnosis (*'irfān*). And when describing how he reaches the state of complete knowledge (*ma'rifa*), Avicenna introduces what seems a new idea. Making use of the same Arabic root meaning to know, he claims that the gnostic gains what he calls a willing acquaintance (*mu'ārifa*) at that stage. His word connotes some sort of reciprocal relationship which, though based on knowledge, implies an exchange and a give-and-take in addition to it. At that limit, he says, all that there is hidden in the gnostic is revealed to him; but if he penetrates into this relationship of acquaintance, it becomes less and less apparent to him, so that he seems to be absent even when present, and travelling far away even when in his place. This acquaintance or mutual knowledge is at first only sometimes arrived at; later

[1] *Ishārāt*, p. 203.

he can have it when he wishes. And he can proceed still farther and reach a stage where it depends no more on his desire. Whenever he notices one thing, he sees another also; and the idea constantly occurs to him to leave this world of illusion and seek the realms of Truth. Once he has passed all the stages of exercise and has truly attained the goal, the intimate of his self becomes a highly polished mirror turned towards the Creative Truth. And pleasures from on high will come pouring down upon him; and he will be overjoyed to find that his soul has traces of God upon it. He takes one look at the realms of Truth and another at his soul; and after that he is hesitant and never sure.

In some of his other works also, Avicenna had spoken of this twofold relation of the human soul—its contact with the heavenly world, and its attachment to the body that it occupies. This dual activity, however, is a common theme in Ṣufī literature; and we find it difficult to agree with the claim that it was an Avicennian contribution. The gnostic who stood with reluctant feet gazing, now at the realms of Truth, then at his own soul, finally relinquishes his self completely; and fixes his eyes solely on the Lord of sanctity. And if he ever turns again to his soul, it is only to see it looking on, and not to appreciate its splendour. It is then and there that he reaches the ultimate goal. 'There is in truth the arrival (*al-wuṣūl*).'[1]

This account of the life-long journey stresses the different stages through which the gnostic has to pass. There is first the state in which he begins to have 'moments'; then come the periods of 'quietude'; after that he achieves 'contact'; and finally he 'arrives' at union with the Creative Truth. Whether the stages are divided into only three, or more, the description of them by Avicenna had a profound influence on his successors; and we find it quoted by Ibn Ṭufail in Andalusia.[2] Here again the problem is posed: Does this exposition prove that Avicenna had a genuine mystic experience? Some have insisted that this is the case;[3] and

[1] *Ishārāt*, p. 204. [2] Cf. *Ḥayy ben Yaqdhān* . . ., edit. Gauthier.
[3] Cf. Gardet, *Pensée religieuse d'Avicenne*, p. 180.

maintain that he is writing of things he passed through himself. They claim in addition that while certain notions are related to Plotinan thought, others are undoubtedly Avicennian. We, however, take the view that he was animated solely by the desire to analyse an experience that he is prepared to accept as profoundly true, but of which he does not claim personal knowledge.

The traveller having climbed to the summit and reached his destination, finds himself completely transformed. His values are changed and his outlook surprisingly altered. Occupation with things that he had most reluctantly renounced now becomes a tiresome and frustrating labour; and dependence on those faculties that he always found so submissive in himself now seems an exasperating weakness. Pride in the qualities that adorned his self appears misguided even though justified; and total abandonment to Him who is creative and true seems the only salvation. There are specific elements in this quest for gnosis which we call mysticism. It begins with separation; then there is a denunciation; then a renunciation; and then a complete refusal. Through the execution of these acts the gnostic succeeds in concentrating on the essential attributes of God, in order that he may profit by them and eventually acquire them, until such time as he arrives at oneness, which is the state of complete unity; and then there is a standstill (*wuqūf*). The separation is from things that might turn him away from his quest; the denunciation is of the things that used to engage and occupy him; the renunciation is in order to gain freedom; and the complete refusal is the neglect of all else save the goal. There are certain degrees to which a gnostic can pass even beyond these, but those are very difficult to understand; words fail to describe them, they can better be imagined, and even then it is not the true thing. To arrive at the proper conception, one has to be a man of contemplation and not of lip-service, of personal insight and not of hearsay; one must be of those who have reached the fountain-head, not of those who have only listened to the tale. This is why the gnostic is so happy and gay; modest and humble withal. He could not be otherwise now that he sees the truth in everything; and finds man an object of pity in search of what is utterly futile.

The gnostic has states in which he cannot bear even the murmur of the breeze, much less such unnecessary preoccupations as might engage him. In those moments when he has turned towards the Truth, should his self raise a veil to separate him, or the intimate of his soul cause a simple motion to disturb him, he is grieved and annoyed. But once he has reached and gained the station of 'arrival' (*wuṣūl*), he then has the choice either to devote himself wholly to the Truth, and sever his relations with all else; or to try to combine the two, devoting attention to this world, and also to the other. He never loses his temper with anyone, nor is he ever very angry. And how could he be when overwhelmed by such a sense of pity for man? Instead of administering blame, he would rather advise and give gentle counsel. He is brave because he does not fear death; generous because he loves no more what he now deems futile; magnanimous because his soul is now too great to worry about the evils committed by his fellow-men; and forgetful of all that was done to him because he is now occupied wholly with God. The gnostics differ sometimes in their modes of life; according to the plans and purposes that they have in view. Some choose to be austere and lead a humble life—sometimes even a miserable one, when they disdain all earthly things. Others do not hesitate to partake of what life can offer. Some continue the religious practices, others neglect them after their 'arrival.'

Avicenna ends this chapter of the *Ishārāt* with the remark that 'what is comprised in this section [of our book] is a source of laughter for the thoughtless, an admonition for the accomplished. He who has heard it and felt revulsion, let him blame himself. Perhaps it does not suit him. And everything has been provided for him who was created for it.'[1]

What of the prodigies usually associated with these mystic divines in the popular imagination? If you hear of a gnostic going

[1] *Ishārāt*, p. 207.

for long periods without food, Avicenna says, or doing something no one else is capable of, or even foretelling a future event, do not be surprised and do not disbelieve it. All these have a perfectly natural explanation. It was seen in the study of psychology that the faculties of the soul are in constant interaction with one another, and that they can for long or short periods render one another ineffective and inoperative. The same applies when they interact with the physical forces and requirements of the human body. A typical case is when fear paralyses sexual passion, or digestion; and prevents the execution of the most ordinary acts. In fact psychic powers directed by the faculties of the soul have complete control over the body; and when the concerted exercise of one faculty prevents the operation of digestion and therefore of hunger, there is nothing contrary to the natural law. These psychic powers can weaken or strengthen the physical forces. Fear and sorrow weaken a man, while hate, rivalry and also joy make him stronger. It is the strength that comes from joy, and confidence and faith in God that make a gnostic capable of doing things others cannot. And the reason why he can foretell the future sometimes is that he gains an unusual capacity to judge from the past and reason things out and thus arrive at a conclusion. Furthermore, it was seen that particulars are engraved in the world of the intellect in a general way and universally; and those who develop the proper disposition can have these particulars engraved upon their own souls to a certain extent. Hence in this case also the process is a natural one, and the explanation not difficult to see.[1]

Besides this analysis of the mystic life, Avicenna has left some tales couched in symbolic language and of semi-mystic, semi-philosophical significance.[2] In their desire to bring about a closer *rapprochement* with religious belief, the Islamic thinkers had claimed that there was an exact correspondence between the different intelligences of which the philosophers spoke and the

[1] Cf. *Ishārāt*, pp. 207–10.

[2] Cf. H. Corbin, *Avicenne et le Récit visionnaire*, 2 vols.

angels about whom religion was so positive. In their account of the cosmos they had argued that each of the celestial spheres had a soul of its own. These souls were celestial beings possessing imagination; and might rightly be called celestial angels. Above them stood the intelligences who might be considered the same as the Cherubim. And as to the Active Intelligence, it was identified with the angel Gabriel. In a dramatized tale[1] we find Avicenna relating how one day he went out for a ramble in the vicinity of a town together with a few companions, and there chanced to meet a man who though to all appearance extremely old, had the full vigour and alertness of youth. According to the interpretation of his pupil who has left a commentary on this tale, he himself represents the seeker after truth; his companions are his senses; and the venerable man (from whom he is to seek information), none other than the Active Intelligence personified. 'My name is "the living," and my lineage "son of the vigilant," ' the old man says, 'and as to my home-town, it is the city of celestial Jerusalem (the sacred abode). My profession is unceasing travel in the regions of the world . . . and my face is always turned toward my father who is "The Living." ' In reply to the request that he should accompany him on his journeys, which symbolize the search after knowledge, the old man remarks that that could not be done while still hampered by the presence of the companions. They cannot be discarded now. The time will come when he (the narrator) will be entirely free and separate from them; and can then embark unimpeded on his quest. There are three directions he could take, though it is not given to everyone to travel the whole way. There are first the regions of the West and the countries beyond it. That is where the light sets. It is the abode of Matter; there it resides for all who seek it. Then there are the realms of the East. It is where the sun rises in all its glory. It is the home and fountain-head of Form. To it must such faces turn as seek illumination. And thirdly are the lands situated between the East and the West, wherein is to be found every-

[1] *Ḥaiy ibn Yaqẓān.*

thing that is composed of matter and form combined. But how is he to find his way; how can he choose between the different paths? Here the rationalist emerges. It is by logical thought and reasoning that he must be guided. That should be sufficient to prevent him from getting lost in the wilderness. That should lead him to knowledge which is an all-revealing source of light. The polar regions should be avoided; they are places of darkness and therefore of ignorance. The people in the West are strangers from distant climes; and they are in constant strife. The East is where the sun dawns; and the sun is the giver of forms, the Dator Formarum. These reflections were expressed in symbolic language a thousand years ago by a philosopher who at the time of writing was actually a prisoner deep in the dungeon of a fortress.

Another such allegorical tale is entitled the *Treatise of the Bird*.[1] Here a bird wings its way from place to place in search of a friend to whom it can confide its secret, and with whom it can share its sorrows; only to find that such beings are rare now that friendship has become a matter of commerce; and that not until a brotherhood is established based on truth and guided from above, can there be free communion among all. The bird calls out to its 'brothers in truth' to share one another's secrets, to remove the veil that separates their hearts, and to join in an effort to seek perfection. It bids them make manifest their inner selves, and hide what has been apparent; to love death in order that they may live; to remain constantly in flight and not hide within the nest lest that may become a trap for them. It is he who can confront his tomorrow with confidence that is truly alive and awake. The bird then begins to relate the story of how once together with other birds it was beguiled into a pleasant place, and there they were all caught in the nets that had been carefully laid for them; and they suffered in their captivity. Until one day the narrator-bird managed to escape from its cage, as some others had done before it, and join them in their flight to lands where they could all be safe. They flew over happy fields and lovely

[1] *Risālat al-Ṭair*, edit. Mehren.

mountains where they were tempted to remain. But they continued till after passing over nine mountains, they finally reached the City of the King. They entered into the palace and were invited into his presence. When their eyes fell on the King they were so overwhelmed that they forgot all their afflictions. He gave them courage and they reported all that they had undergone, whereupon the King assured them that such things would never happen again, for he was sending his Messenger whose mission was to make sure that peace and justice should prevail.

Of the tale of *Salamān and Absāl* there were two versions. One was of Hermetic origin and had been translated into Arabic by Ḥunain; the other, to which he refers in the *Ishārāt*, was by Avicenna himself. The first version has survived,[1] but of the second we only know through the short commentary of Ṭūṣī.

[1] Cf. *Tis'a Rasā'il.*

CHAPTER VII

MEDICINE AND THE NATURAL SCIENCES

THE *Canon of Medicine* is Avicenna's chief medical work, whilst his minor treatises deal with separate diseases and their treatment. Just as his *Shifā* was concerned with all aspects of philosophy, this voluminous undertaking, which was to become equally renowned in both the East and the West, is an encyclopaedia of the medical knowledge of his day. The former was basically Aristotelian with important contributions of Avicenna's own; this comprises in the main what Hippocrates and Galen had taught, together with the results of his medical practice and the experience that he had gained. It also includes what his immediate predecessors had written on the subject. In concept as well as in method there are points of similarity between the two books on which, we are told, he worked at the same time. The *Shifā*, though the whole of it has not yet been edited, has been frequently if not comprehensively studied, but the *Canon* though already printed in full,[1] has been examined only in parts,[2] and still awaits a patient and competent student. Avicenna may not be as great a physician as a philosopher, yet he is commonly referred to as 'the prince and chief of physicians'; and it is supposed that with him Islamic medicine reached its zenith.

Greek medicine reached the Islamic world before philosophy. Already in Ummayad times a Persian Jew by the name of Māsarjawaih had translated the *Pandects* of Ahron, a Christian monk who lived in Alexandria not long before the Arab conquest, into Arabic. In Baghdad, Persian and Indian medicine became incorporated with the Greek. The process had in fact

[1] *Canonis Medicinae*, edit. Carame, Romae, MDXCIII.
[2] Cf. Gruner, *A Treatise on the Canon* ...

already started in Gundīshāpūr, and the teaching at that institution comprised all three elements. Thence a long line of celebrated physicians graduated and spread out over the Islamic world. They became particularly numerous at the court of the Caliphs. Some reached great eminence and even took part in public life; others helped to produce a till then non-existent Arabic literature on the subject. Among the latter, Ḥunain was one of the earliest and most noted. The outstanding contribution that he made to the creation of Arabic philosophical literature, through his numerous translations from Greek, has already been noted. His renderings of medical works, though smaller in number, were no less important. According to his own claim, he translated practically the whole corpus of Galenic writings which ran into some hundred and forty books. He also translated from Hippocrates, including his *Aphorisms*; and some of Galen's commentaries on Hippocrates. In addition, he corrected the translation of the *Materia Medica* of Dioscurides; and made his own renderings of the *Synopsis* of Oribasius, and the *Seven Books* of Paul of Aegina. He did original work as well. He wrote *Questions on Medicine* which became well known; and another work called *Ten Treatises on the Eye* described as 'the earliest systematic textbook of ophthalmology known.' His pupils continued the translation of medical books with just as much interest and care as they devoted to the philosophical works.

It has been observed that after an initial period of translation and minor works, the initiative seems to pass rapidly from the hands of the Christians and Ḥarrānians who were the pioneers, to the Muslims whether Arabs, Turks, or Persians. This is as true in medicine and the natural sciences as it was in philosophy. The time of the translators had hardly drawn to a close when Kindī and Fārābī appeared on the scene, and totally eclipsed them with their original contributions. And the pupils of Ḥunain had not yet finished rendering Greek medical works into Arabic when Muslim physicians, mostly of Persian extraction, came along with the results of their clinical observations and personal experiences. *Pandects* became replaced by substantial encyclopaedias, and aphorisms by hospital reports of much value. The first and, by common consent, the greatest of these was Rāzī, of whose philosophical ideas some mention has already been made. According to a competent critic, 'Rhazes was undoubtedly the greatest physician of the Islamic world, and one of the greatest physicians of all time.' Students of medicine must be grateful that in spite of a large practice and extensive travels, he found time to write about a hundred medical books, not all of which, however, can be classified as learned works. He has a treatise *On the fact that even skilful physicians cannot heal all diseases*; and another *On why people prefer quacks and charlatans to skilled physicians*. His most celebrated work is *On Smallpox and Measles*, two of the most common diseases in the East. And it should be remembered that smallpox had been unknown to Greek medicine. This was translated into Latin and various other languages including English, and was printed some forty times between 1498 and 1866.

This work, supposed to give the first clear account of these two diseases that has come down to us, is eclipsed by his *magnum opus* described as 'perhaps the most extensive ever written by a medical man.' His *al-Ḥāwī*, meaning 'The Comprehensive' and known to the Latins as *Liber Continens*, was an enormous manual giving the results of a life-time of medical practice. This may have been actually finished by Rāzī's pupils and the material afterwards collected by his patron. Only ten out of the original twenty volumes are extant today. 'For each disease Rhazes first cites all the Greek, Syrian, Arabic, Persian and Indian authors, and at the end gives his own opinion and experiences, and he preserves many striking examples of his clinical insight.'[1] In Latin the work was repeatedly printed from 1486 onwards, and its influence on European medicine was considerable.

Besides translations and extracts, Arabic medical literature had included manuals that often took the form of *pandects*. These

[1] Meyerhof: *Science and Medicine*, *Legacy of Islam*, p. 324.

were recapitulations of the whole of medicine beginning at the head and working down to the feet; and there were also the cram books in the form of questions and answers. Now the tendency was to collect all the available knowledge and add the author's own contributions and the results of his practice. (These works differed in size. If the compilation of Rāzī ran into twenty volumes, that of another physician of Persian extraction, known to the Latins as Haly Abbas (d. 994) and called by them *Liber regius*, was far more modest; and so was the *Firdows al-Ḥikma* of Ṭabarī.) There was thus a whole tradition of medical writing in existence when the *Canon* of Avicenna appeared. It cannot therefore claim to be entirely original in form or in subject-matter; but in more ways than one, it was the culmination of all that had been done before in this field. It occupies the same position in medical literature that the *Shifā* has in philosophical writings, and may actually have been meant to be a counterpart of the other. The *Canon* is a highly compact work, giving mainly facts; it rarely indulges in general discussions. It fills a big fat volume, and yet is not unwieldy for the general practitioner to whom it is undoubtedly addressed. Of all his sixteen medical works, this is the one to which the physician can most rapidly refer. One of its distinctive features is the system of classification used; this may be thought nowadays to have been carried too far, and to be rather confusing as a result. It is divided into five books, each of which is then subdivided into different *fanns*, then *faṣl* and then *maqāla*. Book One comprises a general description of the human body, its constitution, members, temperaments and faculties. Then follows a section about common ailments, their causes and their complications. Then one about general hygiene and the 'necessity of death'; and finally one about the treatment of diseases. Book Two deals with *Materia Medica*. Book Three is devoted to separate diseases, and is composed of twenty-two *fanns*. Book Four deals with those diseases that affect the whole system of the sufferer, and not only the diseased part. This book is composed of seven *fanns*. Book Five, which is the last, is on pharmacology, in the form known to the Islamic world as *Aqrabādhin*, a word mutilated and arabicized, corresponding to the Greek *graphidion*, meaning a small treatise; and commonly found in Latin manuscripts as *Grabadin*. This was a subject of some importance when it is remembered that Islamic pharmacology comprised a good deal of original work, and survived in Europe down to the beginning of the nineteenth century.

On the intrinsic value of the *Canon* as a permanent contribution to medical science, we are not competent to judge. Suffice it to say that when translated into Latin by Gerard of Cremona in the twelfth century, it became so highly prized that in the last thirty years of the fifteenth it was issued sixteen times; and more than twenty times in the sixteenth century. This apart from editions of separate parts of the work. In the second half of the seventeenth century it was still being printed and read, and constantly used by the practitioners. And it is supposed to have been studied as a textbook in the medical school of Louvain University as late as the eighteenth century. The medical curriculum in Vienna and Frankfurt on the Oder, in the sixteenth century, was largely based on the *Canon* of Avicenna and the *Ad Almansorem* of Rhazes. The translation of the *Canon* by Andrea Alpago (d. 1520) of Italy was followed by even later versions which were taught in various European universities especially in Italy and France. It superseded to a great extent the *Liber regius*; and it was not until human dissection came to be allowed that European anatomists detected certain anatomical and physiological errors of Galen which had been transmitted to Europe through the works of Avicenna.

On the occasion of the celebrations in honour of Avicenna's millenary in Tehrān,[1] competent judgements were passed on certain parts of the *Canon*. It appears that in pharmacology some of his contributions were original and important; e.g. he introduced many herbs into medical practice that had not been tried

[1] Cf. *Jāshn-Nāmeh*.

before; he seems to have been aware of the antiseptic effects of alcohol, for he recommends that wounds should be first washed with wine. This was probably a common practice long before him, since Zoroastrian rituals had used wine from early times, and had even provided for washing parts of the body with it. Yet Avicenna may have been the first to realize its antiseptic properties. He also recommended the drinking of mineral waters, quite fashionable nowadays. And he suggests that experiments should be made on animals. In the field of chemistry, perhaps his greatest service was the total discrediting of alchemy. This practice had developed a regular tradition in the Islamic world. Kindī and Fārābī had both argued for it as a legitimate pursuit. But it was associated mainly with the name of Jābir, known to the Western world as Geber. The identity of this man has puzzled modern scholars. There was a mystic by that name, yet he could hardly have been the author of some one hundred books on the subject. In any case many had taken up alchemy and wasted their years over it. And when Avicenna came, he repudiated its whole basis clearly and emphatically. 'Its possibility,' he says, 'has not been made evident to me. I rather find it remote, because there is no way of splitting up one combination into another . . . differentiae being unknown. And if a thing is unknown, how is it possible to attempt to produce or destroy it?'[1]

* * * *

We have to return to his philosophical works to take note of Avicenna's views on the natural sciences, which he discusses in the tradition of Aristotle. Large sections of the *Shifā* and the *Najāt* are devoted to such matters and correspond to the *Physica* and other treatises of the Stagirite and frequently bear the same titles. In his classification he had divided the theoretical sciences in true Aristotelian fashion into metaphysics which he calls the higher science, mathematics, the middle science, and physics (*'ilm al-Ṭabī'ī*), the lower science. Again, like his predecessor he

1 *Shifā*; cf. *Risālat al-Iksīr*, edit. Ates.

states that the subject of physics is existing natural bodies that are changeable and that have in them different manners of movement and rest. Unlike metaphysics which is a universal science that has to prove its principles and the correctness of its premisses, physics is only a particular science dealing with specific subjects.

Natural bodies, as the subject of physics, are things composed of matter, which is their substratum, and form which comes into it. And what is common to them all is the three-dimensional form which constitutes extension. These dimensions do not enter into the definition of matter, they are just external accidents and not part of its existence even though they determine its state. In fact natural bodies, in an absolute sense, have only two principal constituents, matter and form; the attributes are accidents accruing from the general categories. Accidents come after matter by nature, and form precedes matter by causality. And that separate principle, which governs all natural bodies, is not the cause of their existence only, but of their two principal constituents as well. To matter it gives permanence through form, and with them both it gives permanence to the natural bodies. It is itself separate, and consequently the state of its nature does not concern natural science. It is to the essence and to the perfections of natural bodies that it gives permanence; and these perfections are either primary or secondary. Without the primary perfections they could not exist, while the secondary perfections are given permanence by means of certain powers or faculties placed in them which produce their actions. It is because of the presence of these powers that they react to outside forces, be they movement or emanation. These powers which are innate in them are of three kinds: (1) natural forces that pervade them and keep their perfections and shapes and natural positions and reactions, and that determine their movement and rest, and that they all have in common; (2) forces that act through different means; without knowledge or will as in the case of the vegetative soul, with knowledge and will as in the case of the animal soul, and with knowledge of the reality of things through thought and investigation as in the case of the human soul. And (3) forces that act independently without the intermediary of any means or instrument, and with a single directing will, and they are called the celestial souls. These forces are all to be found in one or other of the natural bodies affecting their matter and their form. Now every thing that comes to be, after not being, must necessarily have matter as a subject in which or from which or with which it can exist. In natural bodies this can be well perceived through the senses. It must also necessarily be preceded by a state of non-being otherwise it would be pre-eternal (*azalīy*). It must also necessarily have a form which it immediately took with its matter, otherwise nothing would have come to be. Hence, in true Aristotelian fashion, there are three principles attached to all existing natural bodies: form, matter, and privation. Form comes first, then primary matter or substratum, then privation which is only a state. The existence of such bodies has two causes which are in essence external to it, the agent or efficient cause, and the end or final cause. The end is that thing for which it exists. Some count the means and the instruments among the causes, and also the original Ideas, but it is not as they would think it. All natural bodies are led in their existence towards an end and a good, nothing in them is superfluous or by chance 'except in rare cases.' They follow an imperative order, and they have no part that is unused or useless.

The explanation of generation and corruption, or coming into being and passing away, was of interest to philosophers and theologians alike. Aristotle recognized two earlier views, that of the monists who reduced both processes to a qualitative change of the same single substance, and that of the pluralists who explained generation as the association of certain elementary bodies forming a whole, and corruption as their dissociation. It was this theory that was given a more definite form by the Atomists. Yet Aristotle himself had shown in his *Physica* that the belief in atoms leads to some impossible consequences. The theory as developed by the Atomists had an added importance for Avicenna because the Islamic theologians had almost all adopted it as an explanation of generation and corruption, with some slight modifications. It was therefore only natural that he should follow Aristotle and raise the matter in his physics. Some, he says, claim that natural bodies are composed of an aggregate of indivisible parts, and that they can be divided actually and potentially into a finite number of these parts; others believe that their number is infinite; and still others think that bodies are composed of single and composite parts, and that the composite are made up of similar and dissimilar components of those single parts. These single parts actually are not composed of any smaller ones but they have the potentiality of being divided into an infinite number of parts one smaller than the other, though never into an indivisible part. And if none of these three descriptions is correct, then the single body has actually no parts.

An argument which he proceeds to advance in refutation of the atomic theory is this. Whenever a part touches another it makes contact with it, with or without an empty space being left between the two. If, however, it happens that a third part makes contact also with the first, then there must be some empty space left between them, and the same is true if more parts make contact. Hence the aggregate becomes divisible as a whole, and everything that makes contact in this way can be separated from the original part. Taking the contrary case, it may be said a part is indivisible from another when it does not make contact with it except by way of entering into it and becoming completely unified with it to form one single part. And when that happens it does not become the component part of a greater composite body. Consequently indivisible parts cannot go to compose a complex body or a quantity. And again, let us suppose that two indivisible parts are placed on two others with one in between them. Each set is able to move, and neither prevents the movement of the other except by way of friction, for there is no internal or external opposition between them. That being the case, it is possible that they should move together until they meet some obstruction. Supposing they did move and did meet an obstruction, the impact would be either on the middle part or on one of the two extremities. If the obstruction is against either extremity, it will stop it from motion and the other extremity will continue moving; and if the obstruction is against the middle part, then it will become separated itself and will thereby separate the extremities, and that shows that they are divisible. The impact may even make the original sets of two separate from one another. Avicenna adduces various arguments against Atomism and refers to it at length in the *Ishārāt* also, though he had already discussed it in the *Shifā* and the *Najāt* and in some minor treatises. The reason for that is that it was a very live issue among the theologians of the Islamic world, since the Mu'tazelites had adopted the atomism of Democrites and with some modifications applied it to their explanation of God's creations on earth. Atomism thus has a long history in Islamic theology. It made what was originally a purely materialistic theory result from divine wisdom.[1]

Having disposed of Atomism, Avicenna turns to movement and rest, and to time, place and the void, which are thought to be implied in movement. Contrary to his predecessors, Aristotle had maintained both the reality and the continuity of change; and had said that it was 'the actualization of that which is potentially, as such.' Avicenna's definition is not very different and he calls it a change in the state established in the body that is gradual and directed towards something, and that which is to be reached is potentially not actually so. Thus motion is separate from the state of the body, and that state must be liable to increase and decrease. It is for this reason, he says, that it has been said that 'movement is the actualization and first entelechy (completeness) of a thing that is potentially as such.' Thus when a body is actually in one place and potentially in another, so long as it is at rest in its place it is potentially movable and able to reach the other place; and if it moves it attains its first entelechy and

[1] Cf. S. Pines: *Beiträge zur Islamischen Atomenlehre.*

actualization which is the motion itself, and through it attains its second entelechy and actualization which is the reaching to the other place. This is how movement becomes the first entelechy of what is potential. That being the case, the existence of movement is placed in the time between pure potentiality and pure actuality, and is not one of those things that actually take place completely and permanently. All movement is in things that are liable to growth and shrinking, and does not involve substance, which does not suffer such changes. There is, therefore, no movement in substance; and its generation and corruption is not change, because it takes place all at once and not gradually.

Aristotle had said that in order to discover the kinds of movement one must find to which category movement belongs, and had come to the conclusion that there are only three kinds of movement—severally in respect of *quality*, *quantity* and *place*. Avicenna, in considering the same question, decides that in addition there is movement with respect to *position* and falling under that category. This he calls 'our special opinion' and gives as an example the movement of a circular body upon itself. It may not move around anything, but it is in motion all the same and moves round its own position. In a lengthy justification of his view, he examines each of the categories one by one and arrives at the result that it must be conceded that there is no essential movement except in *quantity*, *quality*, *place* and *position*, thus dissenting from the view of Aristotle. As to rest, it is nothing but the privation of movement. But every movement found in a body is due to a cause that originates it. If as a body it moved of itself then all bodies would be in motion. The cause that makes it move is something besides its primary matter and form; it is a force or some other form that creates in it a property which becomes the source of the movement and its principle. Not that the body moves itself by it, but it moves the body, and the property of doing so belongs to it alone. When the cause producing motion is found in a body, it is said that it is a body that moves by itself; and when it is found outside the body then it moves but not of itself. What moves by itself may do so through its will, or by nature; and when that is forced upon it, then it is by force of nature, and when it is by a natural will of its own, it is said to move through the action of the celestial soul.

Besides the kind, there is the form that movement takes. Reasoning from the essential nature of a thing, and from the fact that movement is something separate from it, and that the natural state is not one of movement, and that when a thing is involved in movement it is not in its natural state, but moves in order to return to it, it can be shown that every movement that is 'by force of nature' takes place when the thing is in an uncongenial state. This movement must necessarily be in a straight line if it is with respect to *place*, for it is because of a natural inclination, and that seeks the shortest path, namely a straight line. Hence it may be seen that the movement with respect to *place*, when in a circle rather than in a straight line, as when round an external axis, is not by force of nature. A thing becomes involved in a circular form of motion not because of the forceful exigencies of its own nature, but in consequence of a psychical principle, i.e. a power that moves that particular thing by choice or by will. The same is true of circular motion when it is with respect to *position*. How could it in fact be otherwise when it was seen that every movement that is by force of nature is an escape from a state that is not natural to it? And nature does not work by choice but by force of compulsion. The fact that the movement is not in a straight line but in a circle is evidence that it is not by force of nature. It is rather by choice or will that comes from the moving power of a soul that does not work through blind force. The same may be said of all kinds of circular motion.

Furthermore, movement with respect to place cannot be indivisible as the Atomists claim, Avicenna says. The existence of indivisible units of motion entails the existence of indivisible units of distance, and as this latter idea cannot possibly be entertained, the former must also be rejected. If motion corresponds with distance, and distance can be divided to infinity, then surely there can be no end to the division of motion. If movement were composed of indivisible units of motion, there could not be one movement more rapid than another unless one had less and the other more units of rest intervening in between it. But this could not conceivably be the case because motion is continuous, and if one is rapid and the other slow it is because of the very nature of the motion and not of intervening units of rest. There can therefore be no indivisible units of motion, no matter how rapid it may be. Movement, it should be remembered, may be of a single genus or of a single species or of a single individual. It is of a single genus when it falls under one category or one of the genera coming under it. Growth and diminution, for instance, are one in genus because they both fall under the category of quantity; and there could be examples falling under the category of quality. It is of a single species when it is from one supposed direction to another single direction within a fixed period of time, like rising or falling. And it is of a single individual when even while of a single genus or species it is due to a single individual mover at a single time, and its unity lies in the existence of continuity in it.

From movement Avicenna passes on to consider time. A movement within a supposed distance and at a certain velocity (*sur'a*) is found to differ from another within the same distance but with a different velocity. Hence there is the possibility of its taking place with greater or less velocity, and this has a corresponding measure, and within that measure fall movement and all its parts. Now since movement is continuous that measure must be continuous also, and it becomes a period that is liable to elapse. This period is expected to exist in matter because it has one part coming after another, and all that follows this order has some part that is supposedly more recent, and everything that newly comes to be is in matter or from matter. In this case it could not be from matter, for the union of matter and form do not produce an original creation. It is rather the disposition and the form that do so. And every measure that is found in a matter or subject is either a measure of the matter itself or of the disposition in it.

It is not a measure of the matter itself, for that would mean that with its increase or decrease there would be a corresponding increase or decrease of the matter. This is not the case and therefore it is a measure of the disposition. And there is an established and an unestablished disposition. It is not the measure of a permanent and established disposition following matter. It is the measure of an unestablished disposition which is movement. It is for this reason that time cannot be imagined except in connection with movement. And Aristotle had said that time *implies* change.

Avicenna argues further to show that 'time is not created as a temporal creation (*ḥudūthan zamānīyyan*), but as an original creation (*ibdā'*), in which its creator does not precede it in time and duration, but in essence.'[1] By temporal creation he means that there was a time when it did not exist and that then it came to exist. If it had had a temporal beginning, its creation would have taken place after a period of non-existence, that is after some prior time; and since time by then had not yet come to exist, it must have taken place after a non-existent *before*. It would then have been 'after a before and before an after'; and what is so, is not the beginning of before, and what is not the beginning of before, is not the beginning of all time. Time, then, must have had an original creation, not preceded by anything except its creator. The same might be said of movement: not of all movement, but the circular only, whether it be with respect to place or position. So that time becomes the measure of a circular motion with relation to priority and posteriority, not in connection with distance. And because motion is continuous, time also is continuous. And just as every continuous thing may appear to be divisible to the imagination, time when divided is found to have imaginary limits which we call moments (*ānāt*). Not everything that is with time is 'in time.' Of the things that are 'in time,' there is first its parts which are the past and the future, together with the limits which are the moments; then second, the movements;

[1] *Najāt*, p. 117.

and third, the movables. For the movables are in movement, and movement is in time, so the movables become, in a sense, in time. And moments may be said to be in time in the same manner as there are units in a number; and the past and the future are analogous to division in numbers; and the movables to the things that are numbered. Besides these there is nothing that could be said to be 'in time.' It may be added that just as all continuous amounts of distance when separated and divided fall into numbers, so time when split up in the imagination falls into years and months and days and hours, either by convention or according to the number of movements involved. There are, however, according to Avicenna, certain distinctions to be made. There is first what has been shown to constitute time.[1] There is then that which if compared with time and measured by it, is found to have a permanence corresponding exactly to the permanence of time, and to what is in it. This correlative is called eternal duration (*dahr*);[2] so that it is correct to say that eternal duration encompasses time. And then there is a time which is absolutely fixed and unchanging (*sarmad*).[3] Thus we see that for him there may be said to be three varieties of time (*zamān*), each with a different specification.

Because of its religious implications, the subject of time occupied philosophers and theologians a great deal; and we find them all devoting much space to it, and discussing it from various angles. The Mutakallemūn maintained that it was 'a definitely created thing with which to measure other created things.'[4] Among the *Falāsifa*, Kindī said that 'it was a period determined by movement and of which the parts are not fixed.'[5] Fārābī's definition did not differ much from the Aristotelian conception. The authors of the *Epistles* said that 'it was nothing save the motion of the spheres in its repetitive turnings';[6] though

[1] Cf. χρόνος (*Categ.*, 5a6), *al-zamān.*
[2] Cf. αἰών (*Metaph.* 1075a10), *al-dahr.*
[3] τό ἀΐδιον (*Metaph.* 993b22), *sarmadīyyan.*
[4] Cf. Jurjānī, p. 119. [5] *Rasā'il*, p. 167. [6] Vol. 2, p. 337.

Avicenna insists that 'it is older than the initial movement.'[1] And Suhrawardī, the mystic, claims that it was before the creation of the world. Sajistānī, another Persian mystic, remarks that time cannot be associated with the Deity; and Abū al-Barakāt believes that it is only 'the measure of existence.' We have already seen how Rāzī divided time into the absolute and the limited; and centuries later Averroës says that 'it is nothing except what the mind perceives from the extension inherent in motion.'[2] For some reason, probably connected with the principal beliefs of that heterodoxy, Nāṣir Khosrow, the Isma'īlī poet and philosopher, devotes a long section of one of his books to a discussion of time and its implications. And when it is recalled that there was a religious movement in ancient Persia that considered Time a Deity known by the name of Zurvān,[3] the importance attached to the whole question becomes more comprehensible. As regards *dahr*, we find a lexicographer defining it as 'that continuous moment which is the extension of the divine presence. It is the core of time, and by it unites pre-eternity with post-eternity.'[4]

From the consideration of time we proceed to the consideration of place. Place is the thing in which the body is, and which contains it. And it may also be said to be the thing on which the body settles. The first is the sense in which it is taken and studied by the physicists. It encompasses that which occupies it, and yet is separate from it in movement. Two bodies cannot be found in the same place. Place is not something *in* what occupies it; and primary matter and form are *in* the body that occupies them. Therefore place is neither primary matter nor form. Nor indeed is it the intervening distances that are claimed to separate matter from that which the body has come to occupy. And what of the interstices within the body itself, are they full, as some maintain, or empty, as the believers in the existence of the void insist? Avicenna, like Aristotle, sets himself to disprove the existence of the void (*al-khalā'*). If we were to suppose an empty void,

1 *Tis'a Rasā'il.*
2 *Tahāfot*, p. 89.
3 Cf. Zaehner, *Zurvān.*
4 Jurjānī, p. 111.

he argues it could not be pure nothingness but some essence or quantity or substance; since for every supposed void there is another more or less empty than the first; and it is found to be divisible in itself. What is just nothing cannot be in this state, consequently the void cannot be a nothingness. Moreover, if everything that had these qualifications is a quantity, then the void would have to be a quantity also. And quantity is either continuous or discontinuous. The void cannot be discontinuous. It is the counterpart of 'the full' (*al-mala'*) which is continuous, so the void must be continuous as well. Besides continuity in its parts, it has permanence in itself and spatial directions, and what possesses these is a quantity that has in addition a position. Hence the void is quantity with a position. The void also has the property of extension and well-imagined divisibility, and therefore three dimensions similar to a mathematical body that is divested of matter. Finally, and after various arguments, Avicenna comes to the conclusion that the void as an empty nothingness does not exist and that, in the words of Aristotle, it is an empty thought. But to return to place. It is not matter nor form nor a void nor the interval between limits. Place 'is the limit of the containing body that touches the limit of the contained body' and that is not very different from Aristotle's definition.[1]

What of the problem of the infinite: does it exist? A continuous quantity existing as a whole and having position cannot be infinite. Nor can a number that is *successive* and existing *simultaneously*. On the other hand if the parts of a quantity do not end and are not simultaneous and existed in the past and will exist in the future, then it is not impossible that they should be infinite, provided they are successive. And a number that is not successive in position nor in nature may be simultaneous and at the same time infinite. Examples of the first are *time* and *movement*. There is no end to their parts which are not simultaneous and are infinitely divisible, and there is no end to their successive continuation. Yet in themselves they do not exist as an infinite

[1] τὸ τοῦ περιέχοντος πέρας.

given whole. And an example of the second is a form of angles that are not successive in position or by nature, but seem to exist simultaneously and in an endless number. There are thus things which in one sense can and in another cannot be actually infinite. Number and movement are not infinite in themselves, though they have a certain potential existence in which they could be. Potential not in the sense that they could ever become completely actualized, rather meaning that number theoretically could go on increasing by addition to an endless limit. Finite and infinite are applicable to what is a quantity in itself, and when used with respect to some forms of body, it is only in relation to what is a quantity. We speak of a power as being finite or infinite not because power is a quantity by itself, but because it varies in intensity and duration. Hence the infinite is not an individual substance of its own.

The consideration of the infinite leads to the consideration of space. Every body has a place that it naturally occupies, and that place is in space. Not every place is suitable to it, it has to seek that position in space which conforms best with its nature. And not all spatial points are equally proper for all bodies to occupy. It can be observed that one body moves upwards and another downwards. Hence there must be some inner force that determines the place of a body in space; and that force either possesses choice and will-power, or is simply natural to the body. Whether there is or is not a force possessing choice and will-power, the movement of the body to find its proper place in space is due to a natural force and depends upon its particular species. Now if this natural force is only one, the place that the body shall occupy is determined by it. If it be composed of two equal forces acting contrary to one another, the place of the body will be midway between the two because of their powers of attraction, and if one be stronger than the other then the place is more towards it. Consequently the exact position of the body is determined by the forces acting upon it, and these come to be part of its nature, so that every single body comes to occupy its own particular place which is the space that it makes its own. Similarly every body has a natural shape, since it is finite and everything finite has a limit which may be one or many. And the shape may be natural to it or may be the result of some force. In the latter case it might take different shapes, but when it has a natural figure which is that of simple bodies, it is spherical in shape because there is only one natural force acting in one single matter equally from every direction. It cannot produce an angle on one side and a straight line on the other.

There is no special reason why bodies as bodies should not be continuous. If we find that actually they are not, it is because their forms differ and do not fit into one another. Simple bodies, however, which have similar forms, whether supposedly continuous or otherwise, find the same place in space. And even when they separate they occupy similar positions, since the acting forces are the same. A body cannot occupy two places at the same time, and those that have similar forms and forces by nature find similar positions in space, and their natural directions are also the same. It may thus be gathered that there cannot be two earths in the centre of two universes with two fires and enveloping spaces. By nature there can be no earth except in one universe, similarly fire and all the heavenly bodies. If the simple bodies—whose natural shape is circular—occupy the first places, then beyond them there can be no bodies at all, and the whole constitutes one single universe. If we were to suppose that there is another universe it would be in the same form and order, and in between the two there would necessarily be a void. But it was already shown that there can be no such thing as a void. It is therefore impossible that there should be another universe besides this one. The universe is one and only one. And we, like all terrestrial elements, move in straight lines as compared to the circular motion of simple bodies. The influence of Aristotle's *De Caelo* on these views is evident; they had been further elaborated by Hellenistic commentators; and are here critically restated by Avicenna. Moreover, it should be noted that

Avicenna, like Aristotle, held to the geocentric theory of the universe; and the central position of the earth seemed to him a necessary assumption. (It was Aristarchus of Samos who taught the heliocentric theory, and he is often called the Copernicus of antiquity.)

Corresponding to Aristotle's *Meteorologica*, sections of the *Shifā* and of the *Najāt* are devoted to the consideration of 'the things on high' (*al-āthār al-'ulwīyya*), and of what Avicenna calls the formation of inanimate things. In about 1200 Alfred of Sareshel, an Englishman, translated part of this section of the *Shifā* and paraphrased it into Latin directly from the Arabic and entitled it *De Mineralibus*.[1] The descriptions given there of the formation of rocks and mountains are surprisingly accurate, and show a remarkable insight into geological phenomena. Stones, he says, are generally formed in two ways, one by the formation of porous pottery-like things, and the other by regular solidification (*jumūd*).[2] Clay often dries out of aqueous mixtures, and changes into something intermediate between clay and soft stone, which later turns into hard stone. Agglutinative clay lends itself more easily to the formation of stones; what is not of this kind crumbles before it petrifies. Stones may also be formed out of flowing water, either by solidification as the water falls drop by drop, and here he is obviously referring to stalactites, or during its flow, meaning stalagmites; and still another way is by the deposition from flowing water of things which adhere to the surface of the bed and then petrify. Avicenna illustrates these statements by his own observations along the banks of the Oxus river where he spent his childhood days. He relates that he had seen deposits of clay there which people were in the habit of using to wash their heads, presumably because it contained sodium carbonate, and that some twenty years later he saw all these deposits solidified into stone. He adds, further, that the stones formed out of water are sometimes pebbles of different

[1] Cf. Holmyard and Mandeville: *Avicennae de Congelatione*: . . ., p. 8.

[2] *Congelatio* in mediaeval Latin.

colours, and this is because of the mineralizing, solidifying element of earthiness in them. This earthiness becomes predominant, as with salt when it coagulates, and this is a peculiarity that does not depend on quantity. The reason for the coagulation may be contact with heat, 'or it may be that the virtue is yet another, unknown to us.' Then there is the case of two liquids that when mixed produce a white precipitate, and that they call the Virgin's Milk. And if what they say about the petrifaction of animals and plants be true, then the reason must be the presence of some mineral and petrifying element that manifests itself in stony spots or is released suddenly from the earth during an earthquake, and petrifies everything that comes into contact with it. It is not impossible, says Avicenna, for compounds to be converted into a single element, if that element becomes preponderant and converts the others into its like; and that is how things that fall into fire are converted into fire. The rapidity or slowness of the conversion depends on the nature of the element. In Arabia, a country he had never seen, there was, he tells us, a tract of volcanic land (*ḥarra*) that turned to its own colour everyone who lived in its vicinity, and every object that fell upon it. Then he assures us that he himself had seen a loaf of bread, though petrified, retaining its original colour and showing the mark of a bite in it. He carried it about for a time as a curiosity. These things, he repeats, all have natural causes.

In proof of his wide interests that extended beyond the study of books to the observation of natural phenomena, it may be mentioned that Avicenna asserts that there are certain varieties of stone that are formed during the extinction of fire; and it is not infrequent that ferrous objects originate during thunderstorms. In the country of the Turks, he had seen coppery bodies in the shape of arrowheads fall from the skies amid thunder and lightning. He had once seen a much larger object, dry and coppery, fall and penetrate into the earth close to the shores of the Caspian Sea. Once he himself attempted to fuse a lump of this kind. But it would not melt; only greenish fumes continued to come from it, nothing remaining at last except some ashy substance. In another case, what must have been a large meteoric stone fell to the ground, then rebounded once or twice like a ball, and finally penetrated into the ground again. People had heard a terrifying noise when this happened. And the Governor tried to remove it and send it on to the Sulṭān to whom the news had been carried. But it proved too heavy. After much difficulty they chopped off a piece. The Sulṭan ordered that a sword should be struck from it, but that was found very difficult to do, as the substance was composed entirely of small rounded granular particles closely adhering to one another.

As regards the formation of large stones, this may occur all at once through the effect of intense heat suddenly turned upon a large mass of clay, or gradually with the passage of time. The cause of the formation of hills may be essential or have some accidental reason. Like Aristotle, Avicenna believed that it is winds that produce earthquakes, and that these sometimes cause the sudden formation of hills. Erosion caused by wind and floods is an accidental cause. That is how valleys come to be; and deep depressions. He thinks it is quite likely that this world was not habitable in former days; and that it was actually submerged beneath the ocean (a suggestion going back to the early Greeks, that was later adopted by Aristotle). Through exposure it may have petrified little by little: petrifaction could have taken place beneath the waters due to the intense heat confined under the sea. It is, however, more probable that the petrifaction occurred after the exposure of the earth with the assistance of the agglutinative clay. This is why certain stones when broken have the fossil of some aquatic animal found in them. The Greeks also had observed that seashells are sometimes seen in regions far from the sea; but orthodoxy would not concede the idea that all or certain parts of the earth might have been at one time covered by water, until Leonardo da Vinci courageously reaffirmed it. The reason for the abundance of stones in mountains, is the clay previously submerged and now exposed. Winds and floods carried away what was between them, causing deep hollows. And mountains are at the present time in a stage of decay and disintegration, except where there is still clay deposited upon them. It is also possible that the bed of the sea may have been originally in the shape of plains and mountains, and that when the waters ebbed away, they were exposed. It may be noticed that some mountains are in layers, and this may be because each layer was formed at a different period. The clay forming the bed of the sea is either sedimentary or primeval, and it is probable that the sedimentary is due to the disintegration of the strata of mountains.

Avicenna then considers the mineral substances and their properties. Mineral bodies may be roughly divided into four groups, viz. stones, fusible substances, sulphurs and salts. Some of these are weak in composition and others are strong; some are malleable, others are not; some have the nature of salt, others are oily. He then proceeds to give a description of the properties of some of the minerals.

With regard to the air, he says he has seen it suddenly thicken and change, mostly or entirely, into rain or hail or snow, then clear up again just as before. He had also noticed it turn into clouds or into mist that covers the mountain-tops or even the surface of the plain because of the cold. And then there is frost that forms on cold nights. All these are not due to the water found in the air being attracted to itself as a result of the cold, because water can by nature move only downwards. It is due to the transformation of the air into water because they have some matter common between them; and water by evaporation turns into air. And air when agitated violently develops a burning property, and men make special instruments for this purpose, such as bellows; air can ignite wood and other things, and fire is nothing else than air possessing this property, namely to ignite. Here he adds the reflection that it appears that the elements are actually derived from one another; and that the corruption of one leads to the corruption of another. It is when they actually change in quality that there is alteration and transformation. And when that happens the disposition for the form most suited to it changes and therefore it takes a new form. Water-vapour can rise very high, and the cold of the upper regions turns it into clouds because of condensation. When it turns into drops it falls down as rain. When it settles over the land, and the cold of the night comes, it turns into dew. If the cloud should freeze, it comes down as snow; and if it first turns into rain and then freezes, in that case it is hail.

Avicenna proceeds to record his observations of various natural phenomena, and give an explanation for each. If these do not always conform to modern scientific knowledge, some come remarkably close to it and others are in entire agreement. The reddish and black marks that make a 'dreadful' appearance around the discs of certain stars, are gases that have caught fire because of their constant motion. And when these gases are very thick and trail behind a star, the fire burns fiercely and forms a tail to it and we have a comet. The halo is caused by the reflection of light passing through clouds surrounding the luminary. In the case of the rainbow, the cloud must be opposite the source of light, and then it is the angles in it that cause the reflection. When the sun is on the horizon, the rainbow appears as a complete semicircle to the onlooker, because it is on the same line with him, but when it rises the semicircle diminishes. Winds lose their moisture and become warm after passing over hot land. Water-vapour can become trapped in the earth, and then condense into water, then rise again with force in the form of fountains. Winds are formed when certain regions are cold and others are hot. Cyclones take place when violent winds meet one another, then start turning around. And certain gases when trapped in the earth come to form different minerals according to the place and the time involved, such as gold and silver and mercury and even oil.

* * * *

Much of what Islamic thinkers and scholars knew about astronomy and mathematics came from Greece and India; but there was a great deal of lasting value that they contributed themselves from the 'Abbāsid age onwards. The *Fihrist* contains an impressive list of the books they translated; and those they wrote themselves on these two subjects were just as numerous. There are retained in their Arabic versions some Greek books the originals of which have been lost, such as parts of the *Conics* of Apollonius, the *Spherics* of Menelaus, and the *Mechanics* of Hero of Alexandria. Besides Arab and Persian astronomers and mathematicians at the court of the 'Abbāsid caliphs, there was a Hindu by the name of Manka who introduced the *Siddhanta*, a treatise known in its Arabic translation as *Sindhind*, dealing with astronomy according to Indian methods of calculation and observation. Christian Syriacs as well as Ḥarrānians were active in the translation of Greek mathematical and astronomical works. The *Elements* of Euclid and the *Almagest* of Ptolemy were translated into Arabic a number of times, and became established as standard textbooks. Observatories were erected; and Farghānī's *Compendium* of astronomy gained widespread recognition. It was to be translated during the Middle Ages into Latin and carefully studied. Arithmetic and algebra flourished alongside astronomy, and Khawārizmī (d. *c.* 844) with his many contributions, including a treatise on the Indian method of calculation, became the most famous mathematician of his time. Some of his works were done into Latin by Adelard of Bath and Gerard of Cremona. His *Algebra* has been praised for its lucidity; and we find even an important Italian mathematician of the eighteenth century acknowledging his great debt to him. It has been stated that the use of zero in arithmetic was known to the Arabs at least two hundred and fifty years before the West; and the Latin *cifra* in the sense of zero comes from the Arabic *sifr* meaning empty. Just as Ḥunain was the most accomplished and prolific among the translators of philosophical and medical treatises, Thābit ibn Qurra of Ḥarrān was the most able among those who translated mathematical works into Arabic. Besides the Caliph, he had rich and generous patrons who appreciated his services and handsomely rewarded him. He became known as the master of geometry.

In the account of his life, Avicenna's contributions to the field of astronomy and mathematics have already been noted. Fārābī had refuted astrology, so prevalent in those days, in a separate book[1]; and his successor did not pay any attention to it, though he continued to take a lively interest to his last days in astronomy; unfortunately he did not live to complete all that he had planned to do in association with his pupil. In the *Shifā*, after a section on plants and another on animals, corresponding to what Aristotle had written about them, there are a number of *fanns* concerning mathematics. Avicenna has a commentary on the *Elements* of Euclid and the principles of geometry; and in a complete section gives his views on the *Almagest*, and the new observations that he thought ought to be added to those of Ptolemy because of their deficiency. That is followed by a section on arithmetic, which includes a description of the Indian methods of addition and subtraction, learnt, as he tells us, when as a young boy he was sent by his father to work in a grocery shop specially for that purpose.

Mathematics was a distinctive branch of learning in which a philosopher was expected to be proficient, if not to excel. It was seen that Kindī attached great importance to it, and considered it a preliminary to philosophy. In the classification of the sciences as given by the authors of the *Epistles*, we find it stated as the first of the four branches of true philosophy. Mathematics was itself divided into four, viz. arithmetic, geometry, astronomy and music. Thus the science as such comprised a very wide field, and was then subdivided into various others. Fārābī by one general division differentiates between theoretical and applied arithmetic; and by another divides mathematics into seven subjects. Geometry he also divides into theoretical and applied, or as the

[1] Edit. Dieterici.

Epistles put it, into intellectual and sensual geometry. Astronomy is in one place divided into theoretical and applied and in another into the science of the celestial spheres, the preparation of astronomical tables, and applied astronomy which includes foretelling the future. The science of the celestial spheres was based on the *Almagest*. Besides these there were the mechanical sciences (*'ilm al-ḥial*) which curiously enough are divided by one author into the Greek and the Persian Sāsānian mechanics, thus showing the existence of non-Greek sources. Those that were supposed to have come from Greece, and for which they used the term *mechanike* sometimes, included the science of weights and the science of pulleys; then the science of spheres mainly based on the *Spherica* of Theodore translated into Arabic partly by Qustā ibn Lūqa and the rest by Thābit ibn Qurra; and the science of moving spheres based on a book by Autolycus. There was also the science of optics and the science of stereometry which they called *Al-Mujassamāt*. The mathemathical sciences were studied generally for their practical applications in the construction of buildings and cities; but there were also those who were devoted to the subject itself, and may be called pure mathematicians or scientists.

Avicenna defines music as 'a mathematical science in which there is discussed the state of melody in so far as it is in harmony or it is in discord, and the state of the intervening periods'; and includes such things as rhythm, both simple and compound. So far as is known, it was a member of that remarkable class of clerical writers known as *kātibs*, to whom we attributed the origin of literary prose in the introduction to this book, who wrote the first treatise on the theory of music. Yūnus al-Kātib (d. *c.* 765), a clerk of Persian extraction, was followed by one of the same origin. Al-Khalīl (d. 791) was the man who systematized Arabic prosody and became the first lexicographer of the Arabic language. And the *Fihrist* attests that in addition he was the author of a *Book of Notes* and a *Book of Rhythms.* He was succeeded by an Arab named Isḥāq al-Mūṣelī (d. 850), who recast the old system and put down his theories in a *Book of Notes and Rhythms*.

Arabian music was indigenous, and its principles were based on a Semitic theory and practice of early date, which had also greatly influenced the Greek music, if it did not actually form its foundation. The Pythagorean scale is supposed to have come originally from the Semites.[1] In the early days of Islam, Persian and Byzantine music were engrafted upon the Arab, thus producing something characteristically different from the rest; and they in turn borrowed from it. There seems to have been a free combination of the different elements. Between the eighth and the tenth centuries many of the Greek works on the theory of music were translated into Arabic and had some influence. Nevertheless the Arabian, Persian and Byzantine systems of music remained distinctly different. Kindī's extant works on musical theory are the earliest existing in Arabic, and already show the influence of Greek authors. Some of his pupils continued his work in that field; and Thābit ibn Qurra, the mathematician, and Rāzī, the physician-philosopher, contributed also. But by far the greatest of the Islamic theorists was Fārābī. His *Grand Book on Music* has been the subject of a modern study.[2] He also wrote on the *Styles of Music*, and *On the Classification of Rhythm*; and in popular Arabic literature is known far more for his talent and ability as a musician than for his philosophical works. After him came a mathematician by the name of Būzjānī (d. 998) who wrote a *Compendium on the Science of Rhythm*. And the authors of the *Epistles* had a treatise on music that was widely known. Various other minor figures discussed the subject; though it was Avicenna who, after Fārābī, made the most valuable contribution to the theory of music. He told us in the account of his life that this was because he felt that what had been written by the Greeks was not complete and required additions and clarifications. He treats it in the *Shifā* at some

[1] Cf. the works of H. G. Farmer and Baron d'Erlanger on Arabian music.

[2] Cf. Baron d'Erlanger, *La Musique Arabe*, Vol. 1.

length, and in independent works such as in his *Introduction to the Art of Music*;[1] and in occasional references here and there. One of his pupils named Ibn Zaila (d. 1048) wrote a *Book of Sufficiency in Music*; and his contemporary, the great mathematician and physicist Ibn al-Haitham (d. 1039), compiled two studies based on writings attributed to Euclid, first a *Commentary on the Introduction to Harmony*, and second a *Commentary to the Section of the Canon*.

It has been considered that mensural music was the most important legacy left by Arab and Islamic musicians. And in so far as the theory is concerned, what Fārābī wrote in the introduction to his *Grand Book of Music* has been declared as 'certainly equal, if not superior, to anything that has come down to us from Greek sources.'[2] The names of some of the musical instruments actually come from Arabic; and Avicenna was the first to introduce the Persian names of some of the modes, to be later adopted by his successors. There is no trace in Latin of the musical section of the *Shifā*, though Roger Bacon quotes him on one aspect of the subject that was of much interest to him, and on which he had written with great emphasis. That was the therapeutic value of music, and the effect of different forms of composition on a man's moods. It had been discussed by Fārābī before him, who, it is often related, could put people into a cheerful mood, or drive them to tears, and even put them to sleep through music. Avicenna, who was much more occupied with the theory than the practice of it, maintained that it constituted one of the ways in which the soul was made ready to attain wisdom; and we know that Aristotle had written much along the same lines.

From music Avicenna turns to poetry. This was different from his commentary on the *Poetica* which, as has been said, was considered a part of the *Organon* and therefore of logic. Here he treats it as a subject closely related to music and rhythmic language. 'Poetry,' he says, 'is imaginative language composed of

[1] Cf. M. Hafni, *Ibn Sina Musiklehre*. [2] H. G. Farmer: *The Legacy of Islam*, p. 367.

words that have rhythm, harmonious and equal, repeated according to the metre. . . .'[1] 'What has no rhyme, could hardly be considered poetry by us,' he remarks, referring to the blank verse of Greek poetry. In so far as poetry is language, its study concerns chiefly the linguist and the grammarian; and in so far as it is imaginative, it concerns the logician—but why this, he does not say. As regards metre, its principles and requirements, as well as the reasons for its existence, these are connected with music; while the question of the varieties of metre, as found in the literature of one country and not in that of another, is for the prosodist to explain. With these considerations in mind, Avicenna enters into a discussion of consonants and vowels; long and short syllables; and other matters connected with rhythm and metre, clearly under the influence of Greek works.

* * * *

There are a good many minor treatises attributed to Avicenna, not all of which are authentic. One of these, the authenticity of which has been reasonably established, is entitled the *Book of Politics*.[2] For the Islamic thinkers the term politics (*siāsa*) had different connotations. As the equivalent of the Greek *politiké*, it was sometimes associated with the idea of a man's relationship with his fellow-men in an orderly and well-established society; and the principles that should govern his behaviour. It was on a national and not an international level, for the simple reason that Islamic society was then viewed as one unified entity. It was only gradually that national feeling came to assert itself; and different groups in the empire chose to secede from the supreme authority of the Caliph in Baghdad. Fārābī, who had been interested in politics, had written a treatise with a similar title[3] in which he had discussed the principles that ought to direct a man's relationship with, first, his superiors; then his equals; then his inferiors; and finally with himself. It is quite possible that Avicenna should have seen this short essay, but what he wrote

[1] *Shifā, Fī al-Mūsīqī.* [2] *Kitāb al-Siāsa*, edit. Ma'lūf, Beyrouth, 1911.
[3] *Risālat fī al-Siāsa*, edit. Cheikho, Beyrouth, 1911.

was divided differently. He devoted the first section to the methods by which a man should govern himself; the second, to the way in which he should control his income and expenses; the third, to the basis on which he should place his relationship with his family and kinsmen; the fourth, to the means by which he should guide his son; and the fifth, to the management of his servants. (There was also the treatise of Themistius on politics[1] which had been translated into Arabic and which Avicenna may have read.)

Human beings, Avicenna believes, would have never survived if they were all kings, or all slaves; if all rich or all poor. Their jealousy of one another is so fierce that it would have made them exterminate each other. It is because they are unequal in their social status that they can live together, complement each other's functions in society, and form an orderly group. There must be people 'with more money than brains, and those with more brains than money.' It is when the two combine that something useful results. He does indulge in moralizing, though he realizes that 'advice can burn deeper than fire, and cut sharper than the sword.' Men of merit, he says, should choose one of three professions. Either an intellectual pursuit, and that includes statesmanship; or a literary career; or a life of valour and action in the army or in the administration of large provinces. Although himself a bachelor, he has a charming description of the ideal wife. He wants her especially 'short-tongued.' On the education of children, he advocates strong discipline, and insists that they should begin with the study of religion. Probably because of Greek influence, he prefers the children of the upper classes to be educated separately. They must be brought up among their equals in order that the spirit of emulation may develop in them.

Politics in its academic sense was known to the Islamic philosophers as 'the civic science' (*al-'ilm al-madanī*) which is a literal translation of the Greek. Fārābī, who uses this term, proceeds to explain that it was based on the book on *Politics* of Aristotle,

[1] Edit. Cheikho: *Al-Mashriq*, 1920.

and the book on politics of Plato, which is probably a reference to the dialogue known as the *Statesman*. Avicenna says 'it is known as the management of the city, and it is called the science of politics'; and elsewhere he adds that 'by it are known the varieties of politics and rule and civil organizations . . . they are included in the books of Plato and Aristotle on politics.' And in Persian he states more clearly that it is concerned primarily with the management of the city. There was, however, still another sense to the term politics. For them *siāsa* also meant the form of rule or government. Thus we find Fārābī speaking of 'the rule of the prophet (*al-siāsat al-nabawīyya*) . . . monarchy (*al-siāsat al-mulūkīyya*) . . . democracy (*al-siāsat al-'āmīyya*) . . . aristocracy (*al-siāsat al-khāṣṣīyya*) . . . autocracy (*al-siāsat al-dhātīyya*) . . . and oligarchy (*siāsat al-khīssa*) or (*siāsat al-khasāsa*).' All these are literal translations from the original Greek; and we find them adopted by Avicenna, though he has various others to add, all coming directly from the Greek source.

A closely related subject was the science of 'the management of the house (*tadbīr al-manzil*).' This again was a literal translation of the Greek and stood for economics. It was based on a number of Greek books. The authors of some had their names so badly mutilated when transcribed into Arabic that it is now extremely difficult to ascertain exactly who they were. As a branch of practical philosophy, it had been treated by Aristotle and some of his immediate pupils. After them, a number of Hellenistic authors had taken it up, and their works, when put into Arabic, became very popular. In one such treatise[1] we find the opening lines asserting that the affairs of the house require four things for perfection. The first is wealth, the second is domestic service, the third is a wife, and the fourth is children.

It might be added that although Ethics was generally translated after the Greek original into *'ilm-al-akhlāq*, Avicenna chooses to call it in Persian the science of the management of one's own self, and in Arabic the science of the management of man.

[1] Cf. *Al-Mashriq*, 1921.

CHAPTER VIII

AVICENNA AND THE EAST

OF all Avicenna's successors three stand far above the rest. Ghazālī rose to become the greatest religious thinker in Islam, Suhrawardī the originator of a philosophy of illumination, and Averroës the most competent commentator of Aristotle. The first attacked him damagingly for the 'incoherence' of his system of thought, and his betrayal of the fundamentals of his Faith. The second added to his rational reasoning visions of 'illuminative' knowledge. And the third reproached him for failing to understand the Stagirite and in consequence misrepresenting him. Nevertheless he had a number of followers, and his influence persisted in a continuous tradition down to modern times.

A general reaction against philosophy set in soon after his death. The wave of strict orthodoxy that had already started in Baghdad, spread now all over the Islamic world. The Caliphs tried to retrieve their rapidly waning secular power by reviving the religious spirit and enjoining the necessity of careful adherence to dogma. Nor was the political situation propitious. First came the Seljuk Turks conquering one Emirate after another; then hordes of Mongols poured in, routing and ruining all that stood in their way; until with the sack of Baghdad in 1258 they turned the whole country into desolation. And when the Ṣafavid dynasty restored the old Persian empire, sectarian repression left little room for freedom of thought and speculation.

Avicenna had a number of pupils, though none of them rose to great distinction. We are told that he had one by the name of Kirmānī who was in the habit of arguing with the master continually until it led to an exchange of 'disrespectful' words. Bahmanyār, a Zoroastrian, was more appreciative and his questions were answered in a book that was called *al-Mubāḥathāt* (The Discussions).[1] Ibn Zaila was his favourite because of his keen interest in the subject. And Ma'ṣūmī was the most learned. It was for him that Avicenna wrote the Book on Love. When he became involved in a bitter controversy with Bērūnī, Ma'ṣūmī asked to be allowed to reply in his stead. Some of the writings of Bahmanyār and Ibn Zaila have survived. After them came a host of minor figures[2] who generation after generation occupied themselves with what came to be known as *ḥikmat*—a term originally signifying wisdom, but gradually coming to mean medicine, or philosophy or all sorts of occult sciences. It is safe to say that there was not a single *ḥakīm* after Avicenna who did not come under his influence and incorporate into his own thought a good deal of his ideas. The debt was sometimes acknowledged, but not always. Almost as much may be said of religious thinkers of all shades of opinion. Even when refuting his arguments or denouncing his irreligion, they did not hesitate to retain many of his thoughts and attitudes that had penetrated into all forms of literature including poetry. His philosophical system may have proved most objectionable, yet there was his medical works that everybody appreciated, and his logic which became universally adopted and eventually a subject of careful study in the seminaries. In fact there was always a tendency to separate what they considered useful writings from his disquieting speculations already condemned by religious leaders.

Opposition came constantly from two sides: one the mystic Ṣūfīs and the other the theologians. This was in itself a proof of his widespread influence.

The Ṣūfīs deprecated his faith in human reason as a means to knowledge. His rationalism, they said, veiled the Face of God instead of leading man to Him. Ṣūfīsm was spreading far and wide in those days. And the suffering brought by repeated wars and invasions caused many to choose the mystic path and find comfort in its attitude of resignation. Sanā'ī (d. 1150) in his

1 Cf. *Arisṭū 'ind al-'Arab.*

2 Cf. Baihaqī: *Tārikh al-Ḥukamā'.*

passionate praise of the Almighty, found only pity for Avicenna groping in the darkness of his man-made system. And Jāmī (d. 1492), writing five centuries after the philosopher, when his influence was still strong, exhorts people not to seek the light of the soul from the barren breast of Avicenna, for only those with open eyes can show the rest how and where to find the Light. His *Ishārāt* leads to blasphemy; and his conception of the world fills man with forebodings of evil. His book of Healing (*Shifā*) will surely cause illness; and his book of Deliverance (*Najāt*) betrays a sense of bondage. Even in his *Canon of Medicine* he has nothing new to say.[1] The same unfavourable attitude was taken by other Ṣūfīs who had no use for logical reasoning in man's lifelong quest after God. Not until Ibn al-'Arabī (d. 1240) came to blend philosophy, theology and mysticism together, had there been any attempt to take a more conciliatory view of rational thought. And Jāmī's poem proves that it had been of no avail. The Sūfīs still persisted in denouncing all that Avicenna stood for, though they did not hesitate to copy the form of some of his writings.

The opposition of the theologians was just as violent, but some of them chose to reason and argue. Of these the most eminent thinker was Ghazālī, a countryman of Avicenna, who started as a rationalist, developed into a religious philosopher, and ended as a mystic. In many ways he may be compared to St. Augustine. Coming less than a hundred years after Avicenna, Ghazālī went through the regular form of education in those days, and besides the usual Islamic studies he also delved into the writings of the *Falāsifa*. His early interest in logic is shown by a number of works on the subject. It was not long, however, before he became entirely absorbed by the study of religious law and Muslim jurisprudence, and as a result found himself in total disagreement with the philosophical systems of those days. It was then, while a professor at the Niẓāmiyya College in Baghdad, that he undertook the treatise which he called *The Incoherence of the Philo-*

[1] Cf. *Silsilat al-dhahab.*

sophers. This book proved of profound and lasting influence in the Islamic world—both in the East and in Andalusia. For many it was the final refutation of all that the *Falāsifa* had taught, and there is no doubt that it was highly valued at the time. In Ghazālī the contrast between *Falāsifa* and Mutakallemūn is seen very clearly, each group with a special approach and with a style and terminology of its own. Point by point he repeats the arguments of the former only to give the religious explanation based on the fundamental teachings of the Faith. His method was later adopted by many others.

Accepting Fārābī and Avicenna as representative figures among the *Falāsifa*, he quotes extensively from the latter to show 'the incoherence of their speculations and the contradictions in their statements with regard to the Science of the Divine.' Logic is not their prerogative, he declares, and may be usefully employed by everybody. It is in the field of metaphysics that they have gone astray, denying that religious laws are of divine origin, and assuming that they are traditional conventions established in the course of time. The very basis of their thought is unjustified because they have failed to realize that 'the realities of those matters that pertain to God cannot be attained through intellectual theorizing.' What they have done is to grope 'in darkness upon darkness.' There are certain questions on which there need be no quarrel with them, as in the use of their terminology, and their desire to call God an artificer who is a pure substance not existing in any body nor constituted by anything besides itself. Nor should we make objection to their explanations of natural phenomena like eclipses, because they do not run counter to the principles of religion. It is when they deny that the world was created *ex nihilo*, and refuse to accept the divine attributes, and insist that the belief in the Resurrection is false, that they have to be combated and proved to be in grievous error. With that purpose in view, he takes up twenty different points on which the philosophers have gone against religious teachings, challenging their arguments and condemning their theories.

The first and the most essential point of conflict is the assertion that the world existed since pre-eternity (*azalīyya*) and will last till post-eternity (*abadīyya*). This claim cannot possibly be conceded because 'with Muslims there is nothing eternal except God and His attributes, and all else is created.' Avicenna may ask why, if the world be considered as created, the act of creation took place at a specific time and not before or after. The answer to that is 'that its existence was not desired before that time . . . its existence was accomplished because it came to be desired after being not desired, so that it was Will that came into force.' Moreover, when the world and all therein is placed in the category of the possible by the philosopher, it should be remembered that if its existence was possible, so was its non-existence. 'The world came to be, when it came to be, and in the form in which it came to be, and at the time in which it came to be, through Will (*irāda*).'[1] Nor is Time eternal. That too originated in the act of creation. 'God is prior to the world and to time. He was when there was no world, and He was and with Him a world.' Existence and non-existence of all things depend on two things, God's Will and His Power (*qudra*). It is in these that all things have their source and origin, and it is by them that all existing beings may be explained.

Avicenna has attached undue importance to his division of beings into the possible, the impossible and the necessary. 'These are mental propositions that do not need an existent being in order to be attributed to it.'[2] In other words, they are purely logical considerations that do not necessarily have a corresponding existence in the world. They may be useful distinctions to make in the world of concepts, but their ontological application is a totally different matter. The philosophers are united in the belief that 'it is impossible to prove knowledge, power and will in the First Principle,' and that is why they resort to such ideas. They are prepared to call God the Agent. But an agent is he who commits some sort of act, and if he does so it is because he wishes and he willeth, and if there is choice involved then there must be

[1] *Tahāfot*, edit. Bouyges, p. 37. [2] *Ibid.*, p. 71.

knowledge. And if there is choice and knowledge and will then there must also be the power to consummate the act. Otherwise God would not be 'an artificer nor an agent except figuratively.' Moreover the very meaning of an act is doing something. It denotes 'bringing something out of non-existence into existence.'[1] And that is what is meant when it is said that the world was created. If the philosophers do not think so then 'say openly that God is not puissant enough to commit an act that it may become clear that your belief is contrary to the religion of the Muslims.'[2]

Fārābī and Avicenna proceed, in addition, to explain prophecy rationally by attributing to the prophet unusual powers of insight and imagination through which he is enabled to foresee coming events and foretell things that the common man is unable to detect. They have indeed failed to realize that 'it is by way of inspiration and not by way of reasoning' that God grants knowledge to His prophets. They neither guess nor do they imagine, they are informed directly and not through logical reasoning.

As regards natural philosophy, religious teachings neither accept nor deny its claims. It has no quarrel with the *shar*', which is the religious law, except on certain specific issues over which it is impossible to compromise. It may be thought that the Resurrection of the body is contrary to the principles of natural philosophy. And it may be asked what proof is there of the existence of a Paradise or of eternal fire after death? The answer is that God is omnipotent and therefore capable of providing all and everything that He deems necessary. Thus on three principal points the philosophers have been led into grave error by their speculations. They have claimed that the world is eternal and that the separate substances are so likewise. They have maintained that God has no direct knowledge of particular things and individuals. And they have denied the Resurrection of the body after death. Those who say such things must believe 'that the prophets have lied' and that all that they have asserted so emphatically was meant to make the common people believe in things which they

[1] *Tahāfot*, edit. Bouyges, p. 103. [2] *Ibid.*, p. 102.

thought was good for them. In other words they were not making a statement of fact but of convenience. 'And this is blasphemy.'

Ghazālī's arguments in favour of creation *ex nihilo*, God's knowledge of all particulars, and the resurrection of the dead became widely accepted in the Islamic world, and when translated into Latin was adopted by the Christians and employed in many Scholastic treatises. His clear and forceful reasoning could not fail to appeal to those who took the religious viewpoint. But less than a hundred years after him, Averroës (d. 1198) came to champion the cause of Aristotle against both the theologians and those of the *Falāsifa* who had failed to grasp the true import of what the Stagirite had taught. With no less zeal than Ghazālī, he embarked on an *Incoherence of the Incoherence*,[1] a book known in its Latin translation as *Destructio Destructionis*. This was received in almost complete silence in the Islamic world which tried to ignore it. The Jews of Andalusia and the Latins on the other hand, having a far better opinion of Averroës than the Arabs, gladly took it up and translated it into Hebrew and Latin a number of times. And this made it the subject of innumerable commentaries. The two works taken together epitomize better than any others the essential problems arising from the impact of classical philosophy on religious teachings. Averroës undertakes a restatement of the position of the philosophers. Ghazālī had quoted passage after passage from Avicenna, then showed the supposed incoherence of his arguments; now Averroës quotes passage after passage from the book of Ghazālī to show the incoherence of the *réplique*.

The disputation is rarely violent. If he condemns the 'sophistry' of Ghazālī, he just as often pays tribute to the justified objections of the theologian for some of whose penetrating remarks he shows appreciation. There is nothing puerile or vindictive in what each has to say, and that makes these two books important in the history of Islamic thought. The arguments centre almost

[1] English trans. by S. van den Bergh, 2 vols., 1954.

entirely on the writings of Avicenna—a proof of his dominating position. There is, however, one bold accusation that is worthy of note. Averroës openly states that Ghazālī denounced all that Avicenna had said and all that the *Falāsifa* stood for, not out of conviction, but out of fear lest he be ostracized like all the rest. This is repeated by Ibn Ṭumlūs, his Andalusian pupil; though it is difficult to prove. He also claims that Avicenna modified and sometimes altered the ideas of Aristotle as a concession to the theologians. Again this is not something of which it is easy to find examples, though there was never any doubt of his desire to explore and establish if possible a common ground between the two groups. As a specific case Averroës mentions the state of the human soul after death. Avicenna had taken a middle position between those who thought that the souls of men join with and are reunited into one common soul, and the religious belief that they remain separate and individual, retaining their identity after the death of the body. He said the souls remain distinct, and in consequence are innumerable, but they may not retain the identity of the body which they had occupied. Was this said just 'to delude the common people' as Averroës thinks; or was Avicenna trying to arrive at a compromise between contrary views?

With regard to the division of beings into the possible, the impossible and the necessary, he joins Ghazālī in protesting that these are mental concepts that need not have an actual concrete existence. According to Averroës, Avicenna was not justified in basing his proof for the existence of God on a distinction that is purely logical. The Ash'arite theologians had said that all that is by nature possible, is created out of nothing. And Avicenna taking that notion and combining it with the idea of necessity, had produced his well-known argument. Nor should he be considered a faithful representative of the Peripatetics, because he frequently departs from them and takes a wholly independent course. In psychology he went counter to Aristotle by providing an *estimative* faculty in animals for which there is no special justification.

Averroës then proceeds to take exception to the distinction between essence and existence.[1] Avicenna, he says, considers existence as something super-added to essence as though it were merely an accident; and that would make the existence of God conditional on His essence. This unjustified criticism fails to take into account that in the differentiation between the two, Avicenna had specifically said that in the Necessary Being essence and existence are one. These objections and many similar ones do not lead Averroës to disown the Islamic *Falāsifa* completely. He blames Ghazālī bitterly for claiming that they had committed blasphemy, and for making false accusations against them. This, he says, is a wrong done to the very religion that he pretends to uphold.

After Ghazālī and before Averroës, Suhrawardī (d. 1191) came to attempt an entirely new orientation to the now established tradition of Avicennian thought. As the originator of the Illuminative philosophy (*Ḥikmat al-Ishrāq*) he created a new current that was to run parallel; and though touching the main stream on many points, and on occasions borrowing freely, nevertheless remaining distinct and separate. Subsequent to that we find thinkers in Persia commonly divided into pure Avicennians, who were also sometimes called Peripatetics (*Mashshā'ūn*), and followers of the Illuminative philosophy (*Ishrāqīyyūn*). Suhrawardī added many new elements that were either indistinct or entirely absent in Avicenna. A strong tendency towards pantheism was one of them. But by far the most important development, for which one scholar[2] has found some justification in the writings of his predecessor, is the urge towards a conception of a mystic Orient, the home of light and the dawning-place of knowledge and illumination, a lode-star that attracts the wayward soul in its life-long journey. A reference to that has already been noted in one of the mystic allegories of Avicenna. Suhrawardī makes it a definite goal; and for that purpose borrows

[1] Edit. Bouyges, p. 302.

[2] Cf. H. Corbin: *Avicenne et le Récit Visionnaire*, Vol. 1.

heavily from Persian Pre-Islamic thought, especially the conception of *farrah*[1] for which the early Persians had many terms, and which signified a fountain-head of good fortune and glorious light that elevated and ennobled whomsoever it fell upon. It was the prerogative of great crowned heads for whom Suhrawardī now substitutes the righteous souls. This philosophy, for which he paid with his life, was a highly significant movement. His intellectual background had been the same as all the rest. Basically Islamic, he had gained a sufficient knowledge of Greek learning through the many translations and books of his predecessors; he was steeped in Arabic culture; and he had left his original country and was now a resident of Syria. Nevertheless he turns away from what had absorbed the minds of the philosophers and held such a devastating fascination, and from that doctrinal conformity which the theologians considered essential to a religious life. He faces what he believes to be the primordial 'temples of light' (*hayākel al-nūr*) for which the soul in its 'estrangement' (*ghorba*) must constantly yearn, and bereft of which it can never find peace. He reverts to some early Zoroastrian sources, including what was known as Zurvanism; and he transforms the Angels of God so prominent in religion, and whom Avicenna had equated with the separate Intelligences, into harbingers of Light.

* * * *

Neither Ghazālī's passionate appeal to the fundamentals of religion; nor the reproaches of Averroës for a betrayal of Aristotle; nor indeed the flights of Suhrawardī towards the mystic Orient, put an end to the direct and pervading influence of Avicenna. At the eastern extremity of the Islamic world we find a Persian theologian of distinction, and of the same period as Averroës, rise to ridicule Ghazālī's authority. In spite of some bitter attacks, he comments favourably on a good deal that Avicenna

[1] Cf. H. W. Bailey: *Zoroastrian Probl ems* . . ., Chapter I.

had written. Fakhr al-Dīn al-Rāzī (d. 1209) who considered Fārābī the greatest of the Islamic philosophers, had also a high regard for Avicenna. He did not fail, either, to take into consideration the doctrines of Rāzī, the physician who, as the name shows, came from his home town. He goes to Transoxiana to meet the learned men of that region and finds them all deeply engaged in the study of Avicenna; and using his own commentary on the *Ishārāt* as an aid. In one place he is asked to repay the hospitality of his host for a rather lengthy stay, by explaining the *Canon of Medicine* and some of its obscure terms. And in another, he undertakes a commentary on one of the metaphysical works, copies of which have survived.[1] Shahristānī (d. 1153), the historian of religions and philosophies, had already paid tribute to Avicenna by the space he had allotted to him in his works, without in any way committing himself. But it should not be supposed that all theologians were so tolerant. Some years later we find a religious revivalist going to the other extreme, and condemning all and everything that any of the philosophers had said or written. As a fundamentalist, Ibn Taimīyya (d. 1328) denies that there is such a thing as Islamic philosophy, and that there could be philosophers calling themselves Muslims. Ghazālī had not been averse to logic; and had taken a favourable view of its use as an instrument of thought; he, however, condemns it completely, and incidentally has some very penetrating remarks to make on the subject.[2]

The list of those who were avowed followers, or who in spite of disagreement on some points openly admitted their debt to Avicenna, is long and distinguished. They naturally come mostly from his own country and the neighbouring regions. The extent to which Nāṣir Khosrow (d. 1088) may have been influenced by him has not yet been determined. As a much younger contemporary, he became involved in Ismā'īlī propaganda; and devoted his later years entirely to religious matters. And yet in his philo-

[1] *Sharḥ 'Uyūn al-Ḥikma*, Paris MS.

[2] Cf. *Kitāb al-Radd . . .*; and *Naṣīḥat Ahl al-Īmān . . .*

sophical books,[1] when discussing time and space and the faculties of the soul, often along Aristotelian lines, he shows traces of Avicennian terminology in Arabic and Persian.[2] Like the authors of the Epistles, whose writings he must as an Ismā'īlī have studied, he was anxious to combine Greek thought with religious teachings; and he is much concerned with the refutation of Rāzī, the physician, and his belief in the five eternals. He quotes the Mu'tazelites on occasion; and seems acquainted with the treatises of John Philoponus.

In Andalusia, at the western extremity of the Islamic world, it might be supposed that the influence of Fārābī was on the whole stronger than that of Avicenna. And yet we find Ibn Bāja (Avempace, d. 1138) and Ibn Ṭufail paying tribute to Avicenna and admitting their debt to him. The latter was particularly interested in his mystical works. After them came Ibn Ṭumlūs (d. 1223) with his books on logic in which he draws freely from both Fārābī and Avicenna. And Ibn Khaldūn (d. 1406), the great philosopher of history, is not without admiration for the genius of Bukhārā, though he insists that religion and philosophy are two separate domains and have very little in common.

As regards 'Umar Khayyām (d. 1123), back in Persia, there is a great likelihood that he read Avicenna, whose works must have been fairly well known in his time. And the fact that some of the quatrains in 'Umar's collection have been thought to be actually by Avicenna, shows the resemblance in sentiment and outlook between the two. Mathematics and astronomy could not have prevented the inquisitive 'Umar from delving into some aspects of metaphysics. And Avicenna's ill-concealed fatalism must have proved a balm to the hurt mind of the poet; and urged him to administer it generously and openly to others.

By far the most competent and sympathetic commentator of Avicenna in Persia was Naṣīr el-Dīn Ṭūsī (d. 1273). Though not a creative mind himself, he was an accomplished scholar and

[1] Cf. *Zād el-Musāferīn*; and *Jāmi 'al-Ḥikmatain*.
[2] He mentions him by name in the *Safar Nāmeh*.

one of the most prolific of authors. He gave a fresh impetus to the study of his predecessor by writing the most detailed commentaries on some of his books, and by defending him against his detractors. What he wrote himself was also largely derived from the same source. With philosophy he had combined an interest in mathematics and astronomy rather than medicine; and he spent much time at an observatory recording his observations and preparing astronomical tables. He too had had connections with the Ismā'īlī heterodoxy. In his early youth he was one of their adherents and had written books on their teachings. Then he changed allegiance and accepted the patronage of one of the Mongol chieftains, in whose name he produced the astronomical tables that were to become so widely used. Ṭūsī, like many others in his time, was bilingual and wrote in both Arabic and Persian. In the former language, his commentary on the *Ishārāt* has proved invaluable to modern students of Avicenna. Others before and after him had tried to clarify the obscure points of this book, which is not by any means easy reading; and it should not be supposed that his comments eludicate all the subtleties of the original text. And yet they reflect the state of knowledge in his day, and point to the fact that it had not materially changed after the lapse of some three centuries. Creative thought was gradually being replaced by mere erudition; which eventually reached the stage of tiresome repetition interspersed by meaningless verbiage.

In Persian his writings include a commentary on the whole Aristotelian *Organon* together with the *Eisagoge* of Porphyry,[1] in which he follows the pattern and incorporates the substance of the *Shifā* with very few additions of his own. It is significant that he disregards the attempts of Avicenna and Nāṣir Khosrow to write in pure Persian, and uses instead the full Arabic terminology established by the early authors. This, however, leaves the value of the book unimpaired, even from the literary point of view, because its clear and concise exposition is superior to anything produced before him. Though still favoured by the

[1] *Asās el-Iqtibās*, edit. Raḍawī.

learned, Arabic was losing ground in certain parts of Persia; and we find him specially commissioned to put into the language of the people a book on Ethics by Miskawaih. He chooses to write one of his own[1] based on what his predecessors had contributed on the subject, and that takes him beyond them to Plato and Aristotle. Beginning with the classification of the sciences, like so many others, he actually follows Avicenna in almost all that he has to say. In his early Ismā'īlī days he had written a book on the soul and its faculties[2] in the same tone and manner as the authors of the *Epistles*. Now he revokes all that and turns to Aristotle by way of Avicenna. His versatility had become proverbial, and his interests extended to history and *belles-lettres*. He has an account of the conquest of Baghdad by the Mongol Hūlāgū Khān, to which was added a translation of one of the literary works of Ibn al-Muqaffa' into Persian.[3] But in philosophy as well as in various other matters, his guide is invariably Avicenna.

A nephew of Ṭūsī, commonly known as Bābā Afḍal,[4] continued the tradition of learning in the family, and left a number of works remarkable for their style and substance.[5] He followed the lead of Avicenna and Nāṣir Khosrow in the attempt to write in as pure a Persian as was possible in his days; and he borrowed the terms which they had employed. Why he should have chosen to depart from the practice of his uncle in this respect is not clear. The effort is, however, deliberate and successful. Although he does not coin any new words himself, he arrives at a felicity of expression unusual among authors of philosophical works. There seems to have been some movement in his day to put various books of learning into Persian; and all that he wrote himself was in his mother-tongue; but that initiative suffered a setback not long after him. Some have found traces of Hermetism in his writings; and like Avicenna, with whose works he must have been quite familiar, whether in the original or through the com-

1 *Akhlāq Nāṣirī.* 2 *Taṣawwurāt*, edit. Ivanow. 3 *Al-Adab al-Ṣaghīr.*
4 Afḍal el-Dīn Kāshānī. 5 Cf. *Muṣannafāt Afḍal el-Dīn* . . ., edit. Mīnowī.

mentaries of his uncle, he lays emphasis on the correspondence between celestial souls and angels. This was to become a popular theme in prose and poetry. His interest in translation made him produce a good rendering of Aristotle's *De Anima* from Arabic into Persian, probably for the first time,[1] as well as some pseudo-Aristotelian treatises, like the Book of the Apple,[2] which had become very popular in its Arabic version.

Quṭb al-Dīn al-Shirāzī (d. 1311), a contemporary and associate of Ṭūsī, also supposed to have been a nephew of Sa'dī the poet, was primarily a physician, though his interests extended to philosophy and kindred subjects. He co-operated for some time with Ṭūsī in the preparation of his astronomical tables; and travelled extensively in Turkey and Syria, often dressed as a Ṣufī. A man of wide knowledge, his occupation with medicine led him to undertake a commentary on the Avicennian *Canon*; and among numerous works in Arabic he produced a lengthy exposition of the Illuminative philosophy of Suhrawardī; thus showing the two traditions running parallel. In Persian, besides various treatises on astronomy and the natural sciences, he wrote a voluminous book incorporating the form as well as much of the materials of the *Shifā*.[3] And in a tractate on the principles of physical geography[4] he draws a comparison between the views of Avicenna and Rāzī, the theologian. He has hardly anything new to say in any of his works, but he writes in a clear and simple style; and his published correspondence makes pleasant reading.

There had been many minor theologians during this period who had discussed the philosophical system of Avicenna at length, thus testifying to its pervasive and widespread influence. More important were the numerous manuals of logic that appeared and were taught in the recognized seminaries throughout the country. They were all substantially Avicennian with practically no additions. Some of these handbooks are free of the unnecessary explanations and therefore serve a useful purpose.

1 Edit. Bahār.
2 Cf. Margoliouth: *J.R.A.S.*, 1892.
3 *Durrat al-Tāj . . .*, edit. Mishkāt.
4 *Nihāyat al-Idrāk*.

At the opening of the sixteenth century the Ṣafawī dynasty inaugurated an important period in the political history of Persia. Reviving the sense of Persian nationality, it restored the Empire almost to its ancient Sāsānian limits after the lapse of more than eight centuries; and made of it 'a nation once again, self-contained, centripetal, powerful and respected.' A distinct feature of this revival was that it was based more on considerations of religion than of language and race. Their enmity with the Turkish people on the west was more sectarianly religious than political; and their appeal to their own countrymen was on the same level. In consequence of this—and it has been noted by many scholars—we find that whereas art and architecture flourished to a remarkable extent and there were some great miniature-painters, literature suffered lamentably. All throughout the two centuries that marked the duration of this dynasty, poetry was at a very low ebb; and such literary men as did exist and had any talent of their own, chose to emigrate to India and seek the patronage of the Great Moguls there. The rulers had no use or sympathy for mystics and philosophers, though the greatest emphasis was laid on religious dogma, and the theologians enjoyed every aid and encouragement. Hence it was that 'under this dynasty learning, culture, poetry and mysticism completely deserted Persia, and . . . in place of great poets and philosophers there arose theologians, great indeed, but harsh, dry, fanatical and formal.'[1] It might be added that even of those that turned 'their eyes and feet' towards India none was a thinker or philosopher of any merit, and in fact it was recognized and admitted that this period produced nothing of importance in that field.

And yet within the narrow limits of theology certain developments took place that had their importance in the history of Persian thought. The Shī'a branch of Islam to which the Ṣafawī kings and their subjects zealously adhered, had been always dominated by the doctrine of the Imām, i.e. the vice-regent or leader of the

[1] Mirzā Muḥammad Qazwīnī, quoted by E. G. Browne: *Lit. Hist. of Persia*, Vol. 4, p. 27.

Faith. The first Imām had been 'Alī the cousin and son-in-law of the Prophet; and he had been followed by eleven others from among his descendants, thus making twelve in all. The doctrine of the Imāmate was a fundamental principle and an essential part of religion. And since the founder of the Ṣafawī dynasty proudly claimed descent from the seventh Imām, it was only natural that they should be militant advocates of the doctrine and take every measure for its propagation. Moreover, it was equally natural for the theologians who enjoyed their patronage and benefited from their bounty to devote a great deal of their attention and much of their writing to this subject. Its interest for us here lies in the fact that judging from their works, it has been found that Avicenna exerted a penetrating influence on the religious thinkers of this period; and that many elements of his system were grafted upon the conception of the Imāmate as they propounded it. The same is true in a good measure of Suhrawardī and his views of emanations of Illuminative light. The upshot was a fresh impetus to the study of the works of these two men which left a permanent effect on the authors of the period. Thus at the school of Mīr Dāmād (d. 1632) Avicenna and Suhrawardī helped to produce a religious blend in contrast to the many philosophical blends of which they had been the chief ingredients.

The theologians of the Shī'a branch of Islam may be said to have enjoyed a greater latitude in religious speculation than the others. For them the doors of initiative (*ijtihād*) were wide open; and many were those who taking advantage of that, indulged in a good measure of independent thought. It led them sometimes far astray from strict orthodoxy, but helped to widen their horizon and give them an opportunity to take note of the philosophical movements that had appeared in the country. Under the aegis of the Ṣafawī kings they discarded the usual practice of writing exclusively in Arabic which by the sixteenth century had become a foreign language except to a very few; and began producing works in Persian mostly in the form of popular treatises easily comprehensible to the public. At the same time they became divided into fundamentalists of different denominations, and into what have been called 'latitudinarians.' It is among the latter group that we find those who played a part in grafting Avicennian thought on to some of the religious conceptions of the period. Their minds were more open than the rest, and like Suhrawardī, they fell under the influence of some early Zoroastrian beliefs presented in Islamic garb. Metaphysics came to take a new orientation and traditional cosmology became appreciably modified. On the one hand there was Majlisī, the eminent theologian, and his still more learned and celebrated son, laying down the fundamentals of the Shī'a faith in the most authoritative and uncompromising tone; and on the other various semi-heterodox groupings like the Ṣūfīs with their attachment to pantheism (*waḥdat al-wujūd*), or the Shaikhīs who were now increasing in number.

Those who may be called the philosophers of the period fall into two categories. The majority of them were essentially religious thinkers. Only one or two, as will be seen, allowed themselves to follow their thought wherever it might lead them, and refused to have it conditioned by and subordinated to religious dogma. Of the first perhaps the most famous is commonly known as Mīr Dāmād (d. 1631). He stood in high favour with Shah 'Abbās the Great, and spent most of his life in the capital at Isfahān, where he had a large circle of pupils and admirers. With a taste for natural history and philosophy, he wrote mostly in Arabic, but he wrote poetry in Persian under the pen-name of *Ishrāq*, meaning illumination. The choice of this word betrayed his inclination towards the Illuminative philosophy of Suhrawardī which he could not openly profess. In a work entitled *Qisas al-'Ulamā* (Tales of the Theologians) it is related that Mullā Ṣadrā, his pupil and son-in-law, saw him in a dream and said, 'My views do not differ from yours, yet I am denounced as an infidel and you are not. Why is this?' 'Because,' replied Mīr Dāmād's spirit, 'I have written on philosophy in such wise that the theologians are unable to understand my meaning, which only the philosophers can understand; while you write about philosophical questions in such a manner that every dominie and hedge-priest who sees your books understands what you mean and dubs you an unbeliever.'[1] Mīr Dāmād and his pupils were in fact all very much influenced by both Avicenna and Suhrawardī, though he took great pains, as the anecdote shows, to conceal his views carefully under a veil of religious conformity. He had been attracted by Avicenna's mystic writings and allegories; and letters have survived in which he refers to them and answers questions about them. The opinion then generally held of Avicenna and Suhrawardī is reflected in another little story[2] in which one man sees the Prophet in his dream and inquires what is his attitude to Avicenna. 'He is a man whom God made to lose his way through knowledge,' the spirit replies. 'And what of Suhrawardī?' 'He was just his follower,' he is told.

Notwithstanding this evidence of the prevailing disapproval of what the two men were supposed to stand for, we find a son-in-law of Mīr Dāmād by the name of Seyyid Aḥmad 'Alawī undertaking a voluminous commentary on the *Shifā* entitled the *Key to the Shifā*, in which he amplifies the cosmology of Avicenna by introducing a good measure of Zurvanism from Zoroastrian sources, and frequently invoking the spirit if not the letter of Suhrawardī's writings.[3] He projects the Zoroastrian dualism on to the field of Avicennian thought. In connection with the way in which the multiple could proceed from the one, a subject that Avicenna had treated in his metaphysics, he quotes Pythagoras to the effect that 'if one should proceed from the primal cause, so does not-one'; then goes on to illustrate his point by bringing forward the case of Zoroaster who, he says, taught that if from the First Being there is produced an angel called Yazdān, there is also produced from the shade of that Being a demon called Ahrīman. One stands for the Good and the other for Evil. The

1 Quoted by E. G. Browne: *Lit. Hist. of Persia*, Vol. 4, p. 429.
2 Cf. Corbin: *Avicenne et le Récit Visionnaire*, Vol. 1, p. 282.
3 *Ibid.*, p. 67.

metaphor of the shade implies a necessary consequence of the emanation of light.[1]

Findareskī (d. 1640) was another religious thinker of the period who devoted a good deal of attention to philosophy. Highly esteemed at the court of Shāh 'Abbās in Iṣfahān, he usually went about in the garb of a humble dervish, and fell under the influence of that combination of Avicenna and Suhrawardī which was to incline many towards Zoroastrian ideas. The strict religious conformity that prevailed at the royal court did not suit him, and was one reason for his departure to India where he imbibed a good deal of Zoroastrian as well as Hindu thought. Perhaps for that reason little is known about his later days except that he returned to die in his own country.

The first to occupy himself with serious philosophical thought was Mullā Ṣadrā (d. 1640), 'unanimously accounted the greatest philosopher of modern times in Persia.' Though the only son of an aged father, he left his native Shirāz to study philosophy in Iṣfahān; and there sat at the feet of Mīr Dāmād and Findareskī, among other renowned teachers. Having obtained his authorization to teach, he retired for some time to a little village where he lived an austere life and spent his days in study and meditation. He suffered a good deal at the hand of the orthodox divines, and never relished their company. Many times he made the Pilgrimage to Mecca on foot; and died in Baṣra on the return from his seventh journey, leaving a son who denounced and controverted his father's teachings; and boasted that 'his belief was that of the common people.' He had married the daughter of Mīr Dāmād, who had given him his blessing with permission to expound his works. That did not last long, and he soon parted company with the teachings of his father-in-law. In choosing his own path he became surrounded by a constantly growing number of pupils who held him in great esteem and veneration. He lectured in Iṣfahān and, on his occasional travels, at different centres in the country. It was necessary for him not to be too outspoken in his

[1] Cf. Corbin: *Avicenne et le Récit Visionnaire*, Vol. 1, p. 68.

views, which, needless to say, did not always conform with orthodoxy. A prolific author, his best known works written in Arabic, are his *al-Asfār al-Arbaʿa* (The Four Books) and his *Shawāhid al-Rubūbīyya* (Evidences of Divinity) which have been lithographed in Tehran. He also had a commentary on the Avicennian *Shifā*, and another on the *Ḥikmat al-Ishrāq* which is none other than the philosophy of illumination of Suhrawardī. One book is significantly called *Kasr al-Aṣnām al-Jāhilīyya* (The Breaking of the Idols of Ignorance); and the title of another is *Kitāb al-Hidāya* (The Book of Guidance). Count Gobineau, writing perhaps more from hearsay than personal knowledge,[1] asserts that Mullā Ṣadrā was 'pas un inventeur, ni un createur, c'est un restaurateur seulement.' Actually this is not far from the truth, though the philosopher of Shirāz did not restore the pure Avicennian thought as the French diplomat supposed. It was rather a combination of it with the more congenial orientations of Suhrawardī. To his own countrymen he was known as a man who had denounced the Peripatetic and Stoic elements in Avicenna; and who had restated and in a sense reformed the Illuminative philosophy.[2]

If we take *Asfār al-Arbaʿa* (The Four Books) as representative of Mullā Ṣadrā's work, we find that in spite of Gobineau's disparaging, it has some highly valuable features that distinguish it from many other books of the same kind. First and foremost, it should be noted that unlike his predecessors, he states his authorities for his quotations wherever necessary; and by mentioning their works he not only reveals his sources, but incidentally gives us a very complete picture of the different currents that flowed into the main stream of Islamic philosophical thought. Only from an exposition like this can the variety and complexity of the great synthesis be gauged. He often quotes in order to express disagreement, thereby demonstrating his critical powers; this also furnishes evidence that he had access

[1] *Les Religions et les Philosophies . . .*

[2] Cf. Horten: *Das Philosophische System des Schirazi*, 1913.

to some minor Avicennian treatises, including the correspondence with his personal pupils, that modern scholars have not so far been able to trace. In general outline as well as in subject-matter he follows the metaphysics of the *Shifā*; and for the reader's benefit gives, side by side with the views of Avicenna, those of many others before and after him, not forgetting Suhrawardī and the views of the illuminati (*ishrāqī*) on every problem. To all these he often adds his own, boldly beginning with 'and I say.' Moreover, he frequently refers to Pre-Islamic Persian philosophers, and their conceptions of light as the true essence and reality of existence. He sometimes calls them the 'Pahlawi thinkers,' and in other passages 'the Chosroesians (*al-Khosrowānīyyīn*)' obviously meaning followers of Zoroastrian thought which he did not wish to mention specifically. He also throws light on many disputed points in the Avicennian system, the discussion of which has occupied modern scholars. In the course of a long discussion on contingency which he calls *imkān*, he refutes, with many quotations from Avicenna, the view which has lately been expressed that there is no notion of contingency as distinct from mere possibility in Avicenna. He mentions the subject because he is unable to accept the rigid determinism of his predecessor with regard to the belief that creation takes place necessarily. He is inclined to the religious conception of contingency, which, he complains, is not at all envisaged in the *Theology* that is 'only attributed' to the First Teacher, i.e. Aristotle. While to the distinction between essence and existence and their union in God he gives his full support; stressing at the same time that reality is one and single, and that all else is existent through the illuminations of its light and the effulgence of its essence. Here he quotes an Arabic verse to the effect that 'all things in this world are false appearances or idle imaginings, or just reflections in mirrors and in shades.' God for him as for Avicenna was the Necessary Being, but to this conception he adds a thought that he expressed in the form of an axiom, and that his pupils were very fond of elaborating. 'The

Necessary Being,' he says, 'is a simple reality (*basīṭat al-ḥaqīqa*) extremely simple . . . he is everything . . . and yet . . . not a single thing proceeds from him.'[1] This has been explained in many and sometimes conflicting ways which we need not go into except to say that he was anxious to detach himself from pantheistic ideas often attributed to Suhrawardī. Time and movement, in his view, were not preceded by anything except the Deity and His power and command which some people choose to call His attributes, others angels, and which the Platonists designate as the divine Forms; this is because 'people have their own ways in the things they are enamoured of.' Though he expresses surprise over the heated discussion between theologians and philosophers with regard to the question whether the world was created or is eternal, he very discreetly arrives at the conclusion that matter must be considered eternal. In connection with the theory of knowledge he reveals the fact that Avicenna had been influenced by Stoic thought; and in spite of the outspoken condemnation of that conception by his predecessor, he maintains that knowledge is 'the union of the intelligible with the intelligent.'

From problems of metaphysics he turns to questions of psychology, and distinguishes four kinds of perception. They are: (1) sensual perception, (2) imaginative, (3) estimative, and (4) intellectual perception. These are faculties of the 'simple intellect' (*al-'aql al-basīṭ*) the significance of which, he believes, Avicenna failed to realize, because he would not concede that knowledge is the union of the intelligible with the intelligent. As regards the nature of God's knowledge of the universe, he believes that this takes place because once a knowledge of the cause is attained, then the knowledge of the effects or caused things follows without any difficulty. But there are the varieties of intellect to consider; and here he throws much light on the sources from which the Islamic philosophers obtained their ideas on the subject, and particularly on the disputed fourfold division

[1] *Al-Asfār al-Arba'a*, Vol. 1, no pagination.

of the intellect referred to in connection with the treatise of Kindī in the introduction to this book. Besides the writings of Fārābī and Avicenna, Mullā Ṣadrā makes mention of the *Theology* attributed to Aristotle, then speaks of a treatise *On the Intelligence and the Intelligibles* by Porphyry; and then adds that he has in his possession a book on the intellect by Alexander of Aphrodisias, whom Avicenna was in the habit of calling 'the accomplished among the early ones' and according to which Aristotle had divided the intellect into three varieties which he goes on to explain. Hence the division of Alexander, like that of Aristotle, was threefold and not fourfold as some have understood from his writings. Space does not allow further remarks on the *Asfār al-Arba'a* (The Four Books) the reading of which for a student of the history of Islamic thought and its relation with the Greek sources is highly rewarding. It is full of valuable references, including some to Plotinus whom he calls 'the Greek Shaikh' (*al-Shaikh al-Yunānīy*).

It was probably under Avicennian influence that Mullā Ṣadrā refused to believe in the resurrection of the body after death. His metaphysical ideas found their way into the writings of the semi-orthodox religious school of Shaikhīs, though Shaikh Aḥmad Aḥṣā'ī, the founder of that movement, sharply criticized some of the points in his commentaries.

Mullā Muḥsin Faiḍ (d. 1680), who had been the favourite pupil of his master, whose daughter he married, was considered the most faithful commentator of Mullā Ṣadrā, yet he had very little to contribute, and is hardly read nowadays. Mullā Hādī Sabzewārī (d. 1878), on the other hand, is sometimes called the greatest philosopher of the nineteenth century in Persia. The son of a religious divine, he studied at Mashhad and Iṣfahān, and returned to lecture in his native Sabzewār.[1] He wrote some seventeen books, of which the best known is *Asrār al-Ḥikam* (Secrets of Philosophy). In the traditional manner he has treatises on logic and metaphysics in verse. But he was essentially a commentator

[1] Cf. Iqbal: *Development of Metaphysics in Persia.*

and often used some of the writings of Mullā Ṣadrā as text. It is interesting to note that he also categorically denied bodily resurrection and a material hereafter.

Finally, some mention might be made of the fact that innumerable anecdotes amd legends gathered in the course of time around the name of Avicenna, and have since survived in the form of folklore. These represent him as a boon companion ready to drown all worries in a cup of wine; a resourceful spirit, good to invoke in a desperate situation; a man of hidden powers able to appear in the guise of a sorcerer and inflict endless harm; a physician who can cure an illness and extract many a hidden secret by auto-suggestion; an accursed atheist who can undermine men's faith in the most subtle and unsuspected manner; and an abiding mystic who ridicules life and all that it has to offer. It was clearly his philosophy and the circumstances of his life that gave rise to such notions of him. Many tales have been collected from the countryside by a scholar in Russian Tājīkistān who claims to come from the region where Avicenna was born. Thus centuries after his death he remains to fill some with horror, and to guide others to those distant regions of thought so deeply congenial to the Persians.

CHAPTER IX

AVICENNA AND THE WEST

THE intellectual movement in Western Europe during the twelfth and the thirteenth centuries followed a course in many respects similar to that which took place in the Islamic world. In both cases it developed as a challenge and response process involving concepts and beliefs. The impact of Greek thought had shaken Islamic thinkers by challenging some of the fundamentals of their Faith. Not until modern times and the onrush of Western scientific civilization has there been anything of the same magnitude and significance. The small and much-maligned group of *Falāsifa* rose to the challenge, and braving the formidable opposition of the theologians, engaged in what was to be one of the most far-reaching conflicts in the history of ideas. Their response took the form of synthesis—a fact that needs to be emphasized. Although endowed with gifts not unequal to those of the Greeks, they were handicapped by the absence of that complete freedom of thought and expression which the Athenians had enjoyed. They worked under the constant threat of ostracism. And although they rather falteringly asserted their faith in a divine presence, it is safe to assume that they were rationally cognizant of a religious aspect of truth which the Greeks missed. Some modern scholars may reject their protestations of faith, others may generously give them the benefit of the doubt. There really seems no reason to disbelieve them, for whatever may be said of Avicenna, he certainly did not lack courage.

The struggle was repeated when Arabian and Jewish savants brought Greek thought to the heart of the Catholic world in Western Europe. This was not the first impact of Greek philosophy upon Christianity. Long before the Arabs and the advent of Islam, the struggle had begun; but, strangely enough, it hardly ever became very heated. It was sometimes even friendly, and if not to their mutual benefit, it seemed to their satisfaction. We need not go into all that later Christian beliefs owe to Greek and Gnostic ideas. We only wish to point out that the meeting of the two was not as friendly on the western shores of the Mediterranean as it had been on the eastern. And it is to be stressed that here as in Muslim lands, the response to the challenge took the form of synthesis until it was disrupted by the Reformation and the Renaissance. Some would say this was only a natural outcome, others might contend that it was actually the result of the Islamic synthesis.

The way in which Greek thought first reached Western Europe is not very clear. It is certain that it was by more than one route. But we find that whereas the chief channel by which it reached Baghdad was through the efforts of Jacobite and Nestorian Christians, here it was through the intermediary of Arab and Jewish philosophers in Spain and North Africa, and Islamic writings. Here again Plato was the first favourite because of the works of St Augustine, and was then forsaken in favour of Aristotle, and the final phase was the attempt to reconcile the two. Here also interest in Greek medicine and natural philosophy went side by side with interest in logic and metaphysics. And here the whole movement seemed to culminate in the person of St Thomas Aquinas, whose position corresponds in some ways to that of Avicenna, though they did not always agree.

Boethius was among the first to take Aristotle to the West. His translation of the *Categories* and the *De Interpretatione* reached it very early. Hundreds of years later the *Metaphysica* reached Paris from Byzantium. And the *Ethics*, the *Physics* and the *De Anima* came from Greece in the thirteenth century.[1] By far the most important source, if not the earliest in date, was the Arab. To the medical school at Salerno, Constantine the African carried his knowledge of Arabian medicine, and went to Monte

[1] Cf. Guillaume: *The Legacy of Islam*, p. 246.

Casino to take up translation about the year 1070 and continued until his death in 1087. Although his Latin versions are considered corrupt and confused, he did manage to translate Hippocrates, Galen, Haly Abbas and Rhazes from the Arabic. His work was continued at Monte Casino by Johannes Aflacius. In 1085 Toledo, the greatest of Muslim centres of learning founded in the West, fell to the Spanish Christians. And the first prominent European to come to it was Adelard of Bath, the philosopher and mathematician who translated Euclid in consequence of this visit. And a Spanish Jew baptized under the name of Petrus Alphonsi became the physician of Henry I and was the first to spread Muslim science in England.

An unexpected development that was to have important and lasting results was the establishment of a school of translation at Toledo through the initiative of Archbishop Raymond of Toledo. It continued to flourish down to the thirteenth century, with much work to its credit. This was placed under the direction of Archdeacon Domingo Gundisalvo or Gundisalinus. The school corresponded very closely to the *Bait al-Ḥikma* which the 'Abbāsid caliphs had founded in Baghdad; and the part of the polyglot Christians and Ḥarrānians was now being performed by Jews who spoke Arabic, Hebrew, Spanish and sometimes Latin. These usually helped the Europeans who were really responsible for the Latin versions. Thus the converted Jew known as Johannes Hispanus—or Avendeath or Ibn Dāūd—used to translate from Arabic, and sometimes orally, into a Castilian dialect, from which the matter used to be translated into Latin by Gundisalvo. There was also another assistant by the name of Solomon who was very helpful.

The most prominent and prolific translator at Toledo, however, was the Italian Gerard of Cremona who had one Christian and one Jewish assistant. He occupies the same position in the Western world that Ḥunain held in the Islamic world of Baghdad. Rightly called the father of Arabism in Europe, he was born in Cremona in 1114, went to Toledo, and by the time of his death in 1187 had produced as many as eighty translations as a result of an amazing industry that earned him great renown. Among the authors that he put into Latin were Kindī, Fārābī and also Avicenna who, in consequence, was being studied in European centres of learning not much more than a hundred years after his death. A younger contemporary of Gerard was Mark, Canon of Toledo, who translated works of Hippocrates and Galen from the Arabic. Then at the school of Sicily that was flourishing at that time came Michael Scot (d. 1235) and Berengar of Valencia (d. *c.* 1313). They were both among the translators of Avicenna who were now growing in number. Together with Gundisalvo, Avendeath had translated many mathematical and astronomical as well as astrological books into Latin which were seized upon with keen interest especially at the school of Palermo where those subjects were taught. It has been observed that the Crusaders had surprisingly little to do with the transmission of Arabic and Islamic learning, but really it would be more surprising if they had. The absorption of Arabo-Hellenic learning that had started in Spain in the eleventh century continued down to the sixteenth and seventeenth centuries in various parts of Europe; and we find Andrea Alpago (d. 1520) in Italy deeply occupied with new translations of Avicenna, Averroës and other Islamic authors as late as the beginning of the sixteenth century. Latin versions of Arabic books immediately became the subject of study at Bologna, Montpellier, Paris and Oxford, among other seats of European learning in the twelfth century. Generally it may be said that the first two concentrated primarily on Arabian medicine and possessed most of the manuscripts, while Paris and Oxford were absorbed by their interest in philosophy and theology.

From the list of the translations of Archdeacon Gundisalvo in Spain,[1] it appears that he had rendered a number of the works of Kindī and Fārābī into Latin; and in order to follow the

[1] Cf. A. Alonso: *Traducciones del . . . Gundisalvo, Al-Andalus*, Vol. XII, 1947; Bédoret: *Les Premiers Versions tolédans de Philosophie, Rev. Neoscolastique*, 1938.

historical sequence he had continued by translating parts of the *Epistles of the Brethren of Purity*; and had then arrived at Avicenna. From him he took up the metaphysics of the *Shifā*, besides one or two minor treatises, then proceeded to Ghazālī and various other authors.

It is only lately that European scholars have devoted much attention to the list of the works of Avicenna that were translated into Latin during the Middle Ages. To begin with there was a translation of his autobiography, as recorded by Jūzjānī, made by Avendeath[1] under the title of *Prologus Discipuli et Capitula Avicennae*. Then we have the evidence of Roger Bacon to the effect that the *Shifā* was never translated in its entirety. 'The Latins,' he says, 'possess certain parts of the first which is called the Book of Assipha, that is the Book of Sufficiency.' Of the section on Logic with which the *magnm opus* begins, only the commentary on the *Eisagoge* of Porphyry was translated, again by Avendeath, under the title of *De Universalibus*. The section on Metaphysics was translated in its entirety by Gundisalvo under the title of *Metaphysica Avicennae . . . de Prima Philosophia*. The section on Psychology was translated by Avendeath in its entirety under the title of *Liber de Anima*, and so was the section on plants under the title of *Liber de Vegetalibus*. He also translated the section on Physics under the title of *Sufficientia Physicorum*, but apparently not in its entirety. These two, either jointly or separately, also translated some minor works by Avicenna.[2]

After these early versions there appeared later translations which included the Metaphysics, the Psychology, and other sections of the *Shifā*, as well as the *Kitāb al-Najāt*. There is no evidence that the *Ishārāt* was ever put into Latin, nor the fragment known as the *Logic of the Orientals*; though further research

[1] Cf. Alonso: *Traducciones del Arabe al Latin por Juan Hispano (Ibn Dawud). Al-Andalus*, 1952.

[2] Cf. Alonso: *Ibn Sina . . . Revista del Instituto Egypeio de Estudios Islamicos*, 1953.

may add much to our knowledge.[1] Ghazālī had been mistakenly supposed to be a disciple of Avicenna, and as his writings were translated almost at the same time, many got their knowledge of Avicenna through him.

The medical works did not come any later. The *Canon of Medicine* was translated only by Gerard of Cremona in the second half of the twelfth century, but earlier the *Cardiac Remedies* had been done into Latin by Avendeath. Some two hundred years later the *Canon* was translated into Hebrew. Towards the close of the thirteenth century Armengaud, son of a French physician by the name of Blaise at Montpellier, translated a medical poem by Avicenna from Arabic into Latin and called it *Avicennae Cantice*. This, when printed later at Venice, included a glossary by Averroës. It had been preceded by the translation by Moses Farachi (or Faragut) of *al-Ḥāwī*, the voluminous medical compendium of Rhazes.

These translations of Avicenna, whether of medical or philosophical works, were received with great enthusiasm all over Europe. And when the manuscripts were finally printed—mostly at Strasburg and Venice—they ran into innumerable editions; sometimes separately and sometimes together with the works of Fārābī and Kindī.[2] And there is evidence of their widespread use at various centres of learning.

* * * *

The combination of Greek ideas with Christian teachings which was to form the basis of European Scholasticism could not but be profoundly influenced by the Islamic synthesis not only in form but in substance. The theology of the Church in patristic times had been deeply imbued with Platonism; and the writings of St Augustine which dominated Christian thought up to the twelfth century, had incorporated much of the spirit if not the letter of Neo-Platonism. So that by the beginning of the period

[1] Cf. Mlle d'Alverny: *Archives d'Histoire Doctrinale . . .*, 1952.
[2] Cf. *Gesamtkatalog der Wiegendrucke*, Band III, Leipzig, 1928.

during which Arabic learning influenced Western thought, although they had only the translation of the *Timaeus* in Latin, the general attitude was Platonic in spirit. With the arrival of Arabic versions of Greek texts, and commentaries or original works by Islamic authors, knowledge of Greek thought was immediately enriched far more than had been anticipated; and incidentally interest shifted almost entirely from Plato to Aristotle. The Aristotelianism that had reached the Islamic world had been greatly altered through the many restatements and commentaries of the Hellenistic Age; and what reached Europe by way of Spain was clad in an Arabic and Islamic garb. The case of the actual texts was somewhat different. The Arabic renderings had always been rather awkward and obscure in expression; but were very faithful to the original Greek and that made them valuable. In fact they still retain their usefulness because of that. This extensive Arabic literature which had now been made available in Latin, became a decisive and potent factor in the three cultural developments that were to help the general awakening in the thirteenth century. These were, first the growth of the universities out of the old cathedral schools; second, the discovery and appropriation of Aristotle; and third, the new activity of Dominican and Franciscan monks. Italy had been more interested in law and medicine, whereas at the University of Paris and later at Oxford the chief subjects were theology and philosophy, especially now that the new learning was being rapidly translated from Arabic sources. By 1250 they were in full possession of almost everything that had been transmitted by way of Spain and North Africa; and mediaeval knowledge came to be composed of (1) patristic materials, (2) early Platonic and Aristotelian translations such as those of Boethius, and (3) Arabian works.

Almost all the Islamic *Falāsifa* were represented among the books rendered into Latin, and we find Kindī and Fārābī at the head of them all; but it was Avicenna and Averroës who exerted the greatest influence on Scholasticism whether as commentators on Aristotle or through their own personal views. Of these two, Averroës who is more important in Christian than in Islamic philosophy, became a highly controversial figure. He dominated many but repelled others. His followers who preferred his purer form of Aristotelianism to the adaptations of Avicenna, founded a whole school of Averroism which became the chief intellectual heresy of the thirteenth century, and had its stronghold at the University of Paris.[1] Here Siger de Brabant was one of the leading representatives of the group who drew the fire of St Thomas. These Averroists accepted Aristotle as presented to them by Averroës, particularly on the universal oneness of the human intelligence, the *anima intellectiva*, which involved denial of individual immortality with rewards and punishments; the eternity of the visible world as uncreated and everlasting; and also the determinism which precluded freedom of human action and moral responsibility. Such conceptions were bound to provoke the opposition of many a devout churchman.

The influence of Avicenna, which has lately attracted the attention of many Catholic scholars, preceded that of Averroës and continued long after it, and eventually proved a far more vital force. Yet in spite of all its importance and widespread penetration, it was rather vague and indefinite in form. It did not crystallize into a specific set of doctrines to be accepted by a clearly marked group as did the teaching of Averroës. We find traces of Avicenna in almost every Scholastic author in a form that has been described as 'augustinisme avicennisant.'[2] Although there never developed such a thing as a school of Avicennaism, he is everywhere 'a constant and pervasive excitant.'[3] He was identified with the concept of being which had been the core of his metaphysics. His distinction between essence and existence became widely adopted. His deterministic view that God was

[1] Cf. E. Renan: *Averroës et l'Averroisme.*

[2] Cf. Gilson: *Les Sources gréco-arabes de l'Augustinisme avicennisant.*

[3] Cf. K. Foster, O.P.: *Avicenna and Western Thought in the Thirteenth Century, Millenary Symposium*, edit. Wickens.

the Creator necessarily proved provocative; and his idea of divine Providence, *liberalitas*, survived also. It is therefore best to seek him in individual authors and with reference to some of the special problems that occupied them in that age. It was not easy for people who were invariably clericals to welcome the views of a philosopher who was from the religious point of view an 'infidel' and intellectually an alien. It stands to their credit that they studied him with courage and open-mindedness, and adopted whatever they felt they could sincerely reconcile with the fundamentals of their Faith.

Scholastic thinkers are usually divided according to their religious Orders into Dominicans and Franciscans, but one problem that occupied them all irrespective of the views they held on religious matters, was the reality or non-reality of universals. Do universals as such exist independently and apart? Plato had said that they were real and existed before all things. Aristotle had had two different views, one when combating Plato, and the other when thinking for himself; so that his position seemed equivocal. The problem had reached Western Europe when Porphyry's *Eisagoge*, as an introduction to Aristotle's *Categories* and treating of what came to be known as the five universals, had been rendered into Latin by Boethius. And for some reason it had suddenly become a most pressing philosophical problem in the first part of the twelfth century. For them it was a logical question of knowledge and cognition that came to involve both metaphysics and theology. Roscellin, teaching at Besançon, had said that universals were merely breath and sound, *flatus vocis*. Abelard, who had been unacquainted with the other logical treatises of Aristotle, and only knew the *Categories* and the *De Interpretatione* in Boethius's rendering, said that the universals existed neither in things as such nor in words, they consisted rather in general predicability, which thus repeated what Aristotle had said in the *De Interpretatione*. Things resemble each other, Abelard said, and these resemblances give rise to the idea of universals. But the points of resemblance between things are not in themselves things. Yet universals exist as patterns for creation in the mind of God.

With the arrival of Islamic philosophy and the translation of a large part of the *Shifā*, which included the whole of the Metaphysics and some opening sections of the Logic, Avicenna's views on the problem of the universals became the subject of special study and ended by becoming almost generally adopted with or without criticism and some minor modifications. In a separate chapter of the *Shifā*, the universals and the manner of their existence had been discussed at great length. He had done the same in his commentary on the *Eisagoge* of Porphyry which he had placed at the beginning of the Logic. According to him genera, that is universals, have a triple existence. They are before things, *ante res*; they are in things, *in rebus*; and they are after things, *post res*, at one and the same time. By saying that they exist *before* things, he means that they have some existence in the understanding of God, and later in the active intelligence. If God decides to create man or animal, he must have some idea of what a man or an animal is; and that idea is in this respect anterior to man or animal in the concrete, as was seen in his conception of creation. And by existence *in* things, he means a sensible existence as attached to matter, and in natural objects. And by existence *after* things, he means when the genera are abstracted by the mind from the particulars of sense-perception, and we retain a conceptual notion of their existence. We notice different species of the same genus, we see their likenesses, and even when the experience has passed, there comes to exist in our mind the idea that that genus represents. Betrand Russell remarks that 'this view is obviously intended to reconcile different theories.'

The problem of the universals was actually part of a much wider controversy which divided scholastic logicians into 'realists' and 'nominalists.' Again the source of the dispute was Porphyry and centred round three questions: (1) Are genera and species substances? (2) If substances, are they corporeal or incorporeal? (3) And if incorporeal, are they in sensible things or separated from them? Can we, for instance, say that 'humanity' or 'animality' are real substances found in all human beings and in all animals respectively? The realists maintained that they were indeed substances, whereas the nominalists said that these were merely class names arbitrarily chosen and did not exist as distinct entities. This seemingly sterile disputation was highly important because of its religious implications, and we find every scholastic taking one side or the other. Thus Roscellin, the protagonist of the nominalist party, did not hesitate to apply his logical principle to the doctrine of the Trinity. If, he said, the real is the universal, then the Three Persons are but one thing, and become incarnate with the Son. And if it is the singular that is real, then it is proper that we should speak not of one but of three Gods. This heretical conclusion naturally infuriated the more conservative churchmen who set themselves diligently to refute him. And this conflict acted as a powerful stimulus to the mediaeval mind, and helped the establishment of schools of dialectic on which the conservative theologians frowned, but which nevertheless introduced the dialectical spirit into the teachings of theology itself.

The similarity with what happened in Baghdad is so striking that it is well to remind ourselves that there too interest was first centred on logic, and that logical reasoning gradually invaded the domain of theology which was forced to defend itself, and that the outcome was the development of dialectics which were eventually reduced to sterile disputations. However, Abelard, as with the problem of the universals, attempted to discover a middle way between 'the absurdities of the orthodox realists and the blasphemies of the nominalists.' Yet the dispute continued and not a single author dealing with logic failed to take part. The attitude of Avicenna was, therefore, bound to be of interest and importance to all. The Islamic *Falāsifa* had not been unanimous on this question. There were some who were inclined towards nominalism, as for instance Maimonides, the Jewish philosopher of Spain, who helped to introduce many of their ideas to the Western world. This led some European scholars to assume that they could all be regarded as nominalists. This was certainly not so in the case of Avicenna. As has already been pointed out, sometimes his realism is extremely close to that of Plato, whereas at other times, particularly in logic, he tends towards nominalism. Just as in the case of the universals he is prepared to concede that there is some truth in both conceptions. It is therefore more correct to call him a conceptualist. And this attitude influenced many of the scholastic philosophers who took sufficient interest in his works.

* * * *

John Scotus Erigena, 'the most astonishing person of the ninth century,' does not directly concern us here because he flourished long before the arrival of Islamic philosophy. But it is well to remember that as a competent Greek scholar who was an exponent of the Platonic and Neo-Platonic traditions under the influence of St Augustine, he was among the earliest to revive interest in Greek thought in Western Europe. Coming from Ireland, he spent most of his life at the court of King Charles the Bold of France. He set reason above faith, and did not care for the authority of the ecclesiastics; so that the spirit of his writings is very different from that of any other mediaeval author.

Perhaps the first European to incorporate Avicennian ideas into his own works was Gundisalvo, the translator. He who had been engaged in translating Avicenna into Latin was naturally influenced by him. Although his *De Anima* is inspired by St Augustine, and he takes the old traditional views about most things, he draws on Avicenna freely. Next we find William of Auvergne (d. 1249) deeply imbued by the spirit as well as the letter of the new learning that had been transmitted by way of Spain. By 1225 he is teaching at the University of Paris, and in his writings quoting extensively not only from Aristotelian works, till then unknown to the Western world, but from a host of Arab and Islamic philosophers whose very names must have been new to his pupils. Of Plato he seems to have known only the *Timaeus*, with a good deal of Aristotle which could have reached him only through the translation of Arabic commentaries. He mentions various Islamic authors, among them Fārābī, Avicenna, Ghazālī, Averroës, and Avicebron, for whom he has special praise. The movement away from Plato and towards Aristotle had already started, and we find his preference for the latter being freely expressed. His attitude in connection with the commentaries and independent works of the Arabians is generous and friendly but rather cautious. He does not hesitate to criticize them when he feels they go counter to his principles. He may have been the first scholastic to take up the cudgels against Averroës who was to become the exponent of a heresy frowned on by the Church. He also combated astrology, made popular as a result of some Arabic treatises on the subject.

As to Avicenna, William of Auvergne, though frequently critical of him, throughout shows considerable respect for his views, and does not hesitate to adopt them in some cases. This was typical of the scholastic attitude towards him in the first half of the twelfth century. William denounces Avicenna along with Aristotle and Fārābī for denying personal immortality; and he is violently against Averroës regarding the activities of the *intellect agent*. The religious doctrines to which he strictly adhered could allow him to accept neither Avicenna's theory of creation, the eternity of matter, nor his cosmogony in general, nor his belief that matter was the basis of individuation. Yet when we come to his proofs for the existence of God, we find that though he is influenced by St Augustine, he is far more influenced by the Islamic philosophers, and most of all by Avicenna. The scholastics of the thirteenth century were to come under exactly the same influences, adopt the same position and use similar arguments. On the problem of the universals he was a moderate realist, and this also might have been due to the moderation of Avicenna's attitude. It is above all in his distinction between essence and existence that he owes everything to the Persian philosopher. He is supposed to be the first scholastic to expound this already famous point. In brief, at a time when Platonism, Aristotelianism, Neo-Platonism and Jewish and Arab ideas were clashing with Christian thought, William of Auvergne combated some of the philosophical theses that he thought undesirable and contrary to the doctrines of the Church, yet accepted much that he deemed valid and fruitful.

Almost contemporary with William of Auvergne was Alexander of Hales (d. 1245). His *Summa universae theologiae* was the first scholastic work in which full use was made of the physics, metaphysics and natural history of Aristotle. Pope Gregory IX had lifted the prohibition that had been hanging over the works of Aristotle and the Arabian philosophers, and he openly cites the Metaphysics of Avicenna which proves his acquaintance with that work. He is particularly drawn to Avicenna's Psychology, with his isolating of the *estimative* faculty, to which reference has already been made. This was considered by the scholastics one of Avicenna's most original contributions in this field.

St Bonaventure (d. 1274), though a contemporary of Albertus Magnus, who studied together with St Thomas at the faculty of theology in Paris, was an Augustinian and consequently more of a Platonist; and seems to have come least under the influence of the Islamic thinkers who were mostly Aristotelians. He did not, however, altogether avoid 'the master of those who know,' and because of it he is constrained to remark that 'so it appears that among philosophers, the word of wisdom was given to Plato, and the word of knowledge to Aristotle.' As a religious man it was natural for him to find Plato more congenial, and he could not but take strong exception to the notion of a separate active intelligence that ran counter to his doctrinal beliefs.

In Robert Grosseteste, Chancellor of Oxford and Bishop of Lincoln, on the other hand, the Islamic influence is not totally absent, though very diffuse and indefinite. His interests covered a wide field, but he had a special inclination towards scientific subjects such as optics and meteorology which the Islamic authors before him had brilliantly developed. He, moreover, occupied himself with the translation of Greek texts directly into Latin. Like so many others he found the psychology propounded by the Islamic thinkers something of a stumbling-block; difficult to reconcile with Church doctrines and religious principles. Like St Bonaventure and the other Franciscans, he was a devout Augustinian and therefore profoundly imbued with Platonism; but Roger Bacon, his renowned pupil, took up the study of the new learning with great determination and ended as a great admirer of Avicenna.

With Albertus Magnus (d. 1280) the synthesis that was to form the pattern of all philosophical speculation in mediaeval times gained a broad basis of general knowledge without which it could have made little progress. Born a nobleman, he joined the Dominican Order at Padua; and taught chiefly at Cologne before moving to Paris, in those days a famous school of philosophy, where he became a lecturer. It may be presumed that it was here, where the best manuscripts were available, that he continued the study of the Islamic authors which he had started in Italy. And it was in Paris that he undertook the voluminous writings that were to establish eventually his position as one of the most learned leaders of scholastic thought. With extraordinary industry and massive erudition, he devoted himself to the task of making all branches of science and philosophy, including physics and mathematics, accessible to all who knew Latin; and he had certainly succeeded in placing them all within reach of his contemporaries, whether at Paris or Cologne, when he finally returned to his native land. As the greatest transmitter of the Greek and Islamic systems to the scholastic world, Albertus spent some fifty years in assembling the largest mediaeval storehouses of learning. And while avowedly a follower of Aristotle, he protested against regarding him as infallible. 'He who believes that Aristotle was God,' he says, 'ought to believe that he never erred. If one regards him as a man, then surely he may err as well as we.'[1] And where orthodoxy required it, he disagreed with the Stagirite, and unlike the Averroists did not follow him blindly. Thus we find him insisting that the world was created in time. In fact he was among the few in those days who took the line that philosophy and theology were entirely separate sciences, one concerned with the application of human reason to all problems, and the other with revelation. Of course not everyone agreed with him in this, which was the very same attitude that some of the Islamic philosophers had been forced to adopt. St Thomas was to follow practically the same line. In his writings, Albertus devotes much space to the material that had been collected in Arabic books, and he borrows extensively. He is most indebted to Avicenna and everywhere speaks with admiration and appreciation of him even when not completely in agreement. He was the first to adopt in its entirety what had come to be known as Arabian logic, and incorporate it into the *Schul-logik* of the thirteenth century. Substantially this was the logic of Avicenna. Albertus's *De Anima* is an exhaustive paraphrase of Aristotle and of what his Hellenistic and Islamic commentators had had to add —except where it came into conflict with religious doctrine.

It has been found that the conception of time which he expounds in his *Physics* was deeply influenced by what Avicenna had written on the subject in the *Shifā*[2]—a section which we know to have been already translated at least partly into Latin. And though he quotes Fārābī and Averroës frequently, supposing that he is giving their views, he is in fact reproducing Avicenna's statements, with which he seems in general agreement. On the distinction between essence and existence, however, he is critical; and this must have been due to the influence of Averroës who had taken a contrary position from the very beginning.

With St Thomas Aquinas (d. 1274),[1] the greatest of the scholastics and the author of the most comprehensive synthesis

[1] Quoted by Taylor: *The Medieval Mind*, Vol. 2, p. 452.

[2] A. Mansion: *Le Temps chez les peripatéciens medievaux*, *Rev. Neoscolastique*, 1934.

[3] Cf. F. C. Copleston: *Aquinas*, London, 1955.

in the Catholic world, we arrive at a stage when the influence of Avicenna becomes a recognized element of Christian mediaeval thought, and when his views are treated with much deference whether in agreement or disagreement. So far he had been just another Islamic commentator welcomed chiefly as an aid to the understanding of Aristotle; now he becomes a distinct and vital force not comparable to Averroës or any of the others. St Thomas, by birth an Italian nobleman, is said to have studied philosophy in Naples; but it was probably only after going to Cologne and sitting at the feet of Albertus Magnus that he became properly acquainted with the Islamic thinkers whom his master had so diligently studied. He was to make much use of these materials in his lectures at Paris and in his elaborate system of Thomist philosophy. The Angelic Doctor is commonly regarded as one of the opponents of Avicenna with whom he was certainly in frequent disagreement. While this may be partly true, it did not prevent Thomas from borrowing extensively and quoting constantly from Avicenna. In fact Catholic scholars who have lately studied the subject are finding that Thomas was far more indebted to Avicenna than was previously supposed. Of course there had been some fundamental differences between the two. In St Thomas the religious temperament predominates, while in Avicenna the rational tendency was stronger; though the former preferred the purer Aristotelianism of Averroës to the more critical expositions of the latter. St Thomas may have felt at liberty to criticize, modify or even alter Avicenna's statements, but his work testifies constantly to the latter's influence. To take the conception of God and the proofs for his existence as a specific case; St Thomas, who had maintained that there is nothing in revelation that is contrary to reason, had to advance proofs, since he believed that the human intelligence is capable of proving the existence of God and the immortality of the soul —a conviction that had already been affirmed by Avicenna. And when presenting his proofs, we find in his most influential work, the *Summa Theologiae*, some five points: (1) God as the Unmoved

Mover; (2) God as the First Cause; (3) God as the source of all necessity; (4) God as the source of perfection; and (5) God as the final cause. Of these five, four are clearly of Aristotelian origin, and may have come to him directly or by way of Averroës; but one is manifestly the Necessary Being of Avicenna, only rather differently expressed. And when St Thomas states his conception of God as pure activity—not a body because he has no parts—simple—not a genus—the good of every good—that which cannot be defined, he is just following Aristotle, whose work was available to him either through Arabic sources or from the direct translations from Greek which he had made his friend William of Moerbecke, the Flemish scholar, undertake. Furthermore, when St Thomas says God is *intelligent* and his act of intelligence is his essence, he is quoting verbatim from Avicenna, even though both statements might have been ultimately derived from the Stagirite. He did dissent, however, from both Aristotle and Avicenna when insisting that God was aware of all particular things, *singularia*, directly. And contrary to Avicenna, he asserted that God created out of his own free Will, and not necessarily. Moreover the act of creation was *ex nihilo*, just as it is according to the Scriptures.

William of Auvergne had criticized Avicenna's cosmology, but adopted his psychology. St Thomas in his *De Anima* found himself in opposition to much that Averroës had asserted to be the true views of the Peripatetics, and also to some points that Avicenna had made. He maintained the unity and separate existence of the soul against all forms of division and he insisted upon personal immortality in conformity with religious doctrine. There was no common human soul as the Averroists at Paris had taught, but as many souls as there are men. There is on the other hand much of Avicenna in the *De Anima*. Again, in his conception of angels as separate immaterial substances, there is much of Avicenna's doctrine. It is, however, in his distinction between essence and existence that he is avowedly and most consistently Avicennian. The metaphysics of the *Shifā* in which

Avicenna had expatiated on this distinction had been translated in full into Latin and it may be assumed that St Thomas knew it well. Moreover, earlier scholastics had commented on it and almost invariably adopted it; it was therefore only natural that it should figure in the *De Ente et Essentia* in which he constantly appeals to Avicenna. By opening the gap between essence and existence, Avicenna may have provided the thirteenth century with one of its hotly debated questions, but the outcome had already been foreseen by William of Auvergne. The notion of contingent existence was highly congenial to the Biblical doctrine of creation, while Avicenna's cosmogony, in spite of some deceptive similarities, was utterly different from Christian teachings.[1]

Those who have been engaged in discovering traces of Avicenna in St Thomas are finding an increasing amount of interesting material, all going to show that his impact on the mind of the Angelic Doctor could be considered the most serious and prolonged encounter of Christianity with Islamic philosophy in Europe. That the former should adopt everything that the latter had taught was hardly to be expected; but there is no doubt that it proved extremely stimulating to St Thomas and abundantly profitable in the construction of his Christian synthesis. A case only recently pointed out[2] is in connection with the theory of prophecy which, as has been seen, Fārābī and Avicenna had expounded with some ingenuity. In his *Summa Theologiae* and in his *De Veritate*, St Thomas expresses the belief that there are two kinds of prophecy, one which he calls 'divine' and the other 'natural' prophecy. He strongly disapproves of the explanation that Fārābī and Avicenna had given of the reasons and the way in which Prophets are delegated and the powers that they come to possess. A prophet, he insists, is chosen by God and his special powers are granted to him usually through the intermediary of an angel; and he goes on to give

[1] Cf. Mondaine: *A propos d'Avicenne et de St Thomas*, *Rev. Thomiste*, 1951.
[2] Cf. Gardet: *La Pensée Religieuse d'Avicenne*, p. 124.

the doctrinal view on the subject. It is to be remembered that Ghazālī had done the same thing in a book already rendered into Latin. And yet when he comes to what he calls natural prophecy, we find him making it conditional on exactly those extraordinary faculties of the imagination, insight and clear thinking that Fārābī and Avicenna had said were the distinguishing marks of the prophet. In other words, he felt that their explanation applied to natural and not to divine prophecy.

Of all the great authors of the thirteenth century, the best informed on the life and works of Avicenna is supposed to have been Roger Bacon (d. *c.* 1294). Not much admired in his own day, and, it is thought, sometimes over-estimated in modern times, Bacon was encyclopaedic in his learning and profound in erudition; and that is one reason why the *Doctor mirabilis* has been called the greatest genius of the Middle Ages. It has been determined that he knew Hebrew and Arabic among other languages, though it is not clear whether he learnt them at Oxford or Paris. In the latter place he was under surveillance and some sort of imprisonment because of his suspected heresy. There he met Hermann Allemanus, the translator, and questioned him on many Arabic books. There is no evidence that he translated any Arabic works into Latin himself; but it is known that he strongly disapproved of the language and the lack of faithfulness of some of the versions in common use in those days. There is, however, no reason to suppose that he read Avicenna and Ghazālī in the original.

Bacon was different from St Thomas, and the influence which Avicenna had on him was of an entirely different kind. St Thomas was bent on a system of synthesis, and made use of Avicenna and his arguments to the extent to which he found them suitable. Bacon, on the other hand, was interested in linguistics, mathematics, astronomy, optics and chemistry, and was obsessed with the idea that philosophy as well as all branches of learning should be made to serve theology. Obviously Avicenna could not be of much help in all these matters, and perhaps least in the service of theology. As a man of outstanding originality and insight himself, highly critical of his contemporaries, and not at all concerned to develop a comprehensive system, he must have found Avicenna stimulating as much as instructive, even though he regarded him and Fārābī as mere interpreters of Aristotle.[1] Contrary perhaps to everybody else, he thought logic was useless and that no time should be wasted on it; whilst he found alchemy, which Avicenna had denounced, worth writing seriously about. On the basis of various Arabic sources, he treated of perspective in some detail. Aristotle was for him a great philosopher who had his limitations and should be read critically; and after him came Avicenna 'the prince and leader of philosophy' as he called him. As a result of his wide reading, he quotes freely from Arabic authors and is not at all averse to profiting from them and their knowledge. That makes him cite Fārābī, Avicenna and Averroës in support of his own views on various matters in the course of discussion. In holding that the active intelligence is separate from the soul, he agrees with Avicenna, and like him he has little use for Porphyry.

Some mention may be made here of the Franciscan Roger Marston who studied in Paris and later became a professor at Oxford.[2] He also accepts the Avicennian notion of an active intelligence, and like Bacon identifies it with God who had inspired and illuminated the soul of St Augustine. It is in connection with him and his views that Gilson defines his happy phrase of 'augustinisme avicennisant.' This explains a specific mediaeval doctrine of knowledge and cognition, the essential elements of which had been borrowed directly from St Augustine and also from Avicenna's work, in its Latin form. Fārābī was brought in to support the other two; and Avicenna was taken as the true interpreter of Aristotle, in contrast to Averroës and the Averroists of Paris who had taken him as their guide. Gilson

[1] Birkenmajer: *Avicenna und Roger Bacon*, *Rev. Neoscolastique*, 1934.

[2] Gilson: *Roger Marston: un cas d'augustinisme avicennisant*, *Arch. d'hist. doctr. et litter.*, 1933.

maintains that there may be said to be a case of Avicennizing Augustinism whenever a mediaeval philosopher or commentator teaches that God is the active intelligence or the intellectual agent, and particularly when the author affirms that this can be proved by establishing a true accord between St Augustine and Aristotle as interpreted by Avicenna. In a way this corresponds to the old Neo-Platonic attempt to reconcile Plato with Aristotle. It has been seen that this endeavour had been repeated by the Islamic authors and especially by Fārābī without any very valuable results. And now the Scholastics were making yet another effort which was to prove no more successful. St Augustine had already accepted much from Plato and Neo-Platonism. To add a good measure of Aristotelianism by way of Avicenna could not be an easy task. And yet there were many Avicennizing Augustinians, especially among the lesser figures in the Middle Ages. Of the more prominent men who chose this course William of Auvergne and Roger Bacon deserve special mention because they provoked many to strong opposition. They were followed by a host of minor authors such as Peckham and Vital du Four. None of these, however, had any important contribution to make. They were just good and earnest Augustinians who realizing the increasing popularity and the widespread diffusion of Avicennian thought, came to feel that a reconciliation would be desirable and even fruitful.

Mathew of Aquasparta (d. *c.* 1302), though a follower of St Bonaventure, was nevertheless drawn to Aristotle through his acquaintance with the works of Avicenna whom he frequently mentions in his writings. And Duns Scotus (d. *c.* 1308), while carrying on the Franciscan controversy with St Thomas, attempted a synthesis between philosophy and theology which did not reach the completeness of Thomism nor gain the same measure of acceptance, but which developed under the same influences and was motivated by the same purpose. Although an Augustinian and therefore more Platonic, he was bound to bring in Aristotle in the construction of his synthesis and to make use of the Jewish and Islamic commentators. Like all philosophers after the thirteenth century, Scotus was well versed in both Avicenna and Averroës, and frequently had the difficult task of choosing between their views. Yet it is Avicenna who eventually becomes his *point de départ.*[1]

His *Quaestiones* opens with a discussion as to what constitutes the proper subject of metaphysics. Averroës had claimed that it was God and the Intelligences, and had cited passages from Aristotle's *Metaphysica* in support of his view. For Avicenna it had been being as being. He had argued that no science can prove the existence of its own subject, it has to take it for granted. Metaphysics could not have God as its proper subject because its chief concern is to prove the existence of God. Scotus, who had been hesitant, declares himself in his *Opus Oxoniense* entirely in favour of the Avicennian standpoint, and decides that it is Avicenna and not Averroës who should be considered the true interpreter of Aristotle. All Scotist metaphysics, in consequence, is centred on the idea of being, *ens*, and the Avicennian principle that being is not a genus in itself. As the first object of intellection, it is neither a substance nor accident, nor any of the ten genera that they call categories. And yet it should not be supposed that Scotus copied blindly all that Avicenna had said. There was much in the Persian that was unacceptable for a Christian philosopher. Gilson insists that 'confondre la philosophie de Duns Scotus avec celle d'Avicenne serait une erreur pire que d'ignorer leurs relations.'[2] Avicenna is a starting-point for him, and throughout Avicenna is his chief guide. He studies, discusses, modifies, and with approbation follows him. 'Avicenne doit être sur notre table comme il était sur la sienne,' adds Gilson. This strong predilection may be explained by the fact that there had developed at Oxford a current of Avicennian thought that was becoming a regular tradition, and Scotus, who though born in Scotland studied at Oxford and there became a Franciscan, must have

[1] Cf. Gilson: *Avicenne et le Point de départ de Duns Scotus*, *Arch. . . .*, 1927.
[2] *Ibid.*

been deeply influenced by it. And when he left to spend his later years at Paris, he found the same tradition reigning there too. Only through St Thomas did Avicenna lose some ground.

On the question of the Active Intelligence—a very delicate point, difficult for a Christian to accept—we find Scotus openly contradicting Avicenna and accepting the conclusions of St Thomas. Gilson, who as a noted Catholic scholar admits that the history of Arabian philosophy and Christian thought are inseparable, even if we accept Averroism and the development after St Thomas, likes to remind us that 'entre Avicenne et Duns Scotus il y a saint Thomas d'Aquin.'

The religious element in Scotus made him totally averse to the consmological conceptions of Averroës and his naturalistic tendencies due to Aristotelian influence, and he repudiated the arguments in favour of the eternity of the world. Nor did he regard Avicenna as more helpful. He could not forgo the belief in the ultimate contingence of the world, created *ex nihilo* and out of the gratuitous exercise of the free will of God. Even though Avicenna had conceded that the world was in the category of the possible, creation could not be *ex nihilo*, he had said, and it proceeds from God necessarily. Duns Scotus had also to differ from Averroës over the question of the emergence of the *many* from the *one*. It has already been seen that under Neo-Platonic influence Avicenna explained how from the absolutely simple and transcendent One only one emanation could proceed immediately, but that through a succession of emanations multiplicity eventually follows. Scotus could accept no such theory of emanations and insisted on the doctrinal view of the creation of the whole universe. It was probably for this reason that he ended by declaring that the union of metaphysics and theology cannot be maintained, and henceforth they stand on opposite pinnacles ruling their separate domains. This was a development that did away with a good deal of confusion and rather futile attempts at reconciliation of specific points that seemed obviously irreconcilable.

Some think that William of Occam (d. 1349) was the most important schoolman after St Thomas. First at Oxford, then Paris, he had been the pupil of Duns Scotus and lived to become his rival. His teacher had with his penetrating criticism prepared the way for him by renouncing all attempts to unify philosophy and theology. It is perhaps in his logic that Occam shows best the manner and the degree of Avicenna's entry into the body of Scholastic logic. Albertus Magnus had already repeated his view that the controversy over the question whether logic is a science or an instrument of science is irrelevant. He had also adopted the important distinction between primary and secondary intelligibles (*prima* and *secunda intentio*), and that in the field of logic, where we proceed from the known to the unknown, we are concerned with the secondary intelligibles (*al-ma'qūlāt al-thāniya*). Many followed Albertus in accepting the principle that the function of logic is the application of the *intentiones secundae* to the first intentions, and among them was Duns Scotus. It is not therefore surprising to find this division also in Occam.[1]

Duns Scotus was a realist, but Occam was a nominalist, at least in logic, though he has been called a conceptualist in metaphysics. The nominalists of the fifteenth century considered him the founder of their school. For Occam, logic is an instrument of science and philosophy, and that is the old Peripatetic conception of Alexander of Aphrodisias. It has been said that Occam was concerned to restore a pure Aristotelianism, by removing the misinterpretations of Duns Scotus for which the influence of St Augustine and partly of Avicenna were responsible; and also, it may be added, not least the *Eisagoge* of Porphyry. As a result, logic and the theory of knowledge, *scientiae*, the *'ilm* of the Arabs, had become confused and intermingled with metaphysics and theology. The strict nominalism of Occam was naturally far removed from the Avicennian moderate con-

[1] Cf. Moody: *The Logic of William of Occam.*

ceptualism, and he denied the existence of the universal *in re*, which was one of the three forms that his Persian predecessor had been willing to accept. Nevertheless there remain in his logic more Avicennian conceptions that is generally realized. If he ever deliberately attempted to free himself of all Arabic influences, as some have thought, he certainly did not succeed in the field of logic. Even the maxim which after him is called 'Occam's razor,' can, without too great a stretch of the imagination, be traced back to a principle that Avicenna had clearly laid down in his metaphysics, even though Occam used it for an entirely different purpose. But what is most striking is his use of the concept of *first and second intentions* which is a distinctive Avicennian contribution; and proves for him just as clarifying as it had been for its originator. It helped to place logic, whether it be considered a science or just an instrument of thought, on a firm and justified basis with a definite object in view, and with specified terms and limits of its own. It was not to be regarded as an appendage of the sciences, even when called an instrument. It was a necessary element, a prerequisite in the search after the *first intentions*.

There are also Stoic influences in Occam's logic, as in his statement that propositions about future contingents are as yet neither true nor false, an assertion that the Stoics had already made and discussed at length; now he was elaborating it in spite of its disturbing effect on religious dogma. Whether the thought had come to him directly, from translations of Stoic works, or indirectly by way of Avicennian and Islamic writings, it is not easy to say. The tradition had been continuous and had penetrated all branches of study. In his metaphysics, too, some of the conceptions propounded by Avicenna are not difficult to find. They are obviously modified so as not to conflict too violently with Church doctrine, but they nevertheless betray profound agreement with him. Hence the reason why his teachings have been sometimes described as 'destructive' by theologians; and have earned him the reputation of being one of those who helped to bring about the breakdown of scholasticism. On some points he went even farther than Avicenna and maintained that the immortality of the soul which the Persian philosopher had so elaborately demonstrated was actually indemonstrable; and even that the arguments adduced to prove the existence of God were not entirely satisfying. Nor is Avicenna absent from his psychology. Together with him, he believes that the faculties of sensation and intellection are entirely distinct in man, who with his appetitive power could very well desire something that his sense of understanding and right judgement will reject. He also accepts Avicenna's view that everyone has a soul of his own; and rejects the belief of Averroës that after death they all join one common soul.

*   *   *   *

There were thus four main currents in mediaeval scholasticism. First came what may be called Augustinism, then in historical succession Aristotelianism, then Averroism and finally Avicennaism.[1] This last may not have been the strongest, but it certainly was one of the most influential and enduring, and found its way into almost every field of knowledge. Avicenna's influence was not confined to medicine and philosophy. Together with Averroës he helped to bring about the first phase of that scientific revolution that had its effective beginnings in the thirteenth century. It was already a hundred years since they had begun to translate his works; and by the time of Roger Bacon we find many of his scientific ideas being accepted and favourably commented upon. In what was the first important Western study on the subject, Bacon adopts his wave theory of light, and his explanation of the nature of vision, and of the phenomenon of the rainbow. Bacon also takes from him all that he says about the anatomy and the working of the human eye, and concerning the formation of images behind a lens. He also finds him just as helpful in mathe-

[1] Cf. R. de Vaux: *Notes et Textes sur l'Avicennisme latin.*

matics. That was one of the many reasons why he thought so highly of him; and placed him far above Averroës, whose accomplishments could not come anywhere near those of Avicenna.

And yet the chief concern of the Scholastics were the problems of theology and philosophy which in spite of some dissenting views were generally considered as parts of the same subject, and which were not definitely separated until the Renaissance. In those days theology was naturally supreme; and in the words of St Anselm, the father of Scholasticism, all had to remember that the right course was *credo ut intelligam*, laying down the principle that the human mind must set out from faith and then proceed to knowledge in order to arrive at proper understanding. This had led to the doctrine of the twofold truth to which many had come to adhere, and which has not yet completely disappeared. When it is remembered that up to the thirteenth century practically every educated person in Europe was a cleric, and that lay philosophers do not begin to appear till after the age of Dante, the significance and the effect of the statement of St Anselm becomes apparent. But then came the era of what we have called the new learning, that valuable yet disturbing combination of Graeco-Islamic literature that was to prove so challenging. The theory of intelligences with the Active Intelligence at the head of them, was a thorn in the flesh of official theology. St Augustine had known nothing about this development, and had never taught that God was to be equated with the active intelligence or the intellect agent. Nor was the originally Neo-Platonic theory of emanation, now introduced by Islamic thinkers, any easier to accept. As an explanation of creation it ran counter to some of the most fundamental principles of the Church, and with which even the most liberal-minded of men found it impossible to compromise. Notwithstanding all that, the scholastics eventually adopted a great deal of the new learning in spite of their bitter criticism of many of its teachings. And we find a Western scholar admitting that 'without the influence of Arabian peripatetism the theology of Aquinas is as unthinkable as his philosophy.'[1] And it is this Graeco-Islamic influence which in their view is mainly due to Avicenna; in spite of the cross-current of Averroism. As has been repeatedly stated they curiously enough took the former not only as the true interpreter of Aristotle, but also as the chief exponent of Islamic philosophy.

And yet there were formidable obstacles in the way of accepting Avicenna and all that he stood for. Even William of Auvergne, who had shown great sympathy towards the new learning, had found it impossible for a conscientious churchman to accept the view that the world began in pre-eternity and will extend and last till post-eternity. Or that it came into being through successive stages of emanation proceeding from God. The idea that creation did not depend on God's free will, and was something that took place necessarily, was wholly unacceptable; for this deterministic conception reduced the power of God and the omnipotence which was one of His chief attributes. How could it be conceded that God did not have direct and immediate knowledge of every individual life, since that breaks the long-cherished relation between man and his Creator? And that elaborate cosmogony of which Avicenna was the author even though it had its roots in a host of Greek and Hellenistic truth-seekers, may be interesting but must be wide of the truth, because God creates directly; and these things that he called separate intelligences could not be justifiably equated with the Cherubim, and could not by any means be accepted as intermediaries between God and His creatures. That would carry man away still farther from his Father in heaven, and place him in hands much less puissant. How could that personal worship so essential to the religious life be maintained when it had to pass through the mediation of such pure abstractions as intelligences which are no more than mere concepts? And finally, in the vital question known to the scholastics as 'the principle of individuation,' no one faithful to the teachings of his Faith could accept the Avicennian contention that it depended on matter; that it was simply *matter*

[1] C. R. S. Harris: *Duns Scotus*, Vol. 2, p. 40.

that differentiated one person from another and not *form*, as essential religious teaching held.

These were serious difficulties that with all the goodwill that could be mustered it was found impossible to dismiss or ignore. The beliefs so staunchly held and dearly cherished militated against it at every point. And one has only to look back a little farther and farther afield, to see that the same challenging issues had arisen in the Islamic world. There also religious thinkers with equal charity and devout sincerity had been disturbed and even distressed by what seemed to them new-fangled ideas that could be devastating in their consequences. Some chose to protest, others thought it necessary to denounce all such conceptions together with their author who had been led into error through supposedly excessive and unwise reading combined with futile speculation. In the Christian West there stood over against Avicenna St Augustine and his soul-satisfying message; while in the Muslim East there stood the towering figure of Ghazālī to dispute his arguments, deny the value of his rationalism, and invite men to the realms of faith (*īmān*) with its happy vistas that lead to the only form of knowledge that is worth attaining. There was no ground, they all agreed, for compromise over fundamentals.

It stands to Avicenna's eternal credit that notwithstanding such undeniable and not altogether unjustified opposition he succeeded in reaching the head, if not the heart, of a large and distinguished group in both the East and the West. Even for the most irreconcilable of his detractors he seemed to provide some food for thought that could not be lightly disregarded. In Christian lands we find the author of *De Erroribus Philosophorum* fiercely opposing Averroës, but significantly mild and full of understanding in his criticism of Avicenna. And Dante with unconcealed admiration placed him in Limbo along with other noble souls who had not received the Christian revelation. While in his homeland theologian after theologian paid tribute to him as a great mind.

Nor did his influence end with the Scholastic age and the advent of the Renaissance in Western Europe. Admittedly philosophy began to take an entirely different course; and the increasing authority of experimental science completely transformed the climate of thought. Nevertheless, whenever thinkers looked back to their predecessors of the Middle Ages, they could not fail to encounter his provocative ideas and suggestive methods of inquiry. In medicine and related subjects it has been seen that they continued to study and even teach from his books down to modern times; and in the field of rational and also religious speculation it may be safely said that so long as Thomism is studied in European centres of learning—which at present it increasingly is—the Persian philosopher will continue to be heard.

CONCLUSION

ISLAMIC philosophy has seemed to us essentially a response to the challenge that reached the Muslim world from Greece. In the working out of such processes individuals are often as vitally significant as ideas. Avicenna was one of the most remarkable figures in the history of thought.

Culturally one of the creators of the Persian Renaissance in the tenth century, in the field of philosophy he was the culmination of that momentous movement that started with Kindī and his early associates, and, propagated in the happiest manner by the conscientious and painstaking translators, eventually extended far beyond the limits of Eastern lands. With a wideness of range, a vigour of thought, and a unity of conception unequalled among the *Falāsifa*, he constructed the most complete philosophical system that the Islamic world was to have. The system owed much to his predecessors whether Greek, Hellenistic or Muslim; but he gave to his successors in the East as well as in the West far more than he had ever received. The only man to combine philosophy and medicine with such marked distinction, he built an intellectual edifice that could not be surpassed for centuries after him. A lonely and often suspected figure throughout all his life, a poor player of State politics, he rose to become a leader of thought who has exerted the most profound and lasting influence on his countrymen.

His chosen task was not an easy one. In attempting to harmonize reason with revelation, he was undertaking an impossible task. That is why it is not difficult to detect the internal conflict that permeates all Avicennian thought. It might even be called a crisis of faith. Was he to place his faith in the human mind, which he was temperamentally inclined to do, or submit to the claims of religion? Orthodox dogma obviously could not satisfy him; but neither could all that Aristotle stood for. As a final resort he sought a synthesis. That is the usual outcome whenever major concepts clash. For the Greeks the conflict did not arise, at least not with the same intensity. For the Muslims it was a grave issue; and philosophy continuously competed or collided with religious teachings. Between the idea of contingency, Islamic as well as Christian, and the Greek notion of necessity, he had to steer a perilous middle course. Essentially a metaphysician, but one who made good use of logic, primarily an Aristotelian who took a great deal from Plato and Neo-Platonism, he had to produce a system because that was the only way to bring about his synthesis. And yet he never lived to complete his work. Of that *Oriental Philosophy* which was to contain the results of his mature thought, nothing remains but a few leaves; admittedly full of promise but serving no useful purpose.

The importance of Avicenna today lies more in the problems that he poses than in the solutions that he offers. Is reality as distinct from facts a simple element or the product of two and more; is it an entity or a relation; must we seek it through analysis or synthesis? If we consider it organic and unitary with different facets and articulations, could the method suggested by Avicenna be the right one?

A SELECTED BIBLIOGRAPHY

Bibliographies

G. C. Anawati, O.P.: *Essai de Bibliographie avicennienne*. Le Caire, 1950.

Y. Mehdawi: *Bibliographie d'Ibn Sina*. Tehran, 1954.

General Works

Baron Carra de Vaux: *Avicenne*. Paris, 1900.

A. Soubiran: *Avicenne*. Paris, 1935.

Avicenna, Scientist and Philosopher: A Millenary Symposium: ed. G. M. Wickens. London, 1952.

Z. Ṣafā: *Jashn Nāme-ye-Ibn Sīnā*. An Illustrated Millenary Publication. Tehran. 2 vols. 1331–1334 A.H.

Source-Books on His Life

Ibn al-Qifṭī: *Tārīkh al-Ḥukamā'*: ed. Lippert, 1903.

I. A. Uṣaibi'a: *'Uyūn al-Anbā' fī Ṭabaqāt al-Aṭibbā*: ed. Muller, 2 vols. 1884.

Baihaqī: *Tatimmat Sīwān al-Ḥikma*: ed. M. Shafi'. Lahore, 1351 A.H.

Ibn Khallikān: *Wafayāt al-A'yān*: English trans. de Slane, 1842–1871.

Khondamīr: *Ḥabīb al-Siyar*: 4 vols. Tehran, 1954.

Dastūr al-Wuzarā': ed. Nafīsī. Tehran, 1317 A.H.

Manuscript Texts

Avicenna: *Kitāb al-Shifā*: Bodleian. Oxford. Pocock, No. 109–124. Copied in 1206 A.D. Incomplete.

Kitāb al-Shifā: Bibliothèque Nationale. Paris. Fonds arabes. No. 6829.

Printed Arabic Texts

Avicenna: *Kitāb al-Qānūn fī al-Ṭibb*: ed. Carame. Romae, MDXCIII.

Kitāb al-Nafs: ed. Landauer. Z.D.M.G., 1875.

Tis'a Rasā'il. Constantinople, 1880.

Kitāb al-Shifā. Incomplete. 2 vols. Tehran, 1886.

Al-Ishārāt wa al-Tanbīhāt: ed. Forget. Leyde, 1892.

Tis'a Rasā'il. Cairo, 1908.

Majmū'at al-Rasā'il. Cairo, 1910.

Manṭiq al-Mashrīqīyyīn. Cairo, 1910.

Jāmi' al-Badā'i'. Cairo, 1917.

Kitāb al-Najāt: ed. Kurdī: 2nd edit. Cairo, 1938.

Kitāb al-Inṣāf (Fragmenta): ed. Badawī. *Arisṭū 'ind al-'Arab.* Cairo, 1947.

Asbāb Ḥudūth al-Ḥurūf: ed. Khānlarī. Tehran, 1333 A.H.

Majmū'at al-Rasā'il. Hydarabad, 1354 A.H.

Kitāb al-Shifā. Isagoge: ed. Madhour, Cairo, 1952.

Risālat al-Iksīr: ed. Ates. Istanbul, 1953.

Risālat Fī Māhīyyat al-'Ishq: ed. Ates. Istanbul, 1953.

Fī Ma'ānī Kitāb Reṭorīqa: ed. S. Salim. Cairo, 1950.

Al-Khiṭāba: ed. S. Salim. Cairo, 1954.

K. al-Shifā. Al-Burhān: ed. Badawī. Cairo, 1954.

'Uyūn al-Ḥikma: ed. Badawī. Cairo, 1954.

Risāla al-Aḍḥawīyya: ed. Dunyā. Cairo, 1949.

Traités Mystiques: ed. Mehren. Leyde, 1889–1899.

Printed Persian Texts

Avicenna: *Rag Shināsī*: ed. Mishkāt. Tehran, 1330 A.H.

Dānish-Nāmeh. Risāle-ye-Manṭiq: ed. Mo'īn and Mishkāt. Tehran, 1331 A.H.

Dānish-Nāmeh. Ilāhiyyāt: ed. Mo'īn. Tehran, 1331 A.H.

Dānish-Nāmeh. Tabī 'īyyāt: ed. Mishkāt. Tehran, 1331 A.H.

Risāle-ye-Nafs: ed. M. 'Amīd. Tehran, 1331 A.H.

Panj Risāleh: ed. Yār Shāṭir. Tehran, 1332 A.H.

Ishārāt wa Tanbīhāt. Early Persian trans.: ed. Yār Shāṭir. Tehran, 1332.

Logic

Vattier: *La Logique du Fils de Sina communément appelé Avicenne.* Paris, 1658. French trans. of the Logic of *Najāt.*

I. Madkour: *L'Organon d'Aristote dans le Monde arabe.* Paris, 1934.

Metaphysics

M. Horten: *Die Metaphysik Avicennas*. Halle, 1907.

Ṭūsī: *Sharḥ al-Ishārāt*. Lithographed. Tehran (a commentary in Arabic).

N. Carame: *Avicennae metaphysices compendium* (Latin trans. of the Metaphysics of the *Najāt*). Rome, 1926.

J. Saliba: *Étude sur la Metaphysique d'Avicenne*, Paris, 1926.

M. A. Goichon: *Introduction à Avicenne*. Paris, 1933.

La Distinction de l'Essence et de l'Existence d'après Ibn Sina. Paris, 1937.

La Philosophie d'Avicenne et son Influence en Europe médiévale. Paris, 1944.

Livre des Directives et Remarques (French trans. of *al-Ishārāt*). Paris, 1951.

C. Hernandez: *La Metafisica de Avicenna*. Granada, 1949.

Achena et Massé: *Le Livre de Science* (French trans. of the *Dānish-Nāmeh*). Paris, 1955.

Psychology

M. Amid: *Essai sur la Psychologie d'Avicenne*. Genève, 1940.

Hughes de Sienne (1370–1439): *La Doctrine Psychologique d'Avicenne*. Incorporated in Quadri. *La Philosophie arabe*. French trans. Paris, 1947.

F. Rahman: *Avicenna's Psychology*. Oxford, 1952.

Religion and Mysticism

H. Ghorāba: *Ibn Sīna bain al-Dīn wa al-Falsafa*. Cairo, 1948.

A. J. Arberry: *Avicenna on Theology*. London, 1951.

L. Gardet. O.P.: *La Pensée Religieuse d'Avicenne*. Paris, 1951.

H. Corbin: *Avicenne et le Récit Visionnaire*. 2 vols. Paris, 1954.

Medicine and the Natural Sciences

Hirschberg and Lippert: *Die Augenheilkunde des Ibn Sina*. Leipzig, 1902.

P. de Koning: *Avicenne. Livre Premier du Canon*. Paris, 1903.

K. Lokotsch: *Avicenna als Mathematiker nach dem K. al-Shifā*. Bonn, 1913.

E. G. Browne: *Arabian Medicine*. Cambridge, 1921.
Holmyard and Mandeville: *Avicennae de Congelatione et Conglutinatione Lapidum*. Paris, 1927.
O. C. Gruner: *A Treatise on the Canon of Medicine of Avicenna*. London, 1930.
M. Hafni: *Ibn Sina Musiklehre*. Berlin, 1931.
Baron d'Erlanger: *La Musique arabe*. Vol. 2. Paris, 1935.

Avicenna in the West

G. Quadri: *La Philosophie arabe dans l'Europe médiévale*. French trans. Paris, 1947.
R. de Vaux: *Notes et Textes sur l'Avicennisme Latin*. Paris, 1934.
E. Gilson: *Le Thomisme*. 5th edit. Paris, 1934.
G. Théry: *Tolêde, grande ville de la renaissance médiévale*. Oran, 1944.

Lexicons

Jurjānī: *Kitāb al-Ta'rīfāt*: ed. Fluegel. Leipzig, 1835.
Khawārizmī: *Kitāb Mafātīḥ al-'Ulūm*: ed. Van Vloten. Leiden, 1895.
Ḥājī Khalīfa: *Kashf al-Ẓunūn*: ed. Fluegel. 2 vols. Leipzig, 1835.
Tahānawī: *Kashf Iṣṭilāḥāt al-Funūn*: ed. Sprenger. 2 vols. Calcutta, 1862.
Goichon: *Lexique de la Langue philosophique d'Ibn Sina*. Paris, 1938.
Vocabulaire d'Aristote et d'Ibn Sina. Paris, 1939.
S. Afnan: *Lexique des Termes de Logique en Grec, Anglais, Français, Persan et Arabe*. Edition mimiographiée. Paris, 1954.

AVICENNA'S SUCCESSORS AND COMMENTATORS

	A.H. A.D.
Nāṣir Khosrow	died 481/1088
Ghazālī	505/1111
Ibn Bāja (Avempace)	533/1138
Shahristānī	548/1153
Abū al-Barakāt al-Baghdādī	*c.* 560/1164
Ibn Ṭufail	581/1185
Suhrawardī	587/1191
Ibn Rushd (Averroës)	595/1198
Maimonides	601/1204
Fakhr al-Dīn al-Rāzī	606/1209
Ibn Ṭumlūs	620/1223
Ibn al-'Arabī	638/1240
Al-Abharī	663/1264
Naṣīr el-Dīn-i-Ṭūsī	672/1273
Afḍal el-Dīn-i-Kāshānī	707/1308
Quṭb el-Dīn-i-Shīrāzī	710/1311
Ibn Taimīyya	729/1328
Ījī	756/1355
Taftāzānī	793/1390
Sharīf Jurjānī	816/1413
Dawwānī	908/1503
Mīr Dāmād	1041/1631
Mullā Ṣadrā	1050/1640
Mullā Hādī Sabzewārī	1295/1878

INDEX

A

B

C

D

E

F

G

H

I

GEORGE ALLEN & UNWIN LTD
London: 40 Museum Street, W.C.1

Auckland: 24 Wyndham Street
Bombay: 15 Graham Road, Ballard Estate, Bombay 1
Calcutta: 17 Chittaranjan Avenue, Calcutta 13
Cape Town: 109 Long Street
Karachi: Metherson's Estate, Wood Street, Karachi 2
New Delhi: 13–14 Ajmeri Gate Extension, New Delhi 1
São Paulo: Avenida 9 de Julho 1138–Ap. 51
Sydney, N.S.W.: Bradbury House, 55 York Street
Toronto: 91 Wellington Street West